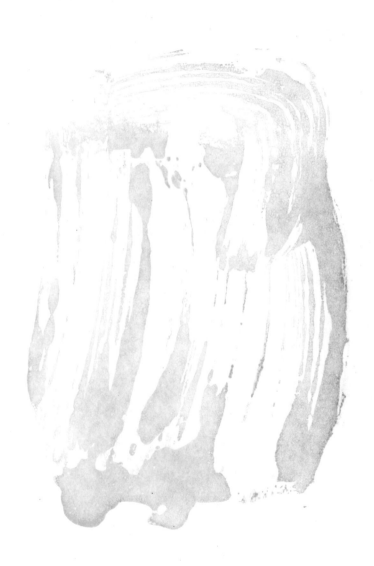

SCALING THE IVY WALL

Getting into the Selective Colleges

HOWARD GREENE and
ROBERT MINTON

ABELARD-SCHUMAN
New York

Designed by Stanley S. Drate

Manufactured in the United States of America
Library of Congress Cataloging in Publication Data

Greene, Howard, 1937–
    Scaling the ivy wall.

    Includes index.
    1. Universities and colleges—United States—
Admission. 2. Universities and colleges—Atlantic
States. I. Minton, Robert, 1918– joint author.
II. Title.
LB2351.G73   378.1′C5′60973   74–9371

ISBN 0–200–04024–3
10 9 8 7 6 5 4 3 2 1

Equality of talents, of education or of wealth cannot be produced by human institutions.

ANDREW JACKSON

The sheepskin is an American invention comparable in importance to the invention of the joint stock certificate.

ROBERT S. BABCOCK
Provost
Vermont State College

In a society devoted to "the career open to talent" the talent testers have become the gatekeepers to opportunity to success, just as the genealogists were in a society based on heredity.

ALLEN BARTON
Director
Bureau of Applied Social Research

Selectivity has replaced exclusiveness as a basis for institutional pride.

PAUL WOODRING
The Higher Learning in America: A Reassessment

Education is now the major route to social mobility in the United States.

S. M. MILLER AND FRANK RIESSMAN
Social Class and Social Policy

Contents

Acknowledgments

This book came about as the result of discussions and indeed arguments between us when Howard Greene, as a consultant to a secondary school, was recommending certain candidates for Princeton to Robert Minton, an alumni representative of the Princeton admissions office. We concluded that the only way to settle our differences in evaluating applicants was to commit our views to paper together. Max Gartenberg, our literary agent who once scaled the Ivy walls of Brown, urged us to write the first book for the general public devoted entirely to selective admissions. Sam Stewart, former editor-in-chief of Abelard-Schuman, who remains convinced despite what we say that he got into Harvard only because he came from Hawaii, decided that we nevertheless might enlighten another generation, and his enthusiasm for the project was highly encouraging. Linda Schjeldahl, our editor, read the manuscript with the eye of one who remembered what kind of advice she might have used when applying for admission to Carleton, and we amended certain passages accordingly.

Several hundred people in some way contributed to our text. The students must remain anonymous. We would like particularly to thank: Bradford Richardson, James Rogers, Edward Wall, Clara Ludwig, Peter Richardson, John and Betsy Wilson, Henry Damon, Russell Mead, Burt Honea, Laurence Sanford, Jr., Mary Anne

Schwalbe, David Evans, Priscilla Wolfe, Robert Kates, James Baker, Edwin Mosher, Carol Halstead, Edward Read, Henry Paley, George Hanford, Fred Glimp, Donald Platten, Dean Witla, Frank Miller, Ted Bracken, Mary Ellen Ames, Joseph Kiebala, Charles Whittemore, Ralph Woodward, Richard and Amy Wilson, Arnold Brooks, Sumner Rulon-Miller III, David Rahr, Franklin Moore, Gerald Finch, Fred Fox, Dudley Blodgett, Sheldon Judson, T. Harding Jones, Royce Flippin, John Smith, Margaret Thorne, Ralph Moye, Fred Neuberger, Robert Holder, Burt Hallowell, David Aloian, John Esty, Richard Moll, David Thomas, Charles Burdick, Dan Stucky, Robert Parsons, Alfred Quirk, Carmen Rinaldi, Lillian Murdock, David Orr, Susan Fedo, Robert Doolan, John Callahan, Edward Hall, Phillip Richards, Paul Saddler, David Worth, Margaret Perry and Timothy Callard.

The generosity and interest in students shown by Sumner Gerstein has helped the authors to gain the experience that has gone into the writing of this book. For research material we are particularly grateful to the College Entrance Examination Board and the National Association of Independent Schools. The cooperation of the National College Counselors Association and the American Association of Collegiate Registrars and Admissions Officers was helpful to us.

The manuscript was impeccably typed by Mrs. Barbara Whipple.

HOWARD GREENE *and* ROBERT MINTON

SCALING THE IVY WALL:
Getting into the Selective Colleges

Introduction: Sizing Up the Ivy Walls

For the Class of 1978, entering college in the fall of 1974, it was the toughest year of all to get into many of the selective colleges. On an average applications were up 10 percent over the previous year. Wellesley had an 18 percent increase in applications. But enrollments remained more or less at the same level at the prestige colleges. Amherst even had 56 fewer places because of an unexpected increase in freshmen in 1973.

Just to cite a bit of the evidence, in 1974 Bowdoin had 4,060 applicants, of which 660 were accepted; for Williams the figures were 4,500 and 888; for Princeton 9,755 and 2,154; for Dartmouth 7,785 and 1,750.

Ivy League, Seven Sisters and other highly selective colleges have restricted their size in order to preserve their character and, incidentally, by doing so they have avoided the financial burdens of expanded facilities and faculty. Keeping close to a scale developed for an era when the country had 50 million fewer people than it has today, these colleges have retained their attractiveness and avoided the loss of identity often attendant on expansion.

A state university official said recently that it could not use alumni to help recruit students because it was no longer the same place they went to, and they would not understand it because of the expansion.

So, despite the fact that it will cost over $6,000 a year at most selective colleges, the applications continue to pour in. Obviously, whatever Harvard or Vassar costs, it seems worth the sacrifice. Princeton, with tuition at $3,500, had an overall 14 percent increase in applications in 1974, and 37 percent in applications to the School of Engineering. Yet it is possible to get a good engineering education at the University of Massachusetts for a tuition of only $300 a year!

The state colleges with their low tuitions, though, are not hurting the selective colleges. It is the hundreds of other private colleges which suffer—applications nationally were off 10 to 15 percent in 1974, just about the same amount by which the public institutions picked up applicants.

Clearly, the competition at a few colleges is so severe that some people look for ways to get around it. Recently the father of an applicant to Dartmouth phoned the admissions office in Hanover, New Hampshire, making it clear it was a long-distance call, an important call. After some pleasantries the father got to the point: "You know I'm in a position to make a considerable gift to the college if my son gets in."

It was not the first time such a broad hint has been made to Dartmouth, and to many another college, too. The admissions officer was neither surprised nor offended.

"I'm glad to hear that," he told the father, "and I hope we both have the same understanding of the priorities."

"What do you mean? What priorities?"

"Well, first we have to see whether we can offer your son admission. Then if he should get in and he enrolls, we have a Parents' Committee who will contact you right away about a gift."

There are some things money cannot buy, and one is admission to colleges where the applications outnumber the openings offered by four or five to one. Recently, a candidate whose grandfather left an Ivy institution $4 million got no special consideration and was not admitted. Some of those admitted to that college that year were not only very poor, they had less impressive academic records than the rich applicant.

Selective admissions is such a complex procedure, that admissions offices have come to accept almost with a smile the most outrageous kinds of pressure. When John Osander was director of admission at

Princeton, one man said he would send him a telegram every day until his son was admitted. "He sent a lot of telegrams," Osander told a journalist. "I don't remember whether the boy got in."

In the past, alumni children were turned down by the selective colleges only if it was obvious that they could not do the academic work. Now, although alumni children do stand a better chance of admission than other applicants to hard-to-get-into colleges, more than half of them are rejected, and most of the rejectees are quite capable of a creditable performance in a top college. Old grads may grumble, but their sense of outrage has had little effect on the final outcome of admissions decisions. The policy, admissions offices can show, is to give due consideration to alumni children.

Why This Book?

There are a number of useful guide books that will help most students determine what college or colleges they will apply to. These are addressed to the high school population as a whole, half of whose graduating seniors now go on to some form of postsecondary education that includes more than 2,100 senior and junior colleges. No book has yet been addressed to the 100,000 or so students who apply to perhaps less than 50 private colleges where admission is most highly competitive.

Because of limitations on enrollment, thousands of qualified applicants must be rejected. This has brought disappointment, resentment and misunderstanding. Inevitably, myths about the admissions process have grown up: to get in you have to be an alumni child, you have to be rich, you have to be poor, you have to be Black, you cannot be Black, you have to be radical, the interview makes all the difference, it's all done by computer, a preppy hasn't a chance—and so on. Such exaggerated statements are the result of an oversimplified view of a very complicated process.

What we have written is based on our experience in college and secondary school education, in admissions work, and in counseling secondary school students. We have extended this personal experience by research. While we have sought to be fair and to avoid sensationalism, we recognize that our subject is an emotional one. Counselors at

Howard Greene Associates find themselves almost daily talking to parents and students agitated and perplexed and dismayed by the kinds of options open to a good candidate for a selective college.

We doubt that we can quell all the anxiety students and parents feel as they go through the long procedures: visits to campuses, tests, interviews, applications and notices of ratings. But it is our experience that the more that people understand about selective admissions, the more they can cope with the difficulties.

For example, the jargon of admissions bureaucracy can be very exasperating. What is the difference between Early Decision and Early Evaluation? What does Admit-Deny mean? We discuss such terms as we go along, and there is a glossary for quick reference, a much shorter glossary, incidentally, than a 64-page book of terms issued by the American Association of Collegiate Registrars and Admissions Officers.

We urge parents, and students particularly, to read the whole book and not just the chapter on tests or on campus visits. This is not a matter of a personal pride. The selective admissions process has a distinct character and cannot be understood merely in terms of test scores or interview behavior. It is important to realize that selective admissions administrators—deans, directors, staff officers—are not employed to keep anyone out of their colleges, and that they have in fact been a vanguard in opening up their institutions so as to allow every possible kind of student a fair chance of being admitted, *whatever his background.* To underscore this change we have presented some historical material showing how selective admissions evolved.

Students should reread the book from time to time as the admission process develops. It will help them to think more and to worry less. In a way a student can develop into a professional applicant, capable of doing the right thing at the right time and thereby helping his chances of admission. We see nothing wrong with ninth-graders reading this book, because it can help them shape their secondary school lives in such a way as to achieve the excellences that selective colleges look for. The competition is severe. Applications to Harvard have more than doubled in the last decade. But it may be some consolation to know that in nineteenth-century China as many as 10,000 students used to compete for only a few hundred university places.

The Most Selective Colleges

If you were to ask anyone at random which of the 1,400 four-year colleges are the most selective, you probably would be told the Ivy League. First of all, the Ivy League is an athletic league of Eastern colleges presumably competing on equal terms in varsity sports. It is composed of Harvard, Yale, Princeton, Dartmouth, Brown, Columbia, Cornell and Penn. Some of these colleges are harder to get into than others. And colleges not in the Ivy League may be harder to get into than some of those in it. Radcliffe and MIT come to mind. And what about Stanford, Duke, Chicago, Amherst, Oberlin or Reed? If anyone were foolish enough to draw up a ranking of colleges according to the difficulty of being admitted, he would begin with Harvard; but then he might be told the following Dartmouth story:

On the eve of a varsity football game with Harvard, Dartmouth coach Bob Blackman told a reporter that a number of Harvard players had been turned down by the Dartmouth admissions office, and he named them. The story was cut out of the paper Saturday morning and pasted in the Harvard locker room to inspire the underdog Crimson team, which it did, and Dartmouth lost the game. Blackman regretted his statement to the press, but the truth of the story was never questioned.

Harvard does admit students other colleges turn down, and not all of them are athletes. Selective admissions means just that, the right to select the students the college wants, and to reject those it does not want—without explanation or apology. C students should not on this account rush their applications to Cambridge, but they ought to know that Harvard is not necessarily harder to get into than some other colleges.

Rather than try to rank colleges on a selectivity scale, we offer three groupings in alphabetical order, with the observation that in our experience the preferences of students fall roughly in the order of groups 1, 2 and 3.

(1) Brown, Dartmouth, Duke, Harvard, Princeton, Radcliffe, Stanford, Swarthmore and Yale; and Cal Tech, MIT and Rice in the category of technical/scientific schools.

(2) Amherst, Bowdoin, Bryn Mawr, Mount Holyoke, Smith, Vassar, Wellesley, Wesleyan and Williams; Cornell and the larger urban colleges, Barnard, Chicago, Columbia and Penn.

(3) Bennington, Brandeis, Carleton, Claremont Colleges, Colby, Colgate, Colorado College, Connecticut College, Davidson, Hamilton, Haverford, Johns Hopkins, Lawrence, Middlebury, Northwestern, Oberlin, Trinity and Tufts.

No doubt there is room for argument on the relative difficulty of getting into these colleges, and cases can be made for extending the list. There are, of course, many more private colleges that are able to select their student bodies to some extent. Something like 70 colleges refuse to handle applications after a certain date, an indication that they are at least getting enough applicants to fill their enrollment. But to include all these colleges in the selective category would, in our view, distort the definition of selective admissions.

What about public colleges? Are they forbidden by law to be selective? No, but in principle they are more open than closed. Let the student enroll and if he can keep up he is welcome. But state universities now have admissions offices, whereas they used to have only registrars, because the demand for places often exceeds the supply at a particular campus. And even where there is open enrollment, there are limits to the numbers that can be instructed at one time. Some students, generally in the lower half of the high school class, must study at another level of the higher educational system, such as a community college. So selectivity of a kind is widespread. It will occur wherever there is competition for place, as in the civil service. The focus in this book is on selection at the upper levels of higher education.

The absence of a college from our list is no reflection on the quality of that college. We simply are saying that in our experience these are the most selective colleges. We have not included art schools, music schools or others open only to the most talented, nor are the various military academies considered here. The cluster of institutions within our purview happens to be that to which the attention of thousands of families is most drawn at the present time, the mid-seventies. The colleges have in common a limited number of places to be distributed among a large number of applicants.

Any college may dispute our list and advise the world that it too is selective in its admissions. We wonder whether this will happen. Selectivity is not necessarily something to be advertised. The public has a love/hate attitude toward selective or prestige colleges. They would love to have degrees from them, and they are proud when their children attend them. They sneer at Ivy Leaguers as snobs, and girls who went to the Seven Sisters are said to be hoity-toity.

". . . the tragic fact remains," Paul Woodring wrote in *The Higher Learning in America: A Reassessment* (1968), "that to many status-seeking Eastern students, failure to be admitted to an Ivy League college seems a fate worse than death." No institution seeks deliberately to build an image on the superficial value of social status.

Because selectivity results in the rejection of many outstanding students, there has been a "spillover" of good applicants that has allowed more colleges to increase their status through selective admissions. Selectivity at the very top has had the effect of strengthening a number of colleges, because an improvement of academic quality coming from the "spillover" students enables administrators to attract better faculties and to raise the money for improved programs and facilities. Another benefit arising from the demand for entrance to prestige colleges is the development of more democratic and meritocratic gauges in determining who will be admitted.

No one is excluded now because of an accident of birth, and rarely is anyone admitted out of sheer favoritism. Selective colleges that used to be exclusive in a class sense no longer are so. Certainly the income level of the parents at all private colleges is higher than at public colleges. This is not because private and especially selective private colleges seek only middle- and upper-middle-class students, but because the educational advantages that the better-off have over the poor make them better students on the whole.

Selective private colleges have wisely broadened admissions policies in order to bring onto their campuses a fairer representation of the students of America. In doing so without greatly expanding enrollment, they have had to turn down students from the traditional pool, pejoratively described as White-Anglo-Saxon-Protestant. Understandably, great disappointment follows the rejection of a student with higher marks than those of a minority student who has been accepted. The University of Washington Law School has been legally challenged in the DeFunis case for rejecting a Phi Beta Kappa white applicant while accepting minority candidates with weaker records. The emphasis on rejection, however, overlooks the fact that the overwhelming majority of those accepted in private colleges are not minority students. At present many selective colleges report a decline in minority applications.

To say that we have great sympathy for anyone rejected by a selective college is of no help, and so we prefer to concentrate our attention on the students who are admitted. Here, it must be granted, lies the reason that the selective colleges can be selective. By long tradition the prestige colleges have attracted top students, men and women who have gone on to prove themselves by their accomplishments. For two generations all but one American president was the graduate of a prestige college: Teddy Roosevelt, Harvard; Taft, Yale; Wilson, Princeton; Coolidge, Amherst; Hoover, Stanford; FDR, Harvard. Kennedy started at Princeton and switched to Harvard. Eisenhower became president of Columbia. Nixon went to Duke Law School. Such colleges have no monopoly on successful alumni, but they do attract many of the country's most able students; more of their graduates than less are in some measure distinguished. The willingness of their students to submit to the intense competitive process signals a drive and motivation that generally leads to success.

This competitiveness becomes all the more essential when applying to graduate school, for the number of graduate students has increased 50 times since the 1920s, while the number of undergraduates has increased only 10 times. Thousands apply for a few hundred places in top medical and law schools. The top selective college graduate is hard to turn down at Columbia Law School or Cornell Medical School.

Probably the most distinctive feature of the selective colleges is not the beautiful campuses, great facilities or marvelous faculties, but the students themselves. "They teach each other" is a sentence you hear over and over from the professors on these campuses. Artful selectivity is in this sense a service to the student. He is assured the stimulation of a diverse group of intelligent and talented peers who challenge his preconceptions and force him to broaden his outlook.

The volume of applications to the most selective colleges has had its impact on many other colleges, which must also deal with an excess of candidates. Overlapping—applying to several colleges—is an almost universal practice of the better students. Thus a college that may have empty spaces (500,000 unfilled openings were reported in 1973) may also have to handle thousands of applications of students who wind up choosing to go elsewhere. Out of this situation has grown up a new occupation: admissions officers constitute a definite corps in college administration, almost a diplomatic corps, because they are the chief representatives of their institutions to that segment of the public from which each new generation of students comes.

Since many people seem to believe that there is something secretive about admissions, it may come as a surprise to our readers to learn that admissions officers talked frankly to us about their work and procedures. The chief confidential information is the applicant's folder, and this contains the key to the decision to admit or reject. No admissions officer will discuss cases in more than general terms. To open admissions records to public scrutiny would result in appeals and recriminations that would make the system impossible to administer. Within this limitation admissions officers answered frankly any question put to them, and all of them were pleased to know that a book of this sort was being written. Aware of the skepticism of some applicants, admissions officers are beginning to describe their operations in detail in the literature they offer, and they welcome searching questions. Candidates are often more direct in their skepticism than adults dare to be, and to a weary admissions officer interviewing many students the challenging questions are the ones they most enjoy handling.

Because of the confidentiality of applicants' folders, the cases appearing in this book, while based on actual cases, have been so presented that no individual can be identified. In discussing students we most frequently use the pronoun "he" rather than "he and she." This is a convenience of style and not a male chauvinist tactic. We are thoroughly committed to the principle of coeducation, and with equal access of boys and girls by most admissions offices, what we have to say applies to either sex, with the exception of course of our remarks on men's athletics.

1

Decisions, Decisions, Decisions

There were more than 8 million students in some form of postsecondary education in the United States in 1974, attending 1,400 four-year colleges and graduate schools and over 700 two-year institutions. How is this enormous student population sorted out and distributed among the colleges? Who slots Johnny for Penn State and Mary for Brown? Is it the College Board? Is it a computer? Is it superman? It would take a superman to do the job, and so in the manner of all institutions which seek to avoid as much responsibility as they reasonably can, much of the burden has been allowed to shift elsewhere—onto the students themselves.

The very phrase "college of your choice" reveals just who decides where Johnny and Mary will study after graduating from high school. It is largely Johnny and Mary. Largely. Maybe Mary's first choice was Radcliffe and Radcliffe turned her down. Nonetheless, Mary had to decide first to apply to *both* Radcliffe and Brown. The more accurate phrase would be *"colleges* of your choice" when applying to selective colleges. But in *any* case it is the student who rates himself, looks over some campuses, leafs through catalogues and finally comes to the decision where he will apply. When he is admitted by more than one college, again he alone decides at which one he will enroll. Going to college is a great privilege, but getting there is not half the fun being there is.

I

It used to be that the biggest worry a college-bound student had was earning sufficient high school credits to qualify for higher education. A high school diploma was a ticket not just to the state college, but to most colleges. What kept college enrollments down was money, not the lack of qualified students. Only 15,000 students took the College Board tests before World War II. In 1974, a million are taking them and over 2 million are taking the American College Testing Program tests. Students are no longer part of an elite minority, they are a mass—and a massive force, it was discovered in the sixties. Even those qualified to apply for selective colleges mount up to 100,000— that is, 100,000 year-in, year-out, 100,000 out of 3.1 million graduating high school seniors. Yet while more and more qualified students were being trained in the postwar period, the enrollments of the most prestigious colleges expanded only slightly, by a few hundred places per college compared with *several thousand more applicants* per college. Selective college applications about doubled in the decade 1964–74, while enrollment remained stable.

Thus good students are faced with agonizing choices in their junior and senior years of high school. They know from their grades and test scores that they are good enough to do the work at the best colleges, but they also know that the admissions offices of the best colleges say that 80 percent of those they reject are qualified to attend. Princeton's admissions report includes the fact that of 735 valedictorians who applied, 380 were turned down. There are other factors besides academic excellence that are weighed in the admissions decision. "Bowdoin is not the right place for everyone," says its admissions brochure. And everyone is not right for Bowdoin even though he be an A student. Bowdoin rejects candidates accepted by Yale and Princeton.

When the Ivy presidents announced the option of some common procedures in 1973, they referred to "the growing complexity" of admissions. It is this complexity that baffles and worries students competing for places in the colleges they have come to believe are the nation's finest. Edward T. Hall, headmaster of St. Mark's School in Massachusetts, who knew the day when he could guarantee large numbers of admissions to Harvard, calls the present situation "that nightmare of college admissions." Burt Honea, college counselor at Concord Academy in Massachusetts, considered tops academically among private schools, says that just about everyone of his 70 seniors hopes to get into the most selective colleges, but only half of them make it.

A typical counselor in a good suburban high school, be it in the East, South, Midwest or on the West Coast, is faced with students who come in with the following questions:

Where should I go to college?
What should I study there?
Where can I get in?
How many colleges should I apply to?
Do I need to visit the campus?
What is more important, College Board scores or grades?
Why do some colleges cost more than others?
Can I qualify for financial aid?
Am I better off in honor sections or regular courses in which I get As easily?
Should I take the SAT again (Scholastic Aptitude Test)?
My dad's a Yalie, but I like Harvard. Can I make it?
Is it better to go far away from home?
What if I take next year off and just think?
Do I *have* to be interviewed?

Few high school counselors have all the answers and none of them has very much time, so what each has to do is, tactfully in the manner of the psychotherapist, force the student to accept the responsibility of finding the answers for himself. "What career choices are you thinking of? . . . Do your grades really justify considering Carleton? . . . Have you been looking at college catalogues? . . . Won't your parents take you to some campuses? . . . What do you think you might major in? . . . How important are athletics to you? . . . If you're nervous about crime in the city, why not look at a smalltown college? . . . Why don't you think you're good enough for the Ivies?"

The student asks questions and he gets not answers but more questions in many cases, because in the heterogeneous high school the counselor cannot know what is right for each of the several hundred students he is responsible for. Sometimes these questions help a student come to grips with his own limits or potentialities, but he or she is still left with the necessity of making out the cumbersome applications to *several* colleges—the average is five but some apply to 10 or 12, at $15 to $20 per application.

The Calendar

(1) JUNIOR YEAR, FALL. But let us follow the sequence of events for college admissions. You can think about college in grade school if you want to, but only in your junior year will any college think about you, and then only to the extent of suggesting that you visit the campus in the spring. It is in the fall of junior year that the first College Board test is taken—*PSAT, the Preliminary Scholastic Aptitude Test,* which is the basis for the National Merit Scholarship Awards. This is something of a watershed for the 100,000 who take this two-hour multiple-choice test of verbal and mathematical aptitude. Some 15,000 are named "semi-finalists," an honor that falls on less than 5 percent of the senior class nationally. This group is of great interest to selective admissions officers, but by no means are all semi-finalists destined to be admitted to the colleges of their choice. The semi-finalists who apply are simply part of the selective "pool," as it is known in the growing lexicon of educational administration.

(2) JUNIOR YEAR, SPRING. In the spring of junior year students take the *SAT*—Scholastic Aptitude Test—a three-hour aptitude test discussed in some detail in Chapter 8. Not all juniors take the SAT, but those who do have the option of taking it again in the fall of senior year, on the chance that their scores will rise about 10 percent the second time—although they could also drop. While a greatly increasing number of high school students rely on their junior year College Board test results for admission, the strong students applying to the highly selective colleges will be encouraged to sit for the examinations in the fall of their senior year because of the quality of the competition.

SAT scores are a critical factor in selective college admissions. But admissions committees have a way of seeing beyond low scores to admit some candidates who look promising despite a mediocre record. For instance, in the Class of 1977 at Amherst College, of 336 enrolled, 217 scored above 600 in the verbal and 273 scored above 600 in the math SAT. But 24 scored below 500 in the verbal and 16 scored below

500 in the math SAT. Median or average SAT scores at most selective colleges are above 600, but this misleads many students who automatically rule themselves out of the competition because they scored below 600. We suggest the reader study the full Amherst 1973 report to secondary schools. Counselors will show students reports of other colleges. We have included Columbia's as a second example. (See Appendix for both reports.)

For this reason, perhaps, Harvard reports the *range* of scores of admitted candidates, which is between 400 and 800. The lowest possible score is 200, and there are special students we know whose language disability puts them in the 200 category and who still got into an Ivy college. This of course is bewildering to high-scoring students who are rejected. We can only say that in the wisdom of selective colleges it is important to give a few disadvantaged students a chance to lift themselves onto a new level of learning.

Test scores are important in the admissions process at many state colleges which have become selective because of the number of applications they receive, particularly from out-of-state students. Michigan, Wisconsin, Virginia, North Carolina, Connecticut, Massachusetts, California, Vermont, New York, New Hampshire, all turn down thousands of students. At UMass-Amherst in 1973 the average SAT scores for the freshman class were 530 verbal and 576 math, and the average freshman ranked in the upper 14.5 percent of his high school class. With only 180 openings for out-of-state students, most of those admitted in this category had some special edge: they were alumni children, athletes or engineers. Even an A student with 700 SAT scores had little chance of getting into UMass-Amherst from out of state unless he fitted the needs of the college.

So the SAT is important for the student whose college aspirations are modest. "It is sad to see a kid who has gotten a B in biology and wants to study biology at UMass-Amherst get SAT scores in the 400s," says Henry Damon, chief counselor at Concord-Carlisle High. To which Robert J. Doolan, director of admissions at UMass-Amherst replies: "I would rather accept a diligent B student with 400 scores than a half-hearted C student who scored in the 600s." And those who may not get into the freshman class, may later transfer in at the junior level after two years in a community college. This prospect is discouraging, of course, to one with his heart set on going away to college right after high school, but the disappointment wears off those with the fortitude to recognize that in American college competition you may lose a round but you do not have to lose the battle.

(3) SENIOR YEAR. After the SAT in senior year come *the three College Board Achievement Tests,* exams that can be taken one, two or three at a time, and even in junior year, though most students wait until senior year because these are not aptitude tests. They are traditional examinations of subject matter learned in a language, math or one of eight other subjects tested. The longer you have studied a subject, the better you should do on an Achievement test. After the Achievements, which are scored on the same 200–800 scale, no more College Boards.

But the good students are studying hard, taking advanced courses generally on a college level that can place them as freshmen in upperclass college courses, particularly in languages and in math. And they are at work on their nonacademic activities—athletics, school government, drama, outside job, social service—which count so much in the judgments of selective college admissions committees.

The Interview. During the fall, if the student has not been interviewed already, he may now be interviewed on campus or by an admissions officer visiting the high school. Or he may be interviewed by an alumnus of the college acting as a volunteer representative of the admissions office. A few colleges, like Wellesley, insist on an interview. Others say it's optional. One dean of admissions told us, "The interview is window dressing to please the candidate and the alumni. It's a public relations tool." But at Harvard we heard an admissions officer say, "The interview can make you or break you." That is to say, if you are on the borderline anyway for whatever reason, a poor interview report might tip the balance against you. But this is a simplistic view of how the admissions process works; no single factor causes a candidate's rejection. It is the whole profile he presents that the admissions committee considers.

The Application. Meanwhile, applications have to be filed. The student quickly learns the different kinds of situations he can opt for, and masters the distinction between *Early Decision, Early Evaluation* and *Early Action.*

All selective colleges but Harvard, Yale and Princeton offer the *Early Decision* option—you apply formally for admission early in the fall of senior year, and if accepted you must withdraw all other applications. In a real sense, you have made a commitment to that college. Under Early Decision you avoid the agonizing wait until April 15 to get the word from the colleges you have applied to.

Early Evaluation is a policy adopted in 1973 by the eight Ivy League colleges (Harvard, Yale, Princeton, Dartmouth, Cornell, Columbia, Brown and Penn) plus MIT—for this purpose the nine call themselves the Ivy Group, Ivy League being strictly a sports league. These colleges send out to every candidate in December and January an evaluation of his or her chances of admission. There are three evaluations that are more or less self-evident, *Likely, Possible* and *Unlikely.* Likely and Unlikely mean just what they say and very few Likelies are rejected and Unlikelies almost never are accepted. Of the Possibles probably one in four or five will be accepted.

The system was started at Princeton and their experience with the Possibles is that one in five make it. With this information in hand, a candidate who is Possible or Unlikely has the time to look hard at other choices of colleges he has applied to or which he has not yet applied to if he decides to go to a place that has *rolling admissions*— that is, no cutoff date for applications.

Early Action is an MIT variant on Early Decision. It simply means that you have been accepted by MIT but are free to apply elsewhere and are not obliged to accept MIT's offer until May 1, the closing date of most selective college acceptances.

Filing applications is time consuming both for candidates and for teachers who are asked to report on the students' qualities. A student who insists on filing ten applications has his work cut out for him and it will cost someone $150 to $200 in fees. Each application may call for as many as three teachers' reports—some teachers use the Xerox; others laboriously write out individual reports for each college. In addition to the application a personal statement must be sent to many colleges, an essay saying whatever the candidate wants to say about himself, his aspirations and capacities. Optional is the College Board's *Student Questionnaire.* This asks the candidate 40 questions about himself and his plans in college. It is an informational data sheet that has nothing to do with admission decisions but is helpful to colleges in determining what to expect from freshmen in the way of course choices and activities.

Financial Aid. That is about all the paper work the student needs to do. But if financial aid is required, the parents must file a *Parents' Confidential Statement* with the College Board, which sends a report to the colleges the student is applying to, suggesting how much the family can afford to contribute to the student's total college costs. A financial-aid office in the college then works out an "aid package" consisting of a combination of a scholarship, a loan, or a campus job —it can be all three, two or just one of these categories. This financial information is provided to families at the time the student is accepted April 15.

During the winter months the candidates go into psychological hibernation while the admissions officers read their "folders," or "dockets" as they are sometimes called, the files, the dossiers consisting of everything that comes in from the candidate and others. These include College Board scores, school transcript, teachers' reports, interview reports, coaches' reports, faculty reports (some candidates talk to the department they plan to major in, and this can lead to a professor urging acceptance), alumni reports, news clippings and many other exhibits and portfolios that the candidate may have sent in. This can be a tape recording of a concerto he has composed or performed, a painting, an album of photographs, a reel of film he has shot or produced.

One thing required of an admissions staff is stamina. For days and nights on end each officer must go through hundreds and possibly more than a thousand folders at least once, and then in committee thrash out an agreement on which candidates not already winnowed out must be rejected and which accepted. It is a specialist's job. At the selective colleges the process is a human affair. The choices are made by discerning men and women and never by a computer, though computers are being used increasingly for statistical purposes: How many alumni sons applied last year by November? the Dartmouth staff can ask the computer, and get the answer in a trice.

Meanwhile, all over the country spring is coming and candidates are getting restless. Some have visited more campuses, talked to alumni, faculty, college students, but seldom to an admissions officer. These generally become available to no one including their families from February on. In the Ivy Group they are pledged to reveal no candidate's chances until acceptance notices go out April 15. Other colleges may indicate to alumni that they want certain candidates, so that the alumnus can subtly influence them to accept offers of admission when they come.

April 15. And on April 15 they come. Perhaps only the election of a new Pope is more dramatic than the collective opening of the envelopes that reach these 100,000 applicants that day—they are supposed to arrive on the 15th unless delayed by the mails. For those admitted to the college of their choice there is possibly a bonanza of acceptances. A boy wrote from boarding school to his family: "I have spread out on my bed what I have worked for for four years, three letters of acceptance from Princeton, Stanford and Penn." Others may be accepted by Princeton, rejected by Yale, accepted by Wellesley, rejected by Radcliffe. And so it goes.

The happy ones have to make a choice—will it be Dartmouth or Bryn Mawr? Less happy are those rejected by the most selective colleges and forced to choose a "backup." The Possibles in the Ivy Group are hit hard by the rejections, and sometimes their parents are hit harder, particularly if their own alma mater turns down their child.

"I wonder how many other Harvard men give less to the college since their kids were rejected," mused a banker we talked to.

May 1. But life must go on, college life too. Once the news arrives, the student has to decide which college to accept and give his acceptance by May 1. There is a limbo for some who are on waiting lists, which means that they might be admitted in the summer or even in September if the college has miscalculated its enrollment. (Yale had a waiting list of more than 200 in September 1973.) In such cases the student has already accepted another college and put down a $200 deposit. He is generally prepared to sacrifice this if he can afford to.

Looking back over the more than two years it took to arrive at college, we might summarize the experience in calendar form, since this is what the College Board does for its series of tests:

JUNIOR YEAR

October	Preliminary Scholastic Aptitude Test (PSAT).
January	National Merit Scholar semi-finalists announced. National Achievement Scholars semi-finalists announced.
April	Scholastic Aptitude Test (SAT).

May	Achievement Tests (one, two or three).
June	SATs, if not taken in April.
Spring	Good time to visit campuses, interviews possible.

SENIOR YEAR

All fall	Visit campuses; interviews by admissions officers or alumni; applications may be filed.
November	SATs.
	Early Decision application deadlines.
December	Application deadlines; teachers' reports; personal statement—all should be filed.
	Parents file the Parents' Confidential Statement if they seek financial aid.
	Secondary schools file candidate transcripts with admissions offices.
	Coaches, alumni, faculty send in reports on candidates to admissions offices.
	Portfolios, films, tapes and other exhibits from candidates pile up in admissions offices.
January	Early Evaluation of Likely, Possible or Unlikely sent to Ivy Group candidates.
	Early Decisions made.
	Achievement Tests (three obligatory if not already taken).
All winter	Candidates can visit campuses, but may not be interviewed.
	Admissions offices read folders, begin eliminating and accepting candidates informally.
April	Around April 1 admissions offices begin sending lists to computer for printout and preparing enormous mailing of acceptances and rejections.
	On the 15th candidates get the news and financial aid information.
May 1	Deadline for deciding whether to accept offer of admission.
	Candidates begin to be taken off waiting list, a process that can last until September.

A Fair System?

While one can sympathize with the disappointment of those rejected by the college of their choice, one would overdo it to cry out against an injustice, because a good number of those rejected by selective colleges still go to excellent colleges. It would insult these places to name them as Ivy reject colleges. The prestige of some places is inordinate and their graduates know it. Ed Wall, a Yale man, dean of admissions at Amherst, freely admits that many of the men Amherst enrolls have applied unsuccessfully to Harvard, Yale or Princeton and there is not a thing he can do about it. He knows that they are excellent students and the Big Three's loss is the Little Three's gain.

Occasionally there are near catastrophes. A Harvard graduate with connections in the administration got a frantic appeal from a father whose son had been rejected there. "He applied no place else and says he just won't go anywhere now." It was arranged for the Harvard admissions office to see the boy, who was assured that the world had not come to an end and he fortunately was placed with highly selective Haverford. His decision to apply only to Harvard was ill-advised, but who knows what forces at home and in his private school fixated his attention so exclusively on number one college?

Students today need to spend more time learning about good colleges where the competition to get in is less intense. Instead of thinking of such places as "safeties" to fall back on, they ought to consider the positive value of going to a college where they will probably do well academically and can take part in extracurricular activities with success. One benefit is an increased sense of self-esteem. It may be a mistake to think that your self-esteem will rise if you get into a more prestigious place. Possibly the competition once you are there will actually lower your judgment of your own competence. Another benefit subsequently may be that from a college where you have excelled you will have a better chance of getting in to a good graduate school than from a prestige college where you squeaked by. These are considerations to think about when applying for college and when deciding what campuses to visit.

Deciding

Decisions, decisions, decisions! The high school student is insufficiently prepared to take full responsibility for his future education. Recognizing this, the College Board has prepared a course called Decisions that is offered to secondary schools to help young people understand how to reach rational conclusions about their plans and to avoid drifting or acting impulsively. The best students often are as much at sea as the average ones, and professional educational counselors find that they have as many clients without emotional difficulties and learning problems as they have with such concerns.

These students need guidance, someone to talk to, to help sort out their plans and help them evaluate their ambitions and goals. Parents are not always able to answer their children's questions because higher education has changed so rapidly that they are out of touch, often misinformed and worried about what is happening on campus. A genuine generation gap. Guidance counselors are overworked and few of them specialize in selective college admissions, because only 10 percent or less of the seniors are applying to these colleges. One of the best sources of guidance is a group of undergraduates of the selective college a student is interested in.

During the oil shortage when Princeton extended the Christmas vacation by two weeks, the Boston alumni committee took advantage of Princeton undergraduates at home studying and brought a number of them together with a group of local candidates for what was scheduled to be a two-hour meeting. It went on an hour longer and ended then only because the facility they were in was closing.

"What can an old grad tell a kid these days?" a committeeman wondered. "They really only understand one another."

High schools might be doing a real service in college preparation by scheduling visits to the school by their recent graduates, currently in college, for talks with juniors and seniors. Just seeing someone who has settled into a college is reassuring and gives young people the confidence in their capacity to make the right decisions.

The admissions procedure at the most selective level is lengthy and complicated. It is like an elaborate chemical process that converts raw material (students) into a product (the class), leaving some blight on the landscape (in the form of disappointed leftovers, who, however, can be converted into the product of another college). Students are not the only ones confronted with decisions. Every selective admissions judgment is a decision. Some judgments are in effect executions.

"We do make mistakes," Clara Ludwig, dean of admissions at Mount Holyoke *admits*. (A witty admissions officer at Choate School once said that an admissions man should be careful what he admits!)

2

College of Your Choice

In 1965, Alden Dunham, then director of admission at Princeton, sounded the manifesto of the new era in selective admissions when he wrote about the need for "diversity" in the composition of the student body: "For the class itself a key word is diversity. . . . the more diverse the student body, the more vibrant and stimulating the residential experience of all." ("A Look at Princeton Admissions," *Princeton Alumni Weekly,* January 19, 1965.)

"Diversity" ought to be emblazoned over college gates in the way *Liberté, Egalité, Fraternité* are emblazoned over public buildings in France.* Another French slogan would also apply, Napoleon's "Careers open to talent." Diversity sounds the death knell for homogeneity at Princeton, Wellesley and a number of other colleges of a once exclusive character. It is now possible for any student to dream about going to an Ivy League college whatever his social status, religion or racial characteristics.

The increase in applications to selective colleges may in part be attributed to the new openness that diversity implies (a huge population jump is obviously a chief cause, as well as the hope that from

*"The most universal quality is diversity." Montaigne (quoted by Daniel Boorstin, *The Democratic Experience*).

selective colleges it will be easier to scale the walls of the graduate schools). Certainly to an egalitarian-minded youth it is important that the student "mix" on campus be as broad as possible. A candidate for an Ivy League college expressed these reservations: "I've heard it's too homogeneous. Who wants to spend four years seeing the same kinds of people all the time?"

But suppose, an alumnus of the homogeneous era asked, the same group of people is highly likable? The candidate replied, "That would be okay, but I'm afraid they might *not* be likable." The alumnus then proceeded to demonstrate that while he thought homogeneity a good thing, in fact his alma mater had vastly altered and you could now change types of friends every six months there if you were so minded.

Diversity is no Princeton monopoly. Columbia goes out of its way to reassure candidates for admission that it plays no favorites:

> Social snobbery, if practiced by a college, would occur in its Admissions Office. First, special favors would be granted to those whose fathers were alumni. Second, it would look kindly upon those whose parents graduated from similar institutions, or were similar in status. . . . Other means of selectively dispensing privileges are more subtle: To particular secondary schools, a college may leak (actually pour!) early word on admissions. . . . Each of the above forms of snobbery, however, has been drastically curtailed, and not simply by Columbia. Five years ago, an alumnus' son would be admitted to the College, and told of his admission well before other applicants, provided he met minimal academic standards. This is no longer so. [Report to Headmasters, Principals and Counselors, 1973]

Diversity at places whose character was determined by alumni children, certain private secondary schools and the upper-middle-class status of student families now makes it more difficult to distinguish which college is best for which student. In the old days a Hotchkiss boy did not agonize, he chose Yale. Now Yale accepts more high school than prep school graduates. Two-thirds of the Ivy League and Seven Sisters students were trained in private schools until the fifties (exceptions are MIT and Mount Holyoke where high school students have traditionally predominated). Now two-thirds in these colleges are trained in public high schools. This is the chief source of diversity. But the private schools themselves have in many instances become as diversified as the selective colleges. The more heavily endowed schools have been able to give scholarships to minority students and to others they believe profit from their intensive kind of education. The ABC program ("A Better Chance"), which began at Dartmouth and is carried on by many colleges, provides a summer of training for minority students destined for private school in the fall. So the diversity the selective colleges seek can also come from private schools now.

"A class is sought that is diverse in many ways—in both academic and nonacademic talents and interests, vocational goals, social and economic and geographical (including foreign) backgrounds—all within a spectrum of academic competence that ranges from good to superb." It is Dunham's definition, but few selective colleges would quarrel with it.

If, then, all the selective colleges seek broadly the same kind of student body, how is a candidate to decide which is to be the college of his choice? The answer is irrational in many cases. One girl told the admission office that she decided on Wellesley because she liked its lake. Aaron Leminick, dean of the graduate school at Princeton, said to 40 visiting candidates: "If you're admitted to the freshman class, your decision to come here or go to Harvard or any place else will be made by your heart not your head. It's a gut decision." Leminick's own son chose Harvard. Clark Kerr, former president of UC-Berkeley, considers choosing a college to be a highly emotional proposition little guided by finding answers to thoughtful questions.

Basis for Choice

On what basis, for example, do so many students decide to go to college relatively close to home? One reason is that they tend to do what others do. In the film *American Graffiti,* the central figure had a terrible time deciding to break away from California to go to an Eastern college on a scholarship, a very believable situation. At an Eastern or Midwestern suburban high school there is nothing unusual about the top students applying to selective colleges. In central city schools and rural schools there may be pressures on bright students *not* to apply to selective colleges.

From the point of view of selective colleges this is a loss; but from that of the colleges such students go to, it is a blessing. It will be a sad day indeed if the selective colleges should succeed in attracting *all* the country's top students. "They take the cream of this area every year," one Midwestern college president has complained of the selective Eastern colleges. The only limit on this skimming-off process is the relatively small enrollments of the top colleges.

Competition for students among colleges, very selective and less so, is fierce, and what this does to the good student's ego is not always healthy. It is not beneficial either to the sense of honor of some candidates, who string alumni along by showing great interest in a college that is not the college of their choice, but which they are anxious to be accepted by as a backup in case they are rejected elsewhere. This happens particularly at the upper levels of selectivity among students applying to Harvard/Radcliffe *and* Princeton, Yale, Dartmouth, Vassar, etc. They want Harvard/Radcliffe, but oh how they plight their troth to Old Nassau!

The "overlapping" of applications obliges selective colleges to take out insurance by admitting two or more applicants for every available place, because half the class goes some place else! This is one of the most disconcerting aspects of college admissions. Here are admissions officers carefully creating a freshman class but never sure *which* class will actually enroll. Harvard comes out the best in this game: only 17 percent of those accepted have the gall to turn Harvard down. There are big universities getting as many as 15,000 applications for a class of 3,000! And they must accept 7,500 in order to get the enrollment they want. Some selective colleges enroll less than half of those they accept.

Where selectivity is not a factor the situation can be simply ludicrous. One Florida college has advertised on the radio that it will give a full scholarship to anyone bringing two paying students to the campus. "Head hunters" charge up to $500 for every freshman they can enroll. But beyond these undignified practices are the solicitations by some very respectable colleges either desperate for enrollment or hungry for top students.

The president of a West Coast college unknown to South Kent, a boarding school in Connecticut, appeared in person one day and made such a strong impression he got five of the seniors to sign up on the spot. This is as valuable to a college as a half-million-dollar endowment. What is a good college like Antioch, founded in 1852, to do when its enrollment falls by 50 percent? The frightening prospect of colleges folding for lack of students is causing excellent institutions to become marketers of their wares and they use the skills of advertising and direct-mail experts to organize campaigns to reach thousands of high school seniors.

Naturally they avoid junk mail, so it costs as much as 32 cents to mail some material to a surprised National Merit semi-finalist, who is urged to consider Georgia Tech, Michigan State and other colleges he may or may not have heard of. The College Board has a service for helping colleges build enrollment. This can be done by increasing the dispersal of applications. *Half of all applications are received by only 10 percent of the four-year colleges.*

In brief, there is a buyer's market in almost all of the private colleges, and where there is a seller's market the college can select those it wants from among its applicants. Calvin B. T. Lee, chancellor of the University of Maryland, Baltimore County, told us: "The selective process is fundamentally a mechanism for responding to market conditions. Where there is greater demand than seats, the selective process is necessary in order to screen the kind of students which the college desires."

The image of the marketplace is not just a metaphor. College admissions offices, including those of selective colleges, are taking part in large "fairs" where several hundred representatives meet several thousand potential candidates. At the 1973 "College Night" at Catholic Memorial High in West Roxbury, Massachusetts, 144 colleges set up tables in the gym and cafeteria, and held sessions in classrooms. Harvard, Smith, Dartmouth, Princeton, Stanford and Notre Dame were mingled with local business colleges and others eager for any student with a high school diploma—or without.

In many cities large "fairs" are now being held annually embracing students in the metropolitan region. Will the day come when students are invited like potential buyers of real estate for an all-expenses-paid trip to the campus? It is already upon us. Princeton and other Ivy League colleges are bringing candidates by bus for a day or for an overnight stay in a dormitory. The candidate pays for his meals, but the bus is paid for by an alumni group. It is indeed the best way for a candidate to look over a college, talk to lots of students, eat with them, go to classes, the theater, a basketball game, even work out in the gym if they want to. In the seller's market you have to sell hard because even at selective colleges one out of two accepted into the freshman class is not buying.

Spreading Selectivity

Selective colleges are few in number but selectivity of some kind is widespread. More than 700 colleges require candidates to take the College Board tests and another 500 require that they take tests of the American College Testing Program. Public colleges particularly have become selective because of pecking orders within state systems. The student rejected by Berkeley is offered a place in another branch of the University of California.

CCNY, the old Harvard of the proletariat in New York City that used to take only the city's top students, is now part of the City University of New York, which has open enrollment, and this obliges CCNY to dip lower into the barrel. But there is a limit here too and CCNY remains selective to the extent that you must have a C average and rank in the upper half of your senior high school class to be admitted. Out-of-state applications for the University of New Hampshire are five times greater than the number of places. Chapel Hill, the main campus of the University of North Carolina, has always been able to choose good out-of-state students because of the demand to get in, and so have the University of Michigan and the University of Wisconsin.

James Reston has contrasted the present situation with his own day in the twenties when he drove his flivver over to the University of Illinois in Urbana and registered *in September*. There was no need to *apply* and there was therefore no admissions office, only a registrar. No college today could just sit and wait like a storekeeper for the customers to show up. Administration is too complex and costly. It is essential to know how dormitory space will be allotted, how many people will be eating in dining halls, what courses students think they will sign up for. A drop of as little as 5 percent in enrollment can put a crimp in the budget.

Public and private colleges alike must operate at maximum efficiency in these inflationary times when the price of meat or heating fuel can soar in the middle of the year and throw out all the carefully planned calculations of financial experts. Hence the pressure by the colleges on students to name the college of their choice. An admissions officer from a selective Eastern college who became director of the admissions office of a good private college in the Midwest had to admit to his former colleagues that he nearly went out of his mind during the summer when they were vacationing. He had to fill a freshman class and he was not allowed to lower standards to do so. Recruiting is a difficult task.

Good Colleges Go Begging for Freshmen

When a college has to go seeking students, it might appear at first glance to have gone down hill. But frequently nothing has happened to the college at all. In fact it may have an improved faculty, new programs and an enlarged library and still have difficulty filling its class rolls. But market conditions are negative. The location may be against the college. The Midwest is particularly out of favor with young people, while the Boston area is particularly "in" these days. New England in general is popular because of winter sports, Cape Cod and proximity to swinging Boston.

A college may be considered too square. Imagine an admissions director talking to high school students in Connecticut about his Midwestern college and saying slyly: "Yes, we do have some drug taking on our campus," in order to give the impression that it was not old fashioned or too traditional!

But probably the greatest cause of declining enrollment is the low tuitions of public colleges, which run from UMass's mere $300 to UCal's $1,000, as compared with $2,000 to $3,400 in the private colleges. Boston University, a private institution, reports a growing number of third-year transfers from the community colleges. This in effect allows a student to get four years' education for the price of two.

It is no wonder that BU's president, Dr. John R. Silber, is one of the most vocal proponents of an increased tuition at the public colleges, on the grounds that the taxpayer is currently subsidizing the education of middle-class students who could afford to pay more. Silber would like to see much higher public tuition for those who can pay, and with some of this money he would create public scholarships for those who are needy.

The influential Committee for Economic Development, a business-supported enlightened research organization, urged in 1973 that public tuitions be doubled around the nation in order to reduce the attrition of private-college enrollments. The Carnegie Commission for Higher Education has warned that many private colleges will collapse if the present trends that rob them of precious student fees continue.

The selective colleges now fear that in the long run they will end up with student bodies composed of a majority of affluent students and a smaller group of scholarship students, while the great middle group goes to the public colleges. A boy admitted on a scholarship to Yale figured he could save his family $300 a year by going to his local community college.

"We just do not know how many students are not applying because of our higher costs," says Clara Ludwig, director of admissions at Mount Holyoke. The wealthiest colleges are able to admit their students regardless of their financial status, and then distribute financial aid afterward, but the mere thought of the rich Ivy League is enough to discourage some impoverished students of great merit from considering these places. This is why it is necessary to recruit such young people by actively seeking them out, particularly with the help of alumni groups that contact remote high schools and look for unusual candidates, who are persuaded to apply.

High schools themselves do not always encourage application to selective colleges. "*You* apply to Mount Holyoke?" a guidance counselor in a rural high school in Pennsylvania said to a bright girl. She ignored him and was accepted. "You can't afford it," he then sneered, and she could not, for Mount Holyoke can afford to put only 17 percent of its girls on scholarship (another 25 percent obtain financial aid from other sources). But her mother got a job and the girl is in the college of her choice despite the discouragement of a narrow-minded counselor. The thought of students going to selective colleges stirs envy and feelings of insecurity in some school personnel, who may have yearned themselves for such an education.

Blue-collar parents too are sometimes without ambition and become upset at the thought of their children learning more than they know, and are fearful of borrowing in order to finance an education. Thus, they actually discourage a school's attempt to help their children capitalize on their scholastic potential.

A New England high school principal trying to increase the percentage of those going to college found that it was a losing battle because of parental discouragement and the belief that you should not be pretentious or grow too big for your breeches. He has moved on to a more middle-class school.

For at least 50 percent of high school seniors it is unnecessary to make a case for going to college. Yet despite the demand for selective college places, not all who are qualified to apply are persuaded that they should do so. For one thing the selective colleges are largely a sectional phenomenon. Most are located in the Northeast.

Mythological Pressure Cooker?

John O'Hearne, a former member of Columbia's admissions staff and now regional director of the College Board in Austin, Texas, calls the mystique of selective Eastern colleges "a mythological pressure cooker" that has little impact in the Southwest. Scouts from the Eastern colleges do succeed in drawing off some of the top students from the big cities, but most want to go to "the state university," meaning the University of Texas in Austin. Because this has become the most desired campus, it too is selective and admits the brighter students, and sends the others to branch campuses.

"Harvard is respected out here, but it is not so important to go there," O'Hearne has noticed. In the thirties some Western families sent their daughters East to Smith and Wellesley for a year or two, and the reports of marriages in the local press would state that "Mary Lou attended Smith College and graduated from the State University."

A very successful Seattle businessman whose father went to Stanford elected to go to the University of Washington because there he would meet the people he would be collaborating with for a lifetime. He was an honors student and could have gone away to college, but doubted the benefits he would derive in another state.

Mary Ellen Ames, director of admission for Wellesley College, tells of visiting a Nebraska High School where a boy she got chatting with said: "You won't get any girls from around here. Chicago is as far as they go. Say, you don't *talk* Eastern. You sound okay." Which is a variant on Senator Sam Ervin's putdown of a North Carolinian who tried to smear him by saying he was a Harvard Law School graduate. "Yeah, but I don't *look* like one," Ervin replied.

Why should anyone bother to get into the competition for admission to the selective colleges when they can get a good education at any of hundreds of the 1,400 four-year colleges? When Ernest Martin Hopkins was president of Dartmouth, he wrote that "the 'prestige colleges,' however influential, represent but a small segment of our great structure of American higher education," and called the Land Grant colleges "the greatest medium of higher education ever devised in the public interest." (Quoted by Frederic A. Birmingham in *The Ivy League Today,* 1961.)

Mary Ellen Ames tells candidates that her college offers "a different educational experience," not a better one. This is typical New England understatement. It is perhaps true that you can learn just as much in one college as in any other. Maryland chancellor, Calvin Lee, holding two Columbia degrees, doubts that you can necessarily learn more at Harvard than elsewhere. It is what he calls "the halo effect" that is conferred on the graduates of the selective colleges that keeps their prestige high.

But whence this halo effect? Of 99 new members of the American Academy of Arts and Sciences in 1973, 50 are attached to so-called prestige colleges. If their faculties are not the best in every respect, they are largely unsurpassed. And the quality of their student bodies has to be higher than on nonselective campuses, which means that social and intellectual stimulus among undergraduates is greater.

"You never hear anyone say anything stupid there," a Radcliffe freshman told her family at Christmas vacation. Harvard claims that it loses no more than *1 per cent* of any class nowadays—that is, 99 percent of freshmen (excluding any who die) finish with a baccalaureate degree. At some colleges the attrition rate runs as high as 50 percent!

Whether the selective colleges should claim credit for the steadfastness of their students is a question. Probably the students are motivated to pile up a record of consistency. They look on transferring as pointless unless they find, as one Wellesley transfer to Princeton found, that she wanted to try for the famous Woodrow Wilson School of Public and International Affairs, of which there is no equivalent at Wellesley.

The point is that these colleges know how to select students who want to stay put, students who will fit the place and enjoy it. There is no question that the selective college campuses are happy campuses —perhaps a more specifically meaningful word to describe them is exhilarated.

The Question of Quality

Faculty who have taught at both a selective and a nonselective campus are loathe to make any statement suggesting that students on the less prestigious campus are being shortchanged educationally. A look at the colleges of the justices of the United States Supreme Court or of those in the *Directory of Directors* is convincing proof that the country's leadership is not dominated by Ivy Leaguers. A Rutgers professor who graduated from and taught at Princeton will only say that he must now deal with more students of lower aptitudes. A professor who resigned from Princeton to teach at Boston University remarked that she could give low grades at Princeton without expecting any protest, while her students at BU who are less diligent give her a hard time if they get less than a B.

The faculties of the most prestigious colleges are full of men and women who did their undergraduate work elsewhere, including state teachers colleges. The president of Princeton, William Bowen, spent his undergraduate years at Denison University in his home state of Ohio, and came to Princeton as a graduate student.

Clearly, the answer to whether the selective colleges are better than others provokes only foggy answers from sensible people. Claims of superiority are better left to dictators and auto manufacturers. When a foolhardy Columbia man wrote an article for *Fortune* called "The Natural Superiority of the Ivy League," he did not endear himself to Ivy Leaguers.

David Evans, a Black on the Harvard admissions staff, tells how at first Black students at Harvard were taken in by prep-school boys who looked as though they were loafing while they got As. It seemed to the Blacks that these fellows were just superbrilliant, when in fact they were really working very hard, but *secretly*.

"You'd be surprised how many faculty here pull the same thing. It's just not fashionable to be caught working hard at Harvard." Black students are now advised to work hard because that really is what is going on at Harvard despite appearances.

Probably the relative educational merits of American colleges can be summed up by saying that the selective colleges are at least as good as the rest. Their distinction arises from a consistent level of excellence to be found in their faculties, student bodies and facilities. The record is very reassuring to employers and graduate schools as they assess candidates. All of this is costly to come by, so tuitions are higher at the selective colleges, but endowments and gifts contributed by alumni, foundations and corporations are also higher at these colleges because of the recognition of their qualities.

Inevitably myths and resentment swirl around these institutions. Some unadmirable values have grown out of the excellences represented by places like Vassar, Cornell, Swarthmore. "I don't care which of these colleges she goes to," said a Midwestern father at Bryn Mawr, ticking off the Ivies and Seven Sisters, "so long as she doesn't go where *I* went."

The prestige often means more to the parents than to the students, though in fairness to parents it should be said that probably few of them would feel as strongly as the Harvard undergraduate recently overheard telling a friend: "If I die tomorrow I will have a distinguished obituary. They will write, 'He was a Harvard man!' " To be able to say, "My boy is at Yale," must reflect positively on a parent, but some parental anxiety is painful. A Princeton admission officer was told by a father: "It's like reliving my own life. I never went to prep school, but my boy's there. Now he's got to make Princeton. Don't you say anything to discourage him. [*Pause.*] And don't you dare tell him I talked to you."

Any college is more than a name. Derek Bok, president of Harvard, reporting to his Board of Overseers for 1971–72, said:

> After fifteen years at Harvard as a student and professor of law, I thought that I was generally familiar with the College. But a detached

familiarity is very different from the immediate awareness of the College that one achieves by working directly with its problems, its personalities, and its enormous range of activities.

So whoever scales the Ivy walls successfully · will find himself wandering through a maze of intellectual and social gardens gradually gaining a detached familiarity with a college, which if it was not *the* college of his choice, is liable rapidly to become so.

3

Spreading Ivy: The Rise of Selectivity

The extensive planting of ivy at the base of college buildings has led to a veneration of that vine that is not universal. Two witty Oxford debaters touring American colleges a few years ago, Jonathan Aitken and Michael Beloff, said in a book, *A Short Walk on the Campus:* "To an American, ivy symbolizes genuine old age which *per se* is to be admired. To a British gardener ivy signifies the destruction by slow suffocation of trees and shrubs."

The unofficial recognition of ivy as the symbol of upper-class higher education occurred in the 1930s, far from any plantings, on the fourth floor of the *New York Herald Tribune.* The sports editor, Stanley Woodward, heard a colleague, Caswell Adams, use the phrase "ivy colleges," and began employing it in his columns. The ambiguity of Woodward's usage perfectly expressed the mixed feelings the general public had about Yale and such places, where college athletics had first developed.

With the growth of football in the Big Ten, the smaller Eastern colleges which had played the game much longer were not in the same competitive class. The Ivy colleges were the weak sisters, the gentlemen colleges that did not play rough Notre Dame or Pitt, and seldom if ever went to the Rose Bowl. In this way many readers could satisfy their annoyance at those "snob colleges for prep school boys." Later Woodward was to say, "Everyone hates the Ivy League."

Before the formation in 1954 of the Ivy League of eight colleges that competed athletically (Harvard, Yale, Princeton, Dartmouth, Cornell, Columbia, Brown, Penn), Woodward meant by Ivy colleges the private colleges in a rather broad sense, including Hamilton, Bates, Colgate, Lehigh, Swarthmore, Stanford, Duke and so on, as well as some state institutions like Rutgers, Virginia and Chapel Hill. It just so happens that many of those colleges which never were very difficult to get into are now able to choose the students they want, although none has the selective advantages of Harvard, Yale, Princeton and Dartmouth—and Harvard has it all over everybody.

By Harvard it is understood now that Radcliffe is also implied; Yale and Princeton have gone co-ed, and so has Vassar. The most selective single-sex colleges now are Wellesley, Smith, Mount Holyoke, Barnard, Bryn Mawr, Amherst and Haverford. Harvard has shifted dormitories around so that the Cliffies now sleep in the Yard, and all students study under one faculty. But Radcliffe retains its own president and its own admissions staff. The change which came in 1972 is known as the "nonmerger agreement," a typical Harvard arrangement.

Since the *Herald Tribune* sports desk did not extensively cover field hockey at Barnard or rowing at Wellesley, in the male chauvinism of those times women's colleges never were stamped with the Ivy brand. The equivalent of the Ivy League were the Seven Sisters (Radcliffe, Wellesley, Smith, Vassar, Barnard, Mount Holyoke, Bryn Mawr). Pembroke has merged with Brown. Other women's colleges that might have been Ivy equivalents if Woodward had recognized such a possibility include Skidmore, Sarah Lawrence, Sweet Briar, Wheaton, Scripps, Hollins, Jackson (a college of Tufts University), Simmons, Bennington, Mills, Sarah Lawrence and Goucher.

It would be a mistake to assume that longevity alone confers the distinction of caste and class that originally was associated with ivy. Of the Seven Sisters only Mount Holyoke was founded before the Civil War, and some very old colleges are not as generally esteemed as Duke (1924), Stanford (1890) or Chicago (1890). Brandeis (1948) is one of the most selective colleges. What is at work in these cases of quick recognition is a great deal of money used to build not social exclusiveness but academic accomplishment.

Genuine scholarship has replaced refinement, manners and exclusivity as the hallmark of today's selective colleges. Plutocracy has been largely supplanted by meritocracy. Harold Hodgkinson, a psychology professor at Berkeley, has added one more step beyond meritocracy by noting that college education has progressed from aristocratic privilege to meritocratic reward to egalitarian *right*. Frank Miller of the National Association of Independent Schools, a former headmaster of Hackley School in Tarrytown, New York, said he watched certain colleges reverse the composition of their student bodies after World War II: "They had heterogeneous intelligence levels and a homogeneous economic level. Now they have heterogeneous economic levels and a homogeneous intelligence level." A bit exaggerated but not a bad encapsulation of an evolution and development on prestige campuses. Ironically, though, this laudable shift in admissions policies has made more colleges more exclusive than ever.

Selectivity Is Not New

It is said that selectivity is a post-World-War-II phenomenon, but this is only relatively true. Selectivity has become more visible because of the enormous rise in college enrollments. As Daniel J. Boorstin notes in *The Democratic Experience* (1973): "While entrance to high school was automatic, or even compulsory, entrance to nearly all colleges remained selective." He was speaking of the late nineteenth century, but from the beginning, when Harvard was founded in 1636, the process of selection was determined by the nature of things. The early colonial colleges were created to train men for the ministry. Although democratic ideas might flourish in these modest colleges— James Madison was a graduate of Princeton, for instance, and Congress sat briefly in Nassau Hall—they were observed by Benjamin Franklin to be exclusive and Old World in character even after they expanded their purpose to include the training of lawyers. Harvard was modeled on Emmanuel College, Cambridge University. Its classical curriculum did not seem to Franklin to offer by itself sufficient higher learning for a republic that would need science and technology for its development. The requirement for admission to Harvard in the 17th century read:

When any scholar is able to read Tully or such like classical Latin author ex tempore, and make and speake true Latin in verse and prose suo (ut aiunt) marte [without any assistance whatever], and decline perfectly the paradigms of nouns and verbes in ye Greeke tongue, then may hee bee admitted into ye college, nor shall any claime admission before such qualification.

There was another qualification in the beginning: citizenship in Massachusetts Bay Colony. And to be a citizen you had to be a Calvinist. When the severity of Calvinism was challenged by Harvard liberals, some ultras departed for New Haven to found Yale in 1701.

To Latin and Greek, which very few boys were trained in, mathematics was added as an entrance requirement. In 1760, the Harvard board of trustees voted that ". . . all who are admitted to the Freshman class shall be acquainted with Vulgar Arithmetic. . . ."

Gradually, after the colonies gained their independence, there was a growth in new colleges that by the Civil War had become cancerous. "By 1860 Ohio had more institutions of higher learning than the German Empire," wrote Merle Conti and Roderick Nash in *Philanthropy in the Shaping of American Higher Education.** Of America's 800 colleges at that time only 180 survived. Such a flourishing of dubious institutions, most of them denominational, made the older colleges more determined to maintain standards, and this seemed to call for more classical preparation, so that by 1900 more Latin and Greek than ever was required for admission.

To meet the needs of the Gilded Era after the Civil War when so much new wealth was piling up, prep schools were formed to train the sons of the rich, particularly in Latin and Greek. An exclusive system was pretty well established before 1900 that conveyed wealthy boys from St. Paul's, Groton, Lawrenceville, Choate to Harvard, Brown, Cornell, etc. Likewise, girls' "finishing schools" began to send their more ambitious graduates to the new women's colleges like Radcliffe, though it was widely held that college was too difficult for delicate maidens. One woman who died of tuberculosis in her late twenties was said to have ruined her health studying at Radcliffe years before. College at the time touched few men and very few women. In

*New Brunswick, N.J.: Rutgers University Press, 1965.

1900, only 4 percent of those of college age went to college, and only 31 percent of the very rich were college graduates.

Indeed, the nineteenth-century colleges did not have much "relevance" to the new industrial America: not until 1844 were algebra and geometry required for admission. In 1870, the University of Michigan added American history to its requirements, and English composition in 1878. Science was so weak in secondary schools that Yale's new Sheffield Scientific School, opened in 1873, had no science requirement for admission.

Because of the limited amount of classics taught in most private and public secondary schools (the first public secondary school was Boston's English High, opened in 1821), colleges trimmed their sails and admitted unqualified candidates. For a number of years they offered a variety of degrees, chiefly the Ph.B. (Bachelor of Philosophy), but also the B.S. (Bachelor of Science) and even a B.L. (Bachelor of Letters). The B.A. stood out by comparison even though students taking other degrees might have more scientific training for the new era. Eventually Harvard, which gave the B.A. and the B.S., had the good sense to lead the way in liberalizing its admissions policy by recognizing that the high schools teaching history, science and modern languages were preparing capable students without the benefit of the classics.

In 1881, 30 percent of Harvard's freshmen were from public schools and Greek was destined to go the way of Hebrew, which became a specialty for the clergy only. Latin, though, was required by the "exclusive" colleges until the 1930s, and thus continued to keep most of the lower-class students from applying for admission. Latin just never seemed to catch on with blue-collar children.

An exception occurred briefly after the Civil War in the South, when some of the freed slaves determined to have their children educated. Their aspirations were mocked, of course, by the whites, who loved to tell the story of the mother screaming at her daughter, "Mandy, has yo did yo Greek?"

The Morrill Act of 1862 made possible the state Land Grant colleges, inspired by Jonathan Turner, a Yale graduate. He wanted working people on the farms and in the factories to have access to higher education, but without the classical curriculum, which was of no use to a man wanting to improve his crops or make things by machine. It was the beginning of mass higher education in practical subjects that required no prerequisites, and admission was open to courses at Kansas State such as Cabinet Making, Scroll-Sawing and Telegraphy. By 1926, enrollment in Land Grant institutions had reached 400,000.

Private vs. Public Colleges

The distinction between public and private colleges became more evident with the creation in 1901 of the College Entrance Examination Board to administer uniform written entrance examinations for colleges who were having trouble administering them individually. No public colleges were among the Board's members because entrance to them was open to any high school diploma holder. This did not mean that there was great competition to enter Yale or Harvard in those days, but it did mean that a candidate had to have passing grades to qualify. A boy could be an average student at Exeter and get into Harvard. A third of the early candidates examined by the College Board were high school seniors. Until World War II, two-thirds of the student bodies of the prestige colleges were private school products.

As America grew rich and powerful, class lines deepened and immigration intensified the sense in the prestige colleges of being apart from the new democracy. This might justify a pride in institutions that were clearly outstanding academically, but the attitudes not only of the millionaires but of the prosperous middle classes and even the not prosperous faculty could be arrogant and vicious.

It seemed important in the early decades of this century for some to go to the "right" college. Rousseau remarked that what counts for such people is not the difference of quality, but the quality of difference. A man who truly understood this was F. Scott Fitzgerald of the Class of 1917 at Princeton, and he revealed it among other places in a trivial short story, "Forging Ahead," which appeared in the *Saturday Evening Post* in 1929. In it a sixteen-year-old Midwest boy named Basil Duke Lee has just learned from his mother that a financial reverse makes it impossible for her to send him to Yale.

His heart tumbled into his stomach; the future, always glowing like a comfortable beacon ahead of him, flared up in glory and went out. His mother shivered, and then emphatically shook her head.

"You'll just have to make up your mind to go to the state university."

"Gosh!" Basil said.

This genteel expletive hardly revealed Basil's true feelings, which Fitzgerald knew so well.

But first, as a sort of gateway to that deep, richer life, there was Yale. The name evoked the memory of a heroic team backed up against its own impassable goal in the crisp November twilight, and later, of half a dozen immaculate noblemen with opera hats and canes standing at the Manhattan Hotel bar. And tangled up with its triumphs and rewards, its struggles and glories, the vision of the inevitable, incomparable girl.

Forced to register at the state university, Basil meets a Japanese named Utsonomia who has turned down chances to go to Harvard, Yale and Princeton because it is "more strong here. More peasants come, with strength and odor of ground." Shortly the Lees recover their fortune and Basil goes to Yale. He also gets the girl in the story, but obviously this is incidental to his passion for Old Eli. The story is ambiguous enough to allow *Saturday Evening Post* readers who went to state universities to feel that Basil is a sap and that Utsonomia is right when he says, "Here I get to know real American peoples." Fitzgerald had a different idea of what "real American peoples" are.

Fitzgerald has been blamed for giving Princeton the reputation of a country club in his first novel, *This Side of Paradise,* published in 1920. New York's swinging mayor, Jimmy Walker, once said in criticism of censorship that he had never known a girl who was ruined by a book, and certainly no book can ruin the name of a university. The critic and scholar Edmund Wilson and the poet John Peale Bishop were classmates of Fitzgerald, and most of the student body was more serious about studying than Fitzgerald, who had to take his entrance exams twice to be admitted and then flunked out because he spent too much time with the Triangle Club, the musical-comedy organization formed by Booth Tarkington. Fitzgerald later gave the twenties one of that era's epithets, "the Jazz Age."

Football and Fraternities

If Fitzgerald's fiction ignored the serious side of academic life, so did many students in the Ivy colleges between 1900 and 1960. And the superficial values of exclusivity, of belonging, belonging to clubs, fraternities, secret societies, of going to house parties, of wearing letter sweaters (turned inside out), club ties, rings and the like, of creating prep school clubs within colleges, all this institutionalizing of social status spread to other campuses as more and more people went to college. Eventually there were 150 fraternities and 65 sororities, some with as many as 100 chapters.

Fitzgerald scarcely created the football hero. One of the earliest assertions of women's rights came in 1885 when the Yale-Harvard game was transferred from the Polo Grounds in New York to New Haven. No nice girl would think of being seen in the rowdy precincts of Coogan's Bluff, but it became fashionable for girls to attend football games at New Haven and cheer on the gladiators. The Yale-Harvard game was one of *the* social events of the fall, and football took a turn for the violent, to such an extent that in 1905 the president of the United States, Theodore Roosevelt, had to convene a White House conference with the athletic directors of Harvard, Yale and Princeton to change the rules and prevent further deaths on the gridiron (18 players had been killed that year).

The older selective colleges that now deplore the commercialization of college football were the first to build vast stadiums in the style of the Roman empire, a practice quickly taken up by the state universities. The Harvard Stadium went up in 1901 and had no trouble packing in 50,000 spectators. Smaller private colleges like Williams and Amherst imitated Yale and Harvard in their athletic rivalry (Wesleyan was the first team to use a forward pass—against Yale), but could not compete for urban crowds, who filled the Yale Bowl or Palmer Stadium, arriving in special trains and wandering among the wealthy folk with their limousines and Stutz Bearcats. Football made the Ivy colleges visible to a large public, a fact that other colleges caught onto as they sought to increase enrollment by publicizing their football teams.

Prohibition and the boom in Wall Street added to the glamour of Ivy men, who sported hip-pocket flasks at football games and made fortunes selling bonds. They were a minority, but they set the tone of exclusivity. The automobile increased the giddiness of college students, and Princeton was finally forced to ban cars not only because they cluttered up the town, but because of accidents and the tendency, as Dean Radcliffe Heermance remarked, of "extending the campus to East Orange and Atlantic City." Jazz plus prohibition equaled "roadhouses" in the suburbs, and nightclubs and speakeasies where college students learned to drink in the cities.

The society pages of Eastern metropolitan papers ensured continuing publicity for the right families in the exclusive colleges by always mentioning the groom's college as well as the bride's if she had indeed gone to college, and this practice continues. Elections to clubs, secret societies and fraternities were faithfully reported in the Eastern press. As recently as 1960 an observer counted 46 Ivy men in 76 weddings reported by the *New York Times* in the month of June. As literacy became universal and Americans read papers and magazines every day, the Ivy college was frequently before the public, who were conditioned to perceive Ivy men and their Vassar or Barnard consorts as a sort of aristocracy. By 1950, it is estimated that half of the very rich men going to college went to Ivy colleges.

"Until 1950," says Bruce McClelland, headmaster of Lawrenceville, "the Ivies depended on class for their student bodies and for their support." Selectivity was possible in the first half of the century for the same reason it is now: there was a surplus of applicants, but nowhere near as large as today. As the plutocracy grew, it sent its children to private schools and hoped they would be admitted to the "better colleges." But not all made it.

In 1924, Dr. William Thayer, headmaster of St. Mark's School, warned his alumni: "The colleges are being faced with the problem of undue pressure at their gates. They cannot give proper care or adequate instruction to the yearly increasing numbers that qualify for admission. Harvard, Yale and Princeton have announced proposed limitations of their freshman classes, by one or another method of selection."

Quotas?

By one or another method of selection! At the time, College Board results were never made known to anyone but the colleges themselves.

No candidate, no parent, no teacher knew how an exam had been marked. The son of an alumnus, a very rich applicant, an athlete, each might flunk and enter by "another method of selection." Did this include racial quotas? It is impossible to know because it is always denied, but except at Harvard there were not many Jews—certainly no more than 5 percent of enrollment—at Ivy colleges before World War II. Even Columbia in New York City was considered anti-Semitic in its admissions policies. And of course there were almost no Blacks in the exclusive colleges, again excepting Harvard, and even there but a handful. There were no Blacks at Princeton until 1948. Today about 10 percent of the student body at Princeton is Black and 20 percent is Jewish. But then we must remember that certain hotels, some even in Miami Beach, refused at the time to let any known Jew register.

One of the rare glimpses of the ugliness and myopia of anti-Semitism in higher education has been recently afforded us by the *Princeton Alumni Weekly,* the only college alumni weekly, incidentally, and one completely independent of the university administration. In "The Curious History of Physics at Princeton," John D. Davies wrote (October 2, 1973): "American academic institutions had been saddled with anti-Semitism. . . . Princeton had once fired an English instructor, the noted Horace Kallen, on the ground that he hadn't *told* the authorities he was Jewish; a Princeton professor today remembers being dismissed, as late as 1940, from an Eastern university because by his presence on the faculty he was holding out to Jewish graduate students a promise they did not in fact have."

In fairness to Princeton it should be noted that when anti-Semitism forced 2,000 German professors out of their posts, 100 came to the United States and Princeton eagerly hired several of them, and of course the Institute for Advanced Studies, independent of the university but closely allied in research, became the home of Einstein and later Oppenheimer. Now Princeton's admission office is one of the few colleges to issue a brochure on Jewish life on that campus.

Financial Aid Develops

If the Ivy colleges were largely attended by sons of the prosperous, the less well off whose sons went to high school could be admitted if they stood high in their classes and did well (it must be presumed) on their College Board exams. By 1940, about a third of the classes at Harvard, Yale and Princeton were made up of high school graduates, most of whom were very bright undergraduates. During the thirties, students on scholarships and "working their way through," as the phrase had it then, made up as much as 40 percent of a class at Dartmouth, Cornell and other Ivy colleges.

But financial-aid policies were radically different from those of today. They were essentially *mandarin.* That is to say, colleges looked for worthy students who could be expected to *rise,* to become leaders in some field, and possibly to become businessmen of note. Money was contributed for scholarships, in short, that would bring new blood into the Establishment, and the awards were made according to the level of performance: the brightest got the biggest amounts of money and the not-so-bright got smaller grants, plus interest-free loans, and had to spend more time on jobs. Thus a brilliant student got a full scholarship that allowed him or her the time to earn a Phi Beta Kappa key or a Rhodes Scholarship, while the student with lower grades was allowed less time to study and was likely to perform below his or her potential.

Some of these weaker students who went to graduate school on the GI Bill got considerably better marks than they had as undergraduates. Now financial aid is not considered a reward for excellence but a right to be accorded everyone who needs it. At those colleges with enough money, every applicant is admitted without regard to his or her financial situation, and only then is financial aid awarded. The amount of aid is never given by a college now on merit, only on the basis of need. Of course, *outside* the colleges there are many scholarships awarded on a competitive basis.

It is a fact that the selective colleges are today in a better position to grant aid to those who need it than are the less selective private colleges and state universities, which have low tuitions but not very much direct financial aid to give out.

The picture of superficial values that Fitzgerald painted, though accurate enough, is only one panel in what should be a series of pictures. The students who attended Ivy colleges in the past may have been essentially middle- and upper-middle-class, homogeneous in their tastes and not very democratic in outlook (at Bryn Mawr dormitory maids lived on the top floor!), but for all their drinking and status-seeking activities they were after all generally bright and very well trained before college. The gentleman's C that was widely accepted as a decent grade (at Princeton Adlai Stevenson got Cs) was probably worth at least a B today, and those who loafed were fired out. The prestige colleges did not get their reputations because they were a group of Union League Clubs that kept out undesirable members. They were prestigious academically, and their graduates went on to the best medical schools, the best law schools, the best business schools, the best engineering schools as well as into their father's insurance firms, brokerage houses and grain elevators.

Roots of Prestige

No one likes to acknowledge elitism as a fact of American life because it strikes the note of stratification leading to privilege, and so its existence is denied. The selective colleges have always trained an elite in the sense that their graduates generally go on to leadership of one sort or another. This opportunity was once limited to a single class; now it is "open to talent."

The old school tie helps to open doors, but the graduates of Dartmouth who have done so well in the advertising business, for example, have been men of great energy and originality. If the diplomatic corps had an unusual number of Ivy graduates, it was because those men, like George Kennan or our first envoy in China, David Bruce, or Henry Kissinger himself, were exceptional; and exceptional as well as ordinary people—well-rounded, they were called—attended these institutions to take advantage of their superb facilities and outstanding faculties.

Widener Library alone entitles Harvard to call itself one of the world's great seats of learning. There is no athletic facility quite like Princeton's Jadwin Cage, and Yale's art museum is worthy of a great city. What made and continues to make possible the provision of the best laboratory equipment, renowned scholars, unique living arrangements like the house system at Harvard is simply money. The selective colleges having attracted the most energetic as well as the most wealthy men and women, have retained their loyalty after graduation and continue to receive their benefactions in vast amounts.

By making certain colleges more substantially endowed, and largely in the twentieth century, philanthropists helped to establish them as selective institutions. Leaving aside the question whether you can learn more at Harvard than at Boston University (some studies seem to indicate you cannot), the attractiveness of Harvard is like that of Oxford or Cambridge. The undergraduate years consist of more than academic learning. They are a unique period of postadolescence in which the student is free for the first time in his life from the direct influence of family, school authorities and the pressures of the larger community, a period of intellectual and spiritual exploration. The Ivy campuses have consistently provided an unequaled climate for this kind of experience, which to some has an air of unreality, of the ivory tower, until they learn about an Archibald Cox who can move from the lecture platform into the heat of politics with more ease than most men of affairs.

The Impact of the GI Bill

The GI Bill of 1944 turned higher education into a truly democratic exercise by offering veterans generous subsidies to continue their education at any level. When World War II began there were only 1.5 million people in colleges and universities. When the Korean War began in 1950 there were 2.4 million, and by 1956 2.3 million veterans had attended college on the GI Bill of 1944. But there were others seeking college training simply because now they could afford it. The Depression was over and the Affluent Society was in the process of becoming the Credentials Society that it seems to be today. Furthermore, this new society could afford better high schools.

The selective colleges were not altogether prepared for the new situation. During the thirties a movement had begun to seek out high school students who would never have thought of applying to places like Dartmouth or Amherst. The New Deal, relying to a great extent for its expertise on professors from Ivy colleges, had made the faculties aware of the narrowness of the student body's composition, and the search for promising talent in small high schools where the curriculums were inadequate had paid off. There was no doubt that high school students could match prep school students, especially after freshman year when the superior training of the prep schools made it relatively easier to catch on to college work.

Enter the High School Applicants

So when large numbers of high school students began applying to the selective colleges in the 1950s, the colleges were rather embarrassed. Bruce McClelland, then on the admissions staff of Williams, recalls: "We really didn't know what to do, how to handle the problem of becoming *very* selective." The problem, of course, was that some of the high school applicants looked better than the prep school boys, the traditional clientele and presumably the ones who would keep these private colleges going in the future with generous gifts and bequests.

One solution was to expand undergraduate enrollment, and this was universally rejected by the selective colleges, making them increasingly selective, though this was hardly the purpose. The decisions not to expand very much were made on the ground that there is a size beyond which a student body in a liberal arts college becomes unwieldy and the quality of the small residential campus is lost. For Harvard apparently the maximum is under 6,000 excluding Radcliffe, and for Wellesley or Amherst it is under 2,000. Enrollments have expanded by 50 to 100 percent in some cases, but this amounts to a few hundred freshman places at most, and the increase in annual applications is in the thousands.

Another reason for not expanding was economic. The selective colleges are expensive to operate and they do everything in a first-class way. Their trustees are men of shrewdness and they know from their own business experience what the risks of capital expansion are during periods of affluence. These colleges are rich but their wealth is not unlimited. Harvard has $1.3 billion (more or less, depending on the state of the stock market) in endowment, but some of its schools struggle for money, including the famous Harvard Law School and the Harvard School of Business. No private institution is in the position of state systems like that of Massachusetts, which increased its operating budget for higher education by $40 million in 1974, a jump of 20 percent.

In view of the difficulties facing most private colleges, the refusal of the wealthier colleges to respond to the demand for admission by taking in all the students qualified to do their level of work is what makes them financially viable today, albeit some of them, like Columbia, are running a deficit. It also makes them exceptionally strong in undergraduate talent, because in the end they gradually have allowed their traditional feeders, the prep schools, to send the bulk of their graduates elsewhere. Only the top students in prep school or high school gain admission to what are called the "top colleges."

Apparently, though, there is always room at the top, because selective admissions have spread considerably in recent years. It is only logical that overlapping applications should create pecking orders among colleges and that those students rejected by their first choice, even though qualified to do the work, will try for what they believe to be an Ivy equivalent. Thus Tufts and Bowdoin appear by the numbers of their applicants to be just as selective as Yale, though some of their students will have been rejected by Yale. As we said earlier, about 40 colleges today can claim to be very selective; there will be arguments about just *how* selective some of them are.

Buttondown Goes West

One of the consequences of postwar affluence and the rise of selectivity in the Ivy colleges was the spread of the "Ivy look" in fashions, especially for men. The movies had tended to ignore the Ivy colleges and their types. Men wearing Brooks Brothers, J. Press and Langrock clothes rarely appeared on the silver screen, and when they did they were no heroes. In the fifties, *The Man in the Gray Flannel Suit* starred Gregory Peck, and Madison Avenue, something of an Ivy preserve, achieved national recognition as the center of marketing. It marketed its own image in the process.

Before the counterculture struck in the sixties, the buttondown collar had become a part of the middle-class male uniform, a quiet tribute to the Ivy men who had started wearing this shirt with their striped ties a generation earlier. Only the narrow bow tie never caught on. You can almost bet that a man wearing a not very neat, small bow tie is an Ivy Leaguer—Archibald Cox is a notable example.

In women's fashions something similar occurred with the spread of the Vassar look, the sweater and skirt, the discreet string of pearls, all of which gave girls a look of being upper-class but at the same time not "stuck up."

Against all of this decorous splendor the modern generation has revolted, and the Ivy campus to some now has "a revolting look." You certainly cannot tell a selective campus by the looks of its students. Old grads are unhappy that the Class of '76 bears so little resemblance to the Class of '36. Selective admissions has resulted, they say, in a very unnatural selection.

The Civil Rights Effect

Actually, what happened is that admissions practices reflected changes in American society as a whole. As more Americans in general went to college, it was inevitable that more high school students would go to selective colleges. As civil rights opened the way to fuller citizenship for minority groups, the colleges reached out to bring in minority groups as they had formerly reached out for the talented but not wealthy students in obscure high schools.

The war against Hitler had made anti-Semitism an embarrassing posture for any college. More Catholics applied to these colleges as the WASP grasp weakened, and that meant Irish, Italians, Lebanese (like Ralph Nader, a Princetonian). In fact any group was now welcome that had been excluded in the past, so that today there will be found on the selective campuses the whole spectrum of American democracy including American Indians and American Eskimos, as well, of course, as the new Utsonomias from abroad—foreign students never were excluded, and Black Africans got a better break than Black Americans.

To accommodate minorities, admissions policies were shaped to recognize that such applicants probably have weaker secondary school training than others, and so they were not forced to compete under a handicap. Ivy alumni often feel it is unfair to turn down a white student with better grades than a Black who is accepted. The strength of the selective colleges is such that they can make their alumni swallow this bitter pill as their institution's contribution to human justice, knowing that no white student rejected will have any difficulty getting a first-class education elsewhere. The Black student, at the same time, must compete for his place in the selective colleges with other Black students, and enters not as an academic cripple but one judged adequate to do the work, which most turn out to be.

The selective colleges in general rejected the option of taking minority groups as special students in need of tutoring. They thus avoided creating academic ghettos, although the minority students themselves have created their own social apartheid to a degree that dismays proponents of integration, Black and white. Having largely put an end to social selectivity on the campus in the form of clubs, fraternities and secret societies, college authorities now find that they can place Blacks and whites in the same dormitory room, but they cannot prevent Blacks from forming discrete social units that tend to exclude whites. The militancy of the sixties has been replaced by a tendency of Blacks to withdraw from the rest in the interest of promoting further racial gains through such unity.

The Growth of Objective Tests

The spread of selectivity has been made possible by the spread of the College Board exams. The public colleges have seen the light, although in the Midwest and Far West they prefer to use the services of the American College Testing Program, a rival to the College Entrance Examination Board, located in Iowa. The objective tests used experimentally in the thirties were immediately put into use during World War II, when the federal government turned to the College Board for testing military personnel and others.

In 1946, the written tests were abandoned and the Scholastic Aptitude Test and Achievement Tests that are scored mechanically took their place. And secrecy disappeared in 1956, so that young people today are like the civil servants of nineteenth-century Russia who wore uniforms with their rank on the sleeve. Board scores have yet to be tatooed on the arm, but so many people are privy to a student's scores which are supposed to be confidential—guidance counselors, parents, admissions officers, alumni committees, coaches, teachers— that students themselves readily disclose them to each other, painful as that may be in cases. An official of the College Board found the effect of knowing where one stands to be generally healthy.

The institutionalizing of selectivity on a national scale has had the curious effect of making the most selective colleges among the most personal in administering admissions, although three out of four applicants have to be turned down. In order to handle the work load, admissions offices have been increasingly staffed by personable and dedicated educators, generally with secondary school teaching experience. They work for their institutions but they are sympathetic to all applicants, and as a result the hard feelings the system creates are somewhat softened by the empathy of admissions officers.

Applicants are encouraged to visit selective college campuses, to be interviewed, to ask questions. Their parents are given a student-conducted tour around the Ivy halls. Alumni committees make contact with candidates and act as liaison for the admissions officers, who also visit hundreds of schools but cannot possibly cover the thousands from which applications are received.

Public systems of higher education cannot possibly get to know applicants because the numbers are so great. Bureaucracy is considered inhuman and Kafkaesque, but it is simply the inevitable outcome of population growth, which makes the cost of individual attention too high. The best that can be expected from a bureaucracy is not warmth but efficiency and fairness. The much maligned computer ensures both—but it still creates that sinking feeling.

When there are more applications than places in a public college, there has to be an arbitrary cut-off point—a C average, upper 50 percent of the class, 550 SATs, or some combination of these three with a weighting of the school attended. The process is swift, automatic and to the candidate absolutely heartless. He feels bent, folded and mutilated.

Is the answer for such a student Open Enrollment? Not quite, because no single institution will be able to accept more students than it has room for, and some sorting out has to be done. Open Enrollment means open to high school graduates in the upper half of their senior class. And once enrolled, the weak student cannot avoid the realization that he is weak because of the brilliant students who also enroll. There is always some sorting out—in college, in life. But Open Enrollment is not to be mocked at, however chaotic its beginnings have been, unless you believe in keeping people in their "place" and denying some the right to explore with teachers new realms of the mind closed to their parents by accidents of birth.

Dr. William J. McGill, president of Columbia, said in a speech in Mexico City that overexpansion of higher education in America is cheapening college degrees. The demand of employers for college graduates for jobs that do not need so much higher education he finds ridiculous. It is perhaps less ridiculous to the degree holder, for whom the baccalaureate is a critical ego bolster and status symbol. Universal high school training would have seemed ridiculous 100 years ago, too.

4

The Selective
Admissions Process

Each selective college has its own unique character, shaped by its particular history, its location, traditions, academic programs and kinds of students who went there. Yet the admissions offices operate in relatively similar ways, which leads you to wonder just how unique any selective college can be. Especially when all these colleges dip into the same applicant pool more or less, and the applicants send in applications to several of them.

Perhaps the distinctions lie in the choices of candidates that are accepted, but if so, no one can tell you how these distinctions arise, nor can any consistent "type" of freshman be found at these colleges. Princeton turns down the number-one student in a high school, Harvard accepts him. But next year Harvard may turn down a student with the same characteristics, and Princeton will accept him. *It all depends on what kind of class a college is putting together.* There is a certain amount of luck involved in acceptance/rejection decisions from the candidate's point of view. And this drives not only candidates up the wall but their teachers, counselors and parents as well. Inconsistency in selective admissions makes it difficult to predict the chances of certain students and impossible to guarantee the admission of anyone. "I don't understand why they took Jack when they turned down Peter," is a not infrequent lament around secondary schools.

Every selective college runs its admissions office slightly differently. At Middlebury the staff interviewer insists on seeing the parents if they have come all the way with the candidate to a fairly remote part of Vermont. At Wellesley the interview is obligatory, but at Brown it is optional. Dartmouth has the most sophisticated computerized information retrieval system. Columbia computerizes its applications for information purposes from the start. But Columbia is just as personal in its selection as any Ivy college.

In the end every selective college admissions office has to do the same thing: *select*. The fact that there are so many cases of overlapping admissions, of candidates being accepted at two, three, five colleges, bears out Edward Wall, Amherst admissions dean, who says, "We're *all* after the same candidates."

The admissions office's function is to attract as many top candidates as it can, pick according to college policy those to be admitted, and finally to get as many of the admitted candidates as possible to enroll. "Basically it comes down to making decisions," is the way James Rogers, Brown's admissions dean, sees it. That is making decisions after you have the applicants. But before you get applicants you have to make sure that the best potential students for your college are interested in applying.

Some qualified high school students never consider applying to selective colleges until invited to do so. An example from personal experience is a boy from Quincy, Massachusetts, who attracted the attention of a Princeton alumnus when he was cited in the *Quincy Patriot-Ledger* as the only high school student at a scientists' meeting on air pollution. He had planned to go to Northeastern University in Boston and was skeptical of Princeton until the alumnus took him to New Jersey and showed him the campus. He eventually went to Princeton on a scholarship and is now doing graduate work at MIT.

Admissions officers like applicants who prefer their particular college, although many candidates do not know which college they prefer. The critical work of admissions comes when the applications have stacked up and have been sorted into manila folders along with comments from teachers, coaches, alumni and others, with SAT scores from the College Board and with any paraphernalia candidates may submit that won't fit into a folder, like a painting or a film or a scrapbook.

With this documentation in hand, the admissions officer is able to make his first judgments rather quickly, rejecting the obviously unqualified 15 or 20 percent, and accepting *pro tem* the obviously outstanding candidates. This leaves perhaps three-quarters of the folders in a limbo of indecision. And the winnowing process is repeated again and again until the staff member is prepared to put his judgments before the admissions committee for ratification or rejection. No candidate is at the mercy of any single staff member, although the weakest are so quickly perceived as such that it can hardly be said that their cases are given more than a cursory scanning.

A selective admissions staff will consist of a dean or director plus six to 15 professional assistants. There is no formal training in admissions work. You learn on the job. Some admissions officers are hired directly after graduation, while others have had a long teaching career or secondary school administrative training.

Worth David, now dean of admissions at Yale, was both a public school and a private school administrator. Ralph Moye, Boston University's admissions director, was a high school principal. Ed Wall of Amherst taught at Andover. Admissions work is considered a specialty in higher education administration and there is an active national organization called the American Association of College Registrars and Admissions Officers that holds regional and national meetings designed to exchange information on admissions problems and procedures. Most of the members of ACRAO are interested in how to attract more enrollment rather than in how to select from among a surfeit of candidates.

A staff member like Laurence H. Sanford, Jr., of Princeton, spends the fall interviewing students either in his office or on the road. His schedule in the fall of 1973 included six weeks of traveling to New England and Canada, visiting 200 schools and talking to 1,000 candidates. He also met with 12 alumni committees involving several hundred men, explained the admissions procedures to new members and discussed strategy for getting top candidates to apply. Princeton has had particular success in attracting girls since it went co-ed, and Sanford put particular emphasis on contacting girls at private schools. Back in the office he divided his time between interviews and reading folders. Princeton has no Early Decision candidates to consider, so the pressure on the staff is not as severe as it is at other selective admissions offices. Still, Early Evaluations of candidates' chances had to be completed largely by the end of December.

The admissions staff meets as a committee when making decisions to accept or reject candidates. Committees include one or more faculty members, but generally faculty members are peripheral because they do not have the time to spend days in concentrated sessions discussing the pros and cons of particular cases. At least one admissions director finds that faculty members are incapable of objectivity in certain instances, say when they want to admit a scholar regardless of a certain drabness of personality, or when the child of a faculty member is a weak candidate!

Discussion occurs not about the obvious rejects or the obvious accepts, but about the great gray mass of candidates who look good enough to be seriously considered, the Possibles, and of these each staff member always has too many. By comparing each other's candidates, admissions officers reach many quick agreements. No staff member has an obligatory quota of admits to produce and he or she generally yields when a better candidate from another region comes up for discussion. E. J. Kahn recounts a Harvard admissions session where the give-and-take got a bit heavy and one man finally said that he did not want to hear any more about a particular candidate because the candidate was not going to get any better by being talked about.

Human nature being what it is, admissions officers who feel particularly strongly about certain candidates avoid being too critical of someone else's candidate, and a subtle, unspoken log-rolling occurs. This does not mean that anything fishy is going on. So many candidates are alike in their qualities, that the margin of difference becomes highly subjective. Feelings run stronger for than against such candidates, so that some lose out not because they have been flatly rejected but because they have not aroused the needed support in the committee.

These judgments vary from committee to committee, since several committees are looking at many of the same candidates. "But Radcliffe took her," a headmaster complained to Princeton. "Let Radcliffe have her," the admissions officer replied. Why should the headmaster care whether two *top* colleges accept a student since she can go to only one? Because he naturally would like to have the school record show as high a number of top college *acceptances* as possible in order to keep up prestige!

Even after the committee as a whole has come to agreement on most candidates, there are still special categories to be dealt with—alumni children, athletes, minorities, special cases—and these too must be sorted out for accepting and rejecting. At the end of March the admissions office has its list of admitted candidates ready for mailing by the April 15 deadline.

If the process sounds complicated, it is, but it works; it is personal, and generally speaking it is just. In a corrupt world it is refreshing to know that admissions to selective colleges are just about impossible to fix. "To a thoughtful outsider," wrote Katherine Kinkead in *The Brightest Ever* (1961), "the Yale admissions procedure is a heartening one." Probably the reason is that the selective colleges have, without consciously thinking about doing so, evolved systems of selection that defy tampering with. Although nominally under the control of the faculty, and ultimately responsible to the college president, the admissions offices are highly autonomous and pride themselves on being unreachable insofar as altering a decision for ulterior reasons goes.

Once President Goheen was consulted, and quite properly, by the Princeton admissions office, on a case that was deemed "sensitive," involving the child of someone important to the university. Goheen returned the query with the remark that it was indeed a tough decision to make and he knew that the admissions office would make the right one. Burt Hallowell, Tufts' president, has found his trustees very useful in heading off attempts to get someone marginal into Tufts. The trustee may call the admissions office's attention to the candidate, but he never promises anyone to do more than that because he cannot. At less selective colleges the president's office sometimes has a quota of candidates he is allowed to admit on his say so. The wife of one president, new to a campus, announced to a surprised admissions office that where she came from the president had thirty places in the freshman class he was allowed to hand out as he pleased. No truly selective college engages in such a practice.

But there are those rare exceptions when judgments are influenced by other criteria. Should not a relative of the president of the United States receive special consideration? Should not the child of an alumnus who has done a great deal for his institution be judged by less rigorous standards? Such instances are so few that they do not invalidate the selective admissions system. Those admitted as a matter of privilege are capable of doing the work. The few people aware of the marginal nature of such candidates' folders shrug their shoulders. The exception really has no bearing on the process as a whole.

5

The Selective Admissions Office

In former times, admissions was pretty much a one-man affair. There was the dean of admissions, a distinguished gentleman and scholar like Radcliffe Heermance of Princeton, who knew most of the headmasters personally and many high school principals. Working with an assistant and a secretary, and relying on the secondary schools to submit good candidates, this one man read all the folders. He looked at the College Board exams, made sure the candidate had sufficient Latin, math and a modern language, and he put together a class before the end of July, quite an accomplishment considering the College Boards were held in June.

In most colleges, as we noted, there was no admissions office, just a registrar to check credentials when the student signed in. Admissions has had to become a small bureaucracy in order to handle with any discrimination the flood of applications. The role of the faculty in such conditions is largely advisory, although in graduate school and in engineering schools the faculty is more deeply involved in admissions than in undergraduate liberal arts colleges. (However, the University of Chicago had 6,000 applicants for 100 Medical School places in 1973. Its faculty naturally must rely on an arbitrary limit of applicants it will consider in depth. The rest are rejected if they fail to reach a competitive academic level in college and on graduate aptitude tests.)

Some modern selective admissions offices look as if they were a group medical practice with a waiting room where parents and their applicant children sit scanning brochures and catalogues until a member of the staff calls in the candidate for an interview. The furnishings are more elegant and the setting is less impersonal. Nonetheless, there is an air of transciency about some admissions setups, reflecting the dynamics of today's college administrations, with their changing presidents and vice presidents and revised organization charts.

Old grads returning to Harvard in 1973 found the admissions office on the ninth floor of a new and rather handsome office building right in the middle of Harvard Square. In 1974, it had moved to Radcliffe! A Harvard candidate, now at Princeton, tells the amazing story of being given a tour of the Harvard campus on a rainy day from the corner windows of the Harvard Square admissions office. "There's the Yard. The big building is Widener Library. Now from here you can see Radcliffe." He never bothered to submit an application.

Brown admissions occupies a town house with red carpeting dating from the last century. Nassau Hall ran out of space years ago, and Princeton admission moved into what used to be the University Store in Old West College. Middlebury admissions occupies an off-campus Victorian house once owned by Emma Willard, founder of the girls' school of that name in Troy, New York. Dartmouth now occupies a set of offices in a former classroom building.

At first glance it all looks very slow paced and easygoing. No visitor gets the impression that time is of the essence, although after thirty minutes the interview is tactfully brought to a close. In fact, admissions staffs are under tremendous pressure to handle the workload. For instance, hours are spent on the telephone with alumni committees, who visit secondary schools and line up candidates, with coaches, with parents.

While we were talking to one admissions director, he took a phone call that sounded like this: "Yes, we're still accepting applications. . . . Can you describe her academic record? . . . Well, I'd have to say she probably wouldn't be admitted here. . . . No, you certainly can let her apply. We're happy to look at a lot of applications. I'm only saying that from what you tell me, she falls below the competitive level here. . . . Well, for obvious reasons I can't do that. Have you talked to her school counselor?"

After hanging up he told us that the girl's father wanted him to recommend a college where she *could* get in, something he would not do with a stranger on the telephone. "If she had applied and he was sitting here, I might have made some suggestions, but if I try to be a placement agent over the telephone, I'll be getting letters of complaint all year long." Matter of fact, he gets them anyway.

Through all the pressures, complaints and flaps these men and women have to keep their tempers and remain judicious. They are in the eye of a hurricane today because of the many constituencies demanding satisfaction—alumni, minority groups, faculty, headmasters, coaches, friends. With Mort Sahl, the admissions officer can ask: Is there anyone I haven't insulted yet?

The Idea of a Balanced Class

The objective is to create a *class*. This is a very subtle concept. If the objective were, as it is in France, let us say, to enroll only the top high school seniors according to academic brilliance, then all the selective admissions staffs would be doing is admitting the 750–800 SAT types and competing with one another for potential Phi Beta Kappas.

But a class consists of just so many extraordinary brains, just so many of the very bright, many of the bright and a few who have yet to shine at all, and in this academic mixture must fall a certain number of athletes, alumni children, minorities, writers, artists, singers, orators, photographers and so on.

There is no placement agency which can tell a candidate: "This year MIT is looking for an experienced coxwain. Dartmouth wants some girl tennis players. Radcliffe needs activities girls." So what happens is that candidates apply to several places and take their chances. They will never know necessarily just why they were accepted by one place and rejected at another. As John C. Hoy noted in *Choosing a College* (1967): "If he [the student] has planned well, he need not worry about how colleges make their decisions. The process of selection is inscrutable." Some examples:

• E. J. Kahn tells of the Harvard band director mentioning to the admissions office a need for a French horn player, and darned if *two* didn't turn up in the next freshman class.

• An Ivy college took a boy recently who was only on the waiting list of a much less selective college. The reason? He was a rower and the Ivy college needed oarsmen while the other had no crew at all.

• During the collapse of the aero-space industry, students became wary of training as engineers, so some colleges (not MIT) with engineering schools had to lower their sights to fill their places.

The idea of creating a class is a way for the admissions office to be a problem-solving center for the college. The first problem is how to give the faculty students that are worthy of *them.* All professors prefer to teach bright students, but only when admission is highly selective can they realize their dreams in large measure.

At MIT the average math SAT of freshmen in the Class of 1978 was 750. This ensures MIT's teachers that they can count on being understood without repeating themselves too often. Although MIT is thought of as an engineering school, a third of it is humanities, economics and architecture. But everyone is required to take freshman calculus, because as Peter Richardson, director of admissions, points out, "A liberal education these days must include mathematics."

The SAT averages at selective colleges are between 600 and 700. These are used like batting averages to show the faculty and the president and the alumni that the academic quality of the student body is superior to that of places which are unable to be as selective.

Christopher Jencks and David Riesman in *The Academic Revolution* point out just how selective a college can be by noting that Stanford draws from the top 2 percent among high school seniors, and Berkeley, in some departments considered academically superior to Harvard (Harvard professors say it's a place they like to spend a visiting year in to relax!), as a state college draws from the top 10 percent of California high school graduates.

But no selective private college can take *all* the bright applicants. *What problem is admissions solving by turning down boys and girls with 700 SATs?*

Let us look at some of the constituencies beside the faculty. There are alumni, on whom the financial security of these colleges heavily depends. Fifteen to 20 percent of the places in each class are reserved for the children of alumni at most selective colleges and while they are not as a group less bright than the average, some are less bright than nonalumni children applying.

As it is, 60 percent of alumni children on an average have to be turned down, but some of the 40 percent who get in are no better than, and, in cases, are weaker than certain nonalumni applicants who lose out.

Athletes in the Class

Another special group that adds up to perhaps 10 percent of the freshman class is athletes—scholar athletes they are called at most selective colleges, to distinguish them from athletes with minimal academic records who have to be rejected. Many athletes tend to do poorly in the secondary school classroom because they put their energies into sports. Selective colleges want the brightest athletes they can get, but compromises are always possible.

The selective admissions procedures are very flexible when it comes to athletes, a subject that is discussed at some length in another chapter. Fred L. Glimp, who used to be dean of admissions at Harvard, freely admits that he sought out athletes and brought them to Harvard despite low grades on occasion. "Athletes give any college a tone it would otherwise miss," he will tell you. "And furthermore they are no real academic risk if you pick the right ones."

No one ever predicted that Bill Bradley, a mediocre College Board tester but good in high school, would do so well academically at Princeton that he would win a Rhodes Scholarship. In most cases the admissions office can admit an athlete without fear of criticism by anybody except some intellectuals or a colleague in another college. *The competition for athletes is fierce.* When Amherst people boast of three of their former players being in the National Football League, you cannot say that the scholar athletes of the Ivies or in this case Little Ivies are of no account. They do tend to be academically stronger than in nonselective colleges.

Minorities in the Class

Another constituency new to all colleges consists of the minority groups, mostly Blacks, but including Latinos, Chicanos, American Indians, Eskimos, disadvantaged whites and disadvantaged Orientals.

It is not surprising that as a group their academic qualities are lower than average, though each year these increase significantly for those admitted to the selective institutions. What may be surprising is that their performance in college is not noticeably different from many of those who have had better secondary school training.

David Evans, a Black staff member of Harvard admissions, explains, "Blacks have problems on campus, but they are emotional problems of adjustment." The Black performance at Harvard is currently a controversial one, discussed in the chapter on minorities.

Selective college minority groups amount to about 10 percent of total enrollment and their spokesmen would like to see this rise. Competition for the limited number of minority places on these campuses has led David Evans to create a referral system of students Harvard does not have room for.

Women in "Men's" Colleges

Women as a separate group concern admissions officers less than they did when men's colleges first went co-ed. The process requires a gradual buildup over a four-year period, at which point a sex-blind or "equal-access" admissions policy can be adopted. The sexual revolution, that has killed *in loco parentis* and made young women responsible for their own bodies without the reinforcement of parietals and chaperones, has solved one problem for colleges: there is no need for separate dormitories for men and women. So if the ratio of men to women changes, the number of beds remains constant. The tradeoff on this one is that by solving a space problem, the authorities have created a controversy that comes under the rubric of "cohabitation," discussion of which is reserved for the chapter on the campuses.

To sum up the problem-solving function in selective admissions, an admissions committee must select large numbers of bright students, but must be flexible enough to admit a percentage of alumni children, athletes and minority applicants. What about ethnic groups that are not disadvantaged, Jews, Chinese, Japanese? For them let the chips fall where they may.

And geographic distribution? Contrary to popular mythology it is no more difficult to get into Harvard from Watertown, Massachusetts, than from Long Beach, California. Selective colleges go out of their way to beat the bushes for candidates from afar and the national character of selective colleges is the result not of studied selection but of a large pool of applicants from the 50 states. Most of the enrollment tends to come from nearer than farther away from any campus. Stanford is a West Coast institution with some Eastern students; Yale is an Eastern institution with some Western students.

The question of why American selective colleges do not simply fill their classrooms with the brightest kids in the land still remains unanswered, because even after satisfying the constituencies mentioned there would be more room for the very bright. Yet some very bright students are turned down by one or more selective college. In 1973, the number-one student of a suburban high school was rejected by Princeton and accepted by Harvard, and several girls accepted by Radcliffe were rejected by Princeton. What is this quality that is required in addition to—or instead of—high academic promise?

The Personal Equation

Here the going gets murky because there is yet no objective test of what is called "the personal side." The personal side. The very casualness of the term has a certain charm that encourages the adrenalin to flow in every parent. "George is a terrific kid! A little weak in his Achievement scores, but let me tell you how he organized the canoe trips at Camp Loonwicket."

The personal side is vague in everyone's mind and suggests that the candidate is being judged for his real self, and not by some impersonal computer incapable of knowing anyone's soul. It is the side that comes out in interviews, in letters, in essays and lately in submission of portfolios and examples of creative work. The talented photographer may suddenly look just as attractive as the would-be lawyer to an admissions officer, not impressive academically but perhaps a future David Douglas Duncan or Richard Avedon.

Jerry L. Avorn, a recent Columbia graduate who wrote the introduction to *Barron's In-Depth Guide to the Ivy League Schools,** calls

*New York: Barron's Educational Series, 1971.

the personal side the X factor in admissions, and suggests, rather unfairly, that an element of whimsy may underlie the rejection of some candidates, who would not feel so inferior if they could but watch an admissions committee at work. Mistakes are made, of course, but not many.

After spending several months in New Haven, *New Yorker* writer Katherine Kinkead concluded: "For in spite of the hundreds of qualified youngsters applying, Yale's selection remains an individual and personal success." Certainly no single admissions officer's prejudices for or against the personal side of a candidate can by themselves affect the chances of admission or rejection. No staff member's moods have any influence on ultimate admissions decisions, and candidates are admitted whom some of the committee may admire without liking personally.

Admissions officers tend to be on the side of candidates because, as noted, most of them have been secondary school teachers or administrators or advisers to college undergraduates. Some, like Robert Ballantyre of Duke, are on the college faculty. Alfred Quirk of Dartmouth taught at the University of New Hampshire. They are personable and understanding people, who can put a nervous candidate at ease, try to not grill anyone in an interview, are diplomatic with teachers and counselors. They are also shrewd and can see through pretensions or can read between the lines of a teacher's praise, alert to words like "however" or "in spite of"—"in spite of Dora's carelessness, she is a brilliant linguist" means she has a good French accent but is lousy at grammar.

Most admissions officers are graduates of the selective college they work for, and a surprisingly large percentage come from private school backgrounds, either as students or teachers. It has been remarked that too few admissions officers come from deprived backgrounds. Yet it is the supposedly rarefied admissions officers who have opened up the selective colleges to high school graduates and to candidates described as underprivileged. Unavoidably, this strikes a professor who grew up on New York's Lower East Side as patronizing. But in time no doubt there will be a certain number of Lower East Siders in selective admissions work.

To get all the work done and to reach out to so many high schools, admissions offices have enlisted the aid of alumni, who act as para-admissions people. They contact high schools, talk to coaches, interview candidates and sell admitted candidates on deciding to accept the offer of alma mater. Princeton originated this system of proconsuls and now has over 2,000 schools committeemen among its alumni, many of them recent graduates. And the latest word is that undergraduates are joining the alumni team on an ad hoc basis to persuade candidates to come to Old Nassau. Thus a selective admissions office has its satellites surveying the territory and relaying its messages to alma mater.

Early Evaluation and Early Decision

Princeton has contributed two other innovations in admissions procedure, the Likely, Possible, Unlikely Early Evaluation, and the rating of candidates on a scale of one to five according to certain academic and nonacademic qualities. Although the Ivy Group has adopted Early Evaluation, Harvard, Yale and Princeton are holdouts so far as Early Decision is concerned.

The Big Three earn nothing but contempt privately among other admissions directors for their aloofness in this regard. For in fact it enhances the competitive edge of HYP by keeping in the competition candidates the others would hope to draw away in an early scramble.

"It would be fairer to the candidate if every college had an Early Decision plan," says Richard Moll, admissions director of Bowdoin. Amherst's Edward Wall says, "We can't move until Harvard, Yale and Princeton shake the trees." Brown has its own way of shaking the trees by trying to spot those of its candidates headed for HYP and denying them admission!

Early Decision is in fact a strategem of selective colleges to counter the pull of Harvard, Yale and Princeton. The reason the Big Three do not have Early Decision is essentially because they would not benefit from it. In the case of Harvard the pile-up of applications would be impossible to process. For Yale and Princeton the crunch in the fall might be less critical, but they would prefer to have one round in which the application pool as a whole can be assessed.

Early Decision has obvious advantages for the candidate. First of all, it makes him reach a conclusion about the college of his choice.

And if he is accepted early, the anxiety is over and done with. If he is not accepted early, he is still in the running and may be admitted in April.

For the college, Early Decision has administrative advantages. It also attracts students who might have gone elsewhere if admitted to several other colleges. The Early Decision freshmen are students who clearly are going to the college of their choice. (Sometimes it is the college of their parents' choice.)

President Kemeny of Dartmouth, addressing a freshman class in September, began: "Now that you have satisfied your parents' need to have you admitted to Dartmouth, we can get on with the more serious purposes of higher education." The students applauded wildly.

Much if not most of the prestige of any institution lies first in the mind of someone who is at least a generation older than the applicant. Fortunately there are wise men and women who are able to so condition students that they are not bedazzled by names of institutions. A lot of such students elect to make Early Decision applications because they *prefer* the college they are applying to. These are the true joy of an admissions office, which no matter how prestigious its college, is somewhat anxious about those it admits. Admissions officers are like lovers, wondering, "Do you *really* love me?"

A Rating System

Princeton's way of rating candidates deserves some discussion because it shows how an admissions office goes about making judgments on the X factor with a certain amount of logic. Or perhaps it should be said that judgments that are inherently subjective are reduced to an objective spectrum of values. Here is how the Class of 1977 was rated:

TABLE I
PRINCETON UNIVERSITY ADMISSION RATINGS
Class of 1977

NONACADEMIC

		1	2	3	4	5	TOTALS
		8	91	246	48	1	394
		100%	97.8%	95.5%	91.7%	0%	
	1	8	89*	235*	44	0	376
		25%	26.9%	39.6%	40.9%	0%	
		2	24	93	18	0	137
		17	473	1512	233	2	2237
		100%	93%	30.2%	17.2%	0%	
A	2	17	440	457	40	0	954
C		52.9%	47.3%	54.7%	70%	0%	
A		9	208	250	28	0	495
D		58	889	1952	204	0	3103
E		100%	27.8%	8.1%	1.5%	0%	
M	3	58	247	158	3	0	466
I		62.1%	59.9%	63.9%	33.3%	0%	
C		36	148	101	1	0	286
		54	824	1132	215	2	2227
		79.6%	21.6%	5.2%	.5%	0%	
	4	43	178	59	1	0	281
		65.1%	67.4%	62.7%	100%	0%	
		28	120	37	1	0	186
		27	194	277	64	1	563
		33.3%	2.6%	0%	0%	0%	
	5	9	5	0	0	0	14
		77.8%	40%	0%	0%	0%	
		7	2	0	0	0	9
TOTALS		164	2471	5119	764	6	8524
		135	959	909	88	0	2091
		82	502	481	48	0	1113

*All students not admitted under these ratings either were foreign or withdrew their applications before admission was offered.

You can grasp the significance of these numbers very quickly. Take the first square at top left, representing the highest ratings. There were eight one/ones, eight applicants who were rated top scholars and tops personally; the eight were admitted (100%), only two of them enrolled (25%).

The next square at the top shows 91 candidates with a one academic rating and a two rating on the personal side. Of these 89 (97.8%) were admitted, and again only a fourth (26.9%), or 24, chose to go to Princeton.

This attrition of top students to Harvard mostly, and to Yale, is worrisome to Princeton and was one of the reasons given by the administration for going co-ed, i.e., to get more acceptances from bright boys preferring a co-ed campus. Now the number of girls applying is increasing at a faster rate than the number of boys.

What do the categories signify? Academically, a one is in the top 1 percent of the senior class in secondary school and has SATs of 730 or higher. Two is in the top 2 to 5 percent of the class with SATs of 670 to 730. Three is in the top 5 to 8 percent of the class, with 650 to 670 SATs. Four is in the top 8 to 12 percent of the class, with 550 to 650 SATs. Five is anyone below four.

On the personal side a one is truly exceptional, a leader, an athlete like Princeton's All-American Dick Kazmeier, a creative talent in music like Harvard's Leonard Bernstein, someone so outstanding that there is hardly any disagreement about the person's star quality. There were but 164 personal ones out of 8,524 applicants in this Princeton class; 135 were admitted and 82 accepted—about 60 percent. By contrast there were more than twice as many rated one academically. But only 37 percent of those academic ones admitted came to Princeton.

A nonacademic two is someone who is excellent in certain areas such as athletic team captain, class president, editor of the paper, top debater, gifted photographer.

There were 2,471 such twos, in the totals at the bottom of the table. But selectivity eliminated 1,512, and more than half those admitted accepted.

Three is described by an admissions officer as "involved, a little excellence but not exciting." You can see that the greatest number of applicants fall into this group—secretary-treasurers of the class, second lead in the senior play, chairman of UN Day, manager of the tennis team, tutor of ghetto kids. Almost the same number of personal threes were accepted from a pool twice as big as the twos.

A four personal rating is almost fatal for admission to Princeton, which rejected 89 percent of such applicants and took only those with high marks, with two exceptions. A four "tends to merge with the group . . . rather dull . . . relatively immature" is how the guideline describes him. Some very brilliant scholars are reclusive and at this age make little impression on an interviewer. They may be shy or they may be arrogant, and in either case unattractive in a drawing room. In college they may continue to remain apart and go on to be people of great distinction in their fields. But these fields are not likely to be diplomacy, life insurance sales, trial law, internal medicine or any calling requiring considerable interaction with other people. Sometimes they become professors, but they are not the lovable kind remembered as inspiring.

Since only six personal fives applied, the process of selectivity can be assumed to have its counterpart in self-selection out of the race. Even an academic rating of one will not help the candidate rated five on the personal side.

This "grid," as it is called, is clinical in appearance, yet it will be the rare reader who has not secretly tried to determine what kind of a rating Princeton might confer on him or her—and conclude in some cases what an abominable system of arbitrary judgments this is. To feel better you have only to put someone else's name down and give it a rating. Willie Mays, a number one on the personal side certainly. Kissinger, surely a one academically. Hitler gets a five on the personal side, and since he was a lousy painter, maybe only an academic three. If the ratings add up to more than six, the chances for admission to Princeton are almost nil.

Candidates, of course, are never told what their ratings are. But students who learn the rating system are quite candid about rating themselves academically, and will give themselves fours unless they score high in the 600s on their SATs. They are so used to being graded that they are conditioned to accept their academic condition.

Their human condition is not always clear to them: the personal rating is liable to be less realistic in the candidate's mind. *The biggest single mistake applicants to selective colleges make is thinking that being very active will impress admissions officers, when actually a long list of activities may suggest some weakness, indecision, lack of commitment.* "We look for commitment, *sincere* commitment," Ed Wall tells Amherst aspirants.

Portfolios

No other college has adopted Princeton's numerical rating system, yet something similar happens in every selective admissions office. John Hoy, ex-dean of admissions at Wesleyan, uses the term "Possible Admit" in describing admissions decision-making. Bowdoin is the only selective college that does not require that SAT scores be submitted and less than half the candidates do submit them. Bowdoin has invited submission of paintings, musical scores, recordings, short stories or anything a candidate feels will shed light on his or her accomplishments and promise for the future.

"It enlivens our discussion sessions to listen to a tape recording to help determine a candidate's worthiness," Dick Moll says.

Bowdoin's admissions offices are somewhat cluttered with boxes and large packages. One box in the fall of 1973 contained a patchwork quilt, submitted by a *boy,* who wrote that he was making a study of American quilting patterns! That would certainly be worth a two at Princeton. Another candidate who specialized in raising raccoons was also a good photographer, and his pictures of raccoons were on display for several days in the office of Moll's secretary.

Bowdoin, as much as Princeton, would like candidates equivalent to academic *ones.* In the Class of 1977 at Bowdoin there were 19 applicants with SAT verbals above 750, and 76 with math verbals above 750. In each case, although more than half were accepted, *only 1.5 percent came to Bowdoin.* The rest were creamed off by the Big Three chiefly. But the percentage of students below the 550 SAT mark is a little higher at Princeton than at Bowdoin—17 and 12 percent respectively.

The Interview

Selective admissions is said to be personal in contrast to admissions by such formulas as taking the top 10 percent into the top branch of the state university. Yet it is not infrequently the case that an applicant is accepted without an interview by the staff or by an alumnus and without visiting the campus. Russell Mead, headmaster of Concord Academy, went to Dartmouth from high school in Denver without knowing much about the Ivy League. "I got a good scholarship and that decided me," he recalls.

It is quite possible that sufficient personal acquaintance will convince the college to turn a candidate down. Failure to impress in an interview, combined with collaborating reports, may be deciding factors when choices have to be made among several good candidates. Folders can be read at the rate of 10 to 15 an hour, which is slower than a computer, but this does not allow the candidate as much attention as he may think he is getting. Visits of admissions staffs to schools, especially private schools, do not allow more than 20 minutes for an interview.

Ted Bracken, formerly at Princeton, says the interview is as much a chance for the candidate to ask questions as it is to make an impression, and it stands to reason that teachers who know the candidate well will probably have more weight in deciding a case than the impression made in an interview. But we know of one boy who wrote a sloppy personal statement, and then appeared arrogant in an interview. His 700 SAT and Achievement scores did not save him from rejection by an Ivy League college.

Committee Work

What do admissions committees debate about in their long sessions? Mostly about which of the middle group to admit when so many look about the same on paper. Here are some examples: A girl with SATs in the middle 600s, daughter of an alumna, on the tennis team of her high school, works in a hospital lab in the summer; a boy who was number one in his class in prep school, middle 600 SATs, valedictorian but not outstanding in an extra curricular way; a hockey goalie with SATs in the low 600s; a potential concert violinist with SATs in the mid 500s.

Here is where balancing of the class determines many decisions. A check with the hockey coach determines that he already has more goalies than he needs. The concert violinist is definitely wanted by the music department even though no credit can be given for any instruction in playing the violin, since this is not a college of practical training. The number-one prep school boy just is not as impressive as the number-10 boy in an urban high school with the same SAT scores who is a good singer and will be an addition to the glee club. The alumna daughter will get in because the tennis coach thinks she would make the team.

"The real art of admissions comes in balancing the class," Arthur Howe, Jr., of Yale once said. But who determines what the balance will be?

Admissions policy formally is set by the trustees, but actually the trustees tend to approve a policy developed by the faculty with the president's approval. Donald Platten, chairman of Chemical Bank and a Princeton trustee, explains the liberalization of Princeton admissions by an essentially conservative board this way: "The board picks the president. If they don't like what he insists on they have to fire him."

Burt Hallowell, Tufts' president, says, "Don't forget that businessmen who are college trustees are dealing with the same pressures in the office that colleges feel—hiring minority personnel, responding to demands for women's rights." At any rate, all the selective colleges have liberalized their admission policies by making the criterion of merit all-important, by establishing what amounts to minimum quotas of minority students and by eliminating any trace of anti-Semitism or racial discrimination.

William Attwood, publisher of *Newsday,* former JFK ambassador to Guinea ("Why did he pick me?" he joked, "I don't even speak Italian!") and a Princeton trustee, wrote a letter to the *Princeton Alumni Weekly* in response to a complaining alumnus, in which he said that the trustees had simply brought Princeton finally into the twentieth century by its admissions policies. Many alumni attribute this liberalization to the student upheavals of the late sixties, and they ultimately blame the "left-wing faculty."

Faculties do tend to be more liberal than conservative, but they really do not have too much time to devote to admissions and are like the trustees in that they must accept the accept/reject decisions of the director or dean of admissions, an untenured administrator, or arrange to have a new one brought in. The amount of time it takes to create a college class even in a small college like Bowdoin simply is not available to college professors.

Although professors are the watchdogs of admissions, and will get edgy if freshman average SAT scores drop (they have dropped nationally in recent years for reasons unclear to anyone), faculty committees are there to support admissions by keeping the director informed of the way students are selecting courses and particularly majors.

Pre-med is the most trendy academic preference these days. As many as 50 percent of freshmen at selective colleges start out planning to go to medical school. This puts pressure on undergraduate science departments. Unless a candidate is very strong, if pre-med is an indicated career preference, the chances of rejection rise.

For a time after the space boom collapsed, wily candidates entered Princeton as engineers because it was a little easier to be admitted, and once there they then transferred to liberal arts in sophomore year. Admissions now screens engineering candidates more carefully and only bona fide engineers are admitted. The engineering faculty, incidentally, is much more deeply involved in Princeton admissions than the liberal arts faculty is, much as medical and law faculties are more involved in graduate school admissions.

The president is very interested in admissions policy. When Nathan Pusey saw Yale run over the Harvard football team 54–0 in 1953, he is said to have growled like a five-star general, "Don't let this happen again." The only way to avoid such disasters is through a deliberate recruiting policy unobstructed by finicky admissions officers. Fair Harvard has room for running backs as well as walking encyclopedias like Henry Kissinger, and the admissions office must see to both needs.

The Alumni Role

Alumni would dearly love to guide the admissions office, reproducing their own kind from one generation to the next. "They sure don't look like the Class of Thirty-five," sighed a Dartmouth man as he watched a group of candidates assemble for a meeting. The spirit of any ancient régime is the same: preserve the status quo.

For all the grumbling, the percentage of alumni children on campuses today is no less than it used to be, between 15 and 20 percent, and many are there because they got a break from the admissions office. There need be no apologies for such cases, since those admitted are all able students and they provide that continuity in selective colleges that is one of their strengths. When they speak of the Bryn Mawr family, they are referring to all the living graduates and their children and relatives in the college. The *New York Times* reporter who visited the Princeton campus in 1973 wrote of the almost mystical sense of loyalty that pervades the students and the alumni. A good deal of this is the result of blood relationships.

Alumni are increasingly useful to selective colleges in helping admissions offices spot candidates. But they are the servants and not the masters, and no amount of devotion to alma mater can get a student accepted whom the admissions committee does not want. Anyone who has worked with an alumni group knows how much frustration and disappointment occurs when the professionals overrule the judgment of the amateurs.

The complaint that not enough alumni children are being admitted by selective colleges does have this merit: there are more alumni children than there used to be, but the colleges have not expanded to reflect this growth, and they have opened their doors to a new clientele. What happens when a college is more liberal in dealing with alumni applicants? Sarah Lawrence enrolls 40 percent alumnae daughters.

From the foregoing it should be clear that there is no way to psych out an admissions committee, and that influence or pressure may be less than useful to a candidate's chances. John Hoy of Wesleyan tells of the admissions officer who received word that a new car would be in his garage the day after a certain candidate was accepted. To make a bribe stick you have to reach a whole committee. Even an acquisitive admissions officer, which is a contradiction in terms given the modest salaries they receive ($12,000–$18,000), is not going to risk his career in education for a few thousand dollars.

There was the case in France of the rich grocer expelled from Algiers, who had the drive and ambition for which the *pieds noirs* are noted. His son was not exactly a chip off the old block. The grocer bribed a teacher to give him a copy of the baccalaureate exam, passing which is the only key to French higher education. The boy passed all right, but he turned out to have something of his father's commercial spirit and sold copies to his friends. The cheating was discovered, a new exam had to be made up, and all the candidates throughout the whole of France sat for a second exam.

The only thing close to that in the United States did not involve corruption. An ambitious football coach in 1973 managed to provide a Texas college with the wrong SAT scores of his favorite player. But this deception was discovered.

A few years ago one of the HYP admissions offices got a phone call: "This is the White House calling." A high staff member wanted inside information on his son's chances for admission. He did not get any information that was not already available to him, and his son was not admitted.

The White House has not always been taken too seriously by our oldest colleges, which came into existence before the District of Columbia had even been surveyed. Recall the Harvard official who answered a query about President Abbott Lawrence Lowell: "The President is in Washington seeing Mr. Wilson."

But it would be only fair to add that within recent years a relative of the president of the United States was admitted to a selective college despite a less than glittering high school record. The remarkable thing is just how rare such favoritism is.

6

High School: Shaky
Ladder on the Ivy Wall

One of the most striking changes in the admissions policies of many selective colleges has been a "tilt" favoring high school applicants over private school applicants. It began in the years following World War II and reached its climax in the mid-sixties, when it was made to seem that a private school student was actually at a disadvantage in applying to Yale, for example.

The American high school was proving superior to the private school. Mass education was perceived to be better than class education. Why waste money sending a child off to prep school, when the prep school could no longer guarantee getting him into any of the top colleges, and when the local high school was sending a dozen graduates into the Ivies every year? For a while many students in private schools disliked the "preppy" image and preferred public school. Admissions officers from upper-class colleges called on boys' clubs on New York's Lower East Side inviting applications from the bright members.

High school is as American as apple pie. But some apple pies are better than others. Not every American high school is the best place to prepare for, say, Duke. And speaking of Duke, a town/gown controversy has been going on there because the faculty want a private school for their children in preference to the blue-collar high schools of Durham, North Carolina. Even liberal senators do not send their children to public schools in Washington, D.C. When selective colleges take two-thirds of their freshmen from high schools, they are taking them mostly from suburban schools, which in a way are subsidized private schools.

Just look at these figures of Princeton admissions in 1973: Stuyvesant High in New York, 33; Bronx High School of Science, 25; nine other New York schools, 49; Scarsdale High in Westchester County, New York, 12. So 104 were admitted from 11 schools in a city of 8 million, and 12 were admitted from a suburban school in a town of 20,000.

Rural schools are no better places to prepare for selective colleges. A study of Brown applicants showed average verbal SAT scores of 600 from suburban, 579 from rural and 574 from urban schools. It is the suburban high schools that have largely benefited from the "tilt" against private schools. In other words, selective colleges are still drawing their student bodies mostly from the white middle class. The "tilt" is more evolutionary than revolutionary, though no more acceptable to private schools, which with some justice see prejudice working against them.

The evolution has occurred because of three factors: greatly increased population, greatly increased affluence, and a private school enrollment that increased only slightly. It is a trend that began at the end of the nineteenth century, but the more recent changes are the most dramatic. Between 1940 and 1970, the number of high school graduates about doubled, from 1.143 million to 2.253 million, but the population rose by only 50 percent.

More students were able to graduate proportionally because of improved economic circumstances. These same economic circumstances allowed the expansion and improvement of suburban school systems paid for by property taxes. The same kind of competition that public colleges give private colleges, public high schools give private day and boarding schools.

A good private school like Belmont Hill outside Boston has been able to create a million-dollar endowment by hard fund-raising for several years. But a suburban town can raise a million dollars a year and then some for its high school capital fund. Private schools simply cannot compete either for money or for enrollment with public schools that are taking so much of the residential tax dollar. Is it any wonder, then, that in the face of a national development of this sort selective colleges would tend to have increasing numbers of high school graduates on their campuses?

It stands to reason that if the increase in the applicant pool is the result of vastly expanded high school enrollment, the selection from this pool would have to come increasingly from the public sector. It is no criticism of private schools that they have lost their swat in this process, any more than it is a criticism of Great Britain that it has lost its world influence to the United States and the Soviet Union. Circumstances cause power to agglomerate in different ways from era to era.

What has been obscured by this "democratization" of exclusive colleges is the continuing presence of 30 to 40 percent private school graduates in the colleges most in demand. If the public high schools are as good as they are cracked up to be, why are the private schools, many of their buildings getting seedy looking, not collapsing?

An answer may be found in *Equality in Educational Opportunity*, the report of James S. Coleman of Johns Hopkins, written in 1966 under federal government sponsorship. Surveying the lack of educational opportunity, the report stated:

> One implication stands out above all: That schools bring little influence to bear on a child's achievement that is independent of his background and social context; and that this very lack of an independent effect means that the inequalities imposed on children by their home, neighborhood, and peer environment are carried along to become the inequalities with which they confront adult life at the end of school.

The college-acceptance record of private schools is impressive by comparison with the high schools; private schools represent about 1 percent of secondary school enrollment, yet they fill 30 to 40 percent of the classes of many selective colleges. *Some private schools place half their seniors in selective colleges.* No high school approaches this. Many good high schools will not send more than 15 percent of their college-bound seniors to selective colleges. In fact, a study published in 1968 of 10,000 high school graduates in Midwest, California and Pennsylvania schools showed that only *7 percent of them went to private nonsectarian colleges,* and most of these, of course, would not be highly selective. (James W. Trent and Leland L. Medsker, *Beyond High School.*)

There are 28,000 high schools in the United States. The selective applicant pool is drawn from 20 percent of them. This does not mean that 80 percent of American high schools are unable to develop students qualified to apply to the Ivies. Most high school students in the South and the West have no interest in selective colleges and prefer state colleges or regional private colleges. It does mean, though, that a student's chances of going to a selective college are improved if he goes to a high school with a record of acceptances by selective admissions offices.*

But like private schools, no high school, not Scarsdale or Newton or Evanston, can guarantee to get any student into any particular college. It is well to remember that in accepting so many high school students, the selective colleges reject three or four times as many as they take, most of them well qualified too. Most high schools send no more than one student to a particular selective college, if indeed they send any at all. Applicants from 5,000 high schools apply to Princeton, but only 2,000 applicants are admitted. Given the multiple admissions of the elite "feeder" high schools—115 high schools had Princeton delegations of three or more in 1973—this means that less than two-fifths of the high schools providing the Princeton applicant pool that year had a candidate admitted. If Princeton is favoring high school candidates over private school candidates, it is also favoring some high school candidates over others.

Charles H. Doebler, former admissions director of Brown, has said: "If there were room at Brown for all the qualified students who applied, there would be no need for such judgments." It is a credit to the many good high schools that they train top students so well.

Growth of Public High Schools

The story of the public high school in America began in Boston in 1821 with the establishment of English High, and grew rather slowly until the end of the century. The public high school stood in contrast to the Latin school, the private academy of the East, which charged

---

*Dartmouth has a file of 20,000 high schools, of which only 10,000 are active. About 700 high schools are represented in any Dartmouth class.

tuition and trained men for college. Only those who could afford it were intended for education beyond the primary grades. Democratic impulses thwarted such segregation. As more colleges opened, more high schools were required, and their purpose was to educate students without the emphasis on the classics. Ironically, when more colleges did away with classics as an entrance requirement, more high schools began offering classical courses!

Originally, high school graduates were expected to go to college, and there was resistance to the demand that the high schools offer terminal programs in manual arts, trades and business to allow graduates to find remunerative employment. As courses in bookkeeping and shop developed, the high school split along class lines, and the college-bound students looked down on the future mechanics and accountants. This was the beginning of what is now called "tracking," placing abler students in demanding academic courses leading to college.

In Europe the egalitarian thrust was confined to slogans like "Liberty, Equality and Fraternity," and the German *gymnasium* or French *lycée* never allowed the lower classes to take instruction in useful arts on their premises. They still do not. In American cities, separate trade schools did grow up, but the suburban and rural high schools are conglomerates of academic and nonacademic training. In 1829, Philip Lindsay, president of Cumberland College (now the University of Nashville), put his finger on the American incapacity to realize the democratic dream: "Our people at first oppose all distinctions whatever as odious and aristocratical; and then presently seek with avidity such as remain accessible."

Until the turn of the century, the numbers graduating from high school were small—3.3 percent of the population aged 5 to 17. By 1940, practically every white American went to high school, though not all graduated. With universal high school attendance, the high school diploma became an essential credential for white-collar jobs. Most students followed the college prep course even though they were not going to college, and it is only natural that they later would hope for their children to have college training. For the few who aspired to the prestige colleges there were special courses that helped them pass college-entrance exams. Thus there were three levels: the top students, the average, and the nonacademic taking shop, business and home economics.

High schools soon offered subjects that had once been taught only in college—arithmetic, then algebra, and calculus. With the explosion of scientific knowledge, high schools had to provide elaborate laboratories, and with all the new paraphernalia and apparatus of modern education, the one-room school house became a joke.* Small communities could not afford a high school, and their children were sent to the nearest big-town school. In recent years communities have combined to build regional high schools and share the costs.

There is no doubt that the modern high school is a highly sophisticated institution by contrast with its origins. Brookline High in Massachusetts offers 450 courses, including 62 electives in English and 30 in history, as well as graphic arts, industrial arts, forestry and food service (students work alongside the chef at the Ritz Carlton). There are only 15 in a class, and there is a counselor for every 130 students. Of course there is a staff psychiatrist.

The Limitations of High Schools

The student unrest of the sixties did not spare the high schools, and subsequently there have been so many critiques, so many calls for reform, that if half of them were responded to, the high school would have disappeared as an institution by now. For better or for worse, high schools are all that most of us have in the way of secondary education, and it were best not to be too harsh in our judgments lest we lose all faith in the enterprise.

It is possible for a determined student to develop his mind in high school, to master some subjects and to mature personally. But parents especially ought to be aware of the obstacles their bright children face even in the good high schools of the suburbs. The essential quality of high school curriculums in the view of Charles E. Silberman, author of *Crisis in the Classroom*, is "mindlessness," and the values transmitted are "docility, passivity, conformity and lack of trust."†

A less radical critic, already mentioned, James S. Coleman, found in visiting many Midwestern high schools in the sixties a universal

---

*Good elementary one-room schoolhouses are dying out now, to the great regret of their alumni, who loved them and were pleased with the personal training a single teacher can give over the years.

†New York: Random House, 1970.

appreciation for the athlete and far less admiration for the scholarly student. He notes in *Adolescents and the Schools* (1965):

> My research included . . . one elite suburban school from which 85 per cent of the graduates attended college; even in this school good grades were certainly *not* an important means of prestige, and extra effort devoted to scholastic matters brought on the usual kidding or ridicule.

Since many colleges make no great academic demands on applicants, the majority of students in high school can go along with the group, enjoying themselves and not making the sacrifices that have to be made by those headed for selective colleges. Our own experience is that even the best high schools really benefit only the top 10 percent of the students academically, and the quality of these top schools is the result of a self-fulfilling prophecy, since they draw students from highly successful parents with the strongest motivation to send their children to the best colleges.

Trent and Medsker found that three factors accounted for successful completion of four years in *any* college: (1) the importance the student attaches to a college degree; (2) the decision in at least sophomore year of high school to go to college after graduating; (3) the desire of parents that the child go to college.

The only thing to add to this for selective-college-bound students is that the desire must be there to enter the top competition. The worst high school atmosphere cannot stop the highly motivated student from reading his assignments diligently and acquiring the learning skills he will need in college. Such a student will probably be encouraged not by his fellow students, but by someone, a teacher, a counselor, a coach or by his parents.

What we are saying to parents is that secondary education is too important to be left solely in the hands of the high school. You must take an interest in your child's schooling, let him know what you expect of him academically, see that he is allowed to develop good study habits, away from TV, radio and record player or tape recorder.

A father we know once said to his daughter, who thought that the Beatles represented the summit of all wisdom, "If you have any problems, don't come to me, just call the Beatles." A subtle hint that a child may find the values of the family more enduring than the pop fads of "the group." The student who is simply "sent" to high school, who is not not highly motivated, has no particular talent for athletics or extracurricular leadership, is liable to develop a hedonistic, fun-loving attitude that the high school will not discourage unless it becomes destructive or obstreperous. Or worse, he may become de-pressed, withdrawn, self-destructive and antisocial. Those who believe the obligatory age for remaining in high school should be dropped from 16 to 14, see high school as destructive to some children, who would be happier at work. The rise of professional school counseling outside the schools is in part the result of a demand by parents for help in solving problems that have developed in high schools. The blame may be partly the parents', but parental values come out of the culture the parents live in.

Some Examples

Let us look briefly at an actual suburban high school we shall call Winslow. Located in a town of 18,000 near Boston, it enrolls 1,700 in a four-year program. Its new principal has a doctorate in education, and his candid opinion is that Winslow deserves only a rating of fair. The 1973 class profile printed in several thousand copies shows that 57.9 percent of the class went to four-year colleges, a jump of nearly 8 percent in four years. Of 423 seniors, 30 went to 21 highly selective colleges. Of the Ivy League, only Columbia was not represented, and of the Seven Sisters, Barnard, Mount Holyoke and Wellesley were not represented. Average SATs were 479 verbal and 522 math, well below selective college averages of 600 and up. Only 11 students scored above 650 on the advanced math College Board Achievement test, but 40 scored above 650 on the regular math achievement test. Essentially these 40 students are the most interesting to selective colleges, but there were 26 who scored between 600 and 650, and they too had a chance at the top schools, providing they had strong personal quali-ties.

A Winslow student considering where to apply might compare his school's 1973 profile with that of Middlebury College. Most of the Middlebury class of 1977 were from the top 10 percent of their second-ary school class, but about half the class had SATs in the 500s, and half in the 600s. However, Middlebury rejected two out of three applicants with SAT scores in the 600s!

This is the reality of selective admissions. A student may see himself in a college class profile based on his academic record, but the college may not see *him* for one reason or another. The competition is fierce, and a guidance counselor has no easy job in helping a Winslow student decide where to apply, given the natural tendency of students to overrate their chances at better colleges.

Guidance at Winslow is good as far as it goes, but six counselors have 1,700 students to guide, and they simply do not have time to devote to the thorough college admissions service such as better private schools can afford. The kind of adequate counseling that every high school needs is provided by Boston Latin, which is a sort of public prep school with competitive admissions open only to Boston children. Edwin Mosher is the college guidance counselor for 373 seniors, *all* of whom go to four-year colleges. Probably too many apply to Harvard—75 in 1973—but Mosher cannot stop students from hoping against hope, and anyway it is, of course, the student's right to apply where he likes. Harvard took 19 from Boston Latin that year, Dartmouth took 4, Cornell 6, MIT 8, Tufts 21, Penn 9, Yale 2 and Wesleyan 2. But the biggest numbers went from Boston Latin to: Northeastern, in Boston (65), UMass (Amherst 120, Boston 90), Boston College (43) and Boston University (38). Those Harvard applicants that did not make it, certainly made out all right.

Brookline High also has it all over Winslow in college counseling. The program includes three meetings with parents of juniors. About 17 percent of the four-year college group are accepted at highly selective colleges from Brookline High. Yet there is a gap between Brookline High and Boston Latin, since the city of Brookline (60,000) guarantees every child a secondary education, while Boston Latin takes only 325 of the 4,000 applying, the top scorers in the School Scholastic Aptitude Test (SSAT). Only a few schools are as academically sharp. Boston Latin offers no practical arts, only traditional subjects. It is, like Bronx High School of Science in New York, an exception among public schools, an elite school along Continental lines, dating back to 1637 and catering now mostly to modest families. Among its students were Benjamin Franklin, John Hancock, Ralph Waldo Emerson, George Santayana and Joseph P. Kennedy.

If there were a pecking order among public schools, Boston Latin would be the equivalent of Harvard, Brookline might be a Penn or Columbia, and Winslow might be near the bottom of the list of the first 100. The tax rate in Winslow is the same as in Brookline, and certainly Winslow is superior to most high schools in Massachusetts. But any family that has a choice of places to live in the Boston area and wants the best high school for its children might hesitate to move to Winslow. It will certainly pay dividends these days to spend some time investigating the schools of the community a family is moving to. For those already settled, only concerted pressure on school boards will keep high schools at a challenging level.

The Trouble with Counselors

Few high schools can afford to assign a counselor to deal with admissions exclusively. So most counselors have several hundred students in their charge, from three or four different grades, from a multitude of backgrounds, and with a range of problems that include pregnancy, dope addiction, family troubles, personal depression and of course academic difficulties. Counselors, though overworked, are trained to be understanding and supportive, and the high schools would be more chaotic and disturbed without them.

Nonetheless most counselors are generalists trained to deal with average students from modest backgrounds. They are not social workers, and they quickly turn really disturbed youngsters over to professionals. And at the other end of the spectrum, they are not very knowledgeable about or interested in selective colleges. Suburban schools may have counselors who are by sheer exposure acquainted with hard-to-get-into colleges, but even these counselors are themselves seldom graduates of such colleges. Furthermore, the turnover in personnel makes if difficult for a counseling department to assign a specialist to the small group of students qualified to apply to the top colleges.

Unless a counselor is held responsible for misguiding students in their college applications, he has no incentive to encourage the better students to apply to the tougher places. Most high schools, even in the suburbs, are content to see 50 or 60 percent of their seniors go to some college, including two-year colleges. Democratic pressures keep high schools from proclaiming their success in getting students into the Ivy League institutions, and, in listing the colleges last year's seniors went to, specific numbers going to Harvard or Oberlin are omitted generally, so that these colleges appear in a list together with the local community college and junior colleges.

Who would have it otherwise? Why should families be made to feel inadequate by proclamations indicating that an elite group went to the so-called better colleges? This being so, counselors feel no obligation to push students into a competitive race they may lose. It is much easier to look over the student's grades and scores and try to slot him mechanically according to the statistics.

Another limitation is the lack of personal knowledge of selective colleges among most high school counselors. They have not visited very many of these campuses or familiarized themselves with their differences. There is too much else to do; they have many other responsibilities for really serious adjustment problems to worry very much about the well-adjusted, comfortable student who is wondering whether to apply to Cornell or Hobart.

Some high schools recognize this situation, and a few that can afford it hire professional counselors to handle college admissions. Some parents go to professional counselors (if there are any in their community) because they are dissatisfied with the counseling provided by the high school. Others would do well to accept the limitations circumstances impose on counselors trained more likely in schools of education and uneasy with selective college admissions problems. This means talking to someone more knowledgeable, such as the alumnus of a selective college working on an admissions committee. Or, if the family can afford it, transferring the student to a private school that has excellent college counseling. The chances of getting a change in high school counseling practices are few—and anyway, by the time they might occur, it will be too late to help the student who needs it now.

The Impact of Federalism

The unevenness of high school quality is the result of the federal character of our government that puts control of public education at the community level, subject to standards set by each state. Countries with centralized governments have developed centralized school systems that can set national standards. The standards, though, apply only to students selected for the college-level track (as early as age 11 in England), and these students tend to be middle class or higher.

It is obviously true, as S. M. Miller and Frank Riessman point out in *Social Class and Social Policy* (1968) that "Education is now the major route to social mobility in the United States," but public schools and public colleges unfortunately are not altering the tiering of people into a class structure, but actually are reinforcing it. "It is not rich and poor that divide Americans; it is educated and uneducated," wrote David B. Wilson, a *Boston Globe* columnist (February 3, 1974).

Recognition of the disadvantages suffered by those in poorly funded school systems has aroused more than indignation. Recent court cases in Texas, California and Virginia have challenged the basis of school inequality: the property tax. The wealthy community has better schools than the poor community. But telephone service is uniform, roads are as good through rural slums as through districts of rich estates. Why should there not be a national standard, a minimum per-pupil cost for all schools? Until there is, the wise parent will pay close attention to his children's education if he expects them to do well in the selective admissions competition.

Here are some impressions from the diary of a bright ninth-grader in a New York high school:

> Everyone in the class was talking, so the English teacher, Mr. Lax, ran out of the room—like a child—and didn't come back. After he left, my class, on its own, went on with the lesson. Actually it was even better than with the teacher. . . . I have just realized that the teachers disturb the class much more than they say the children do. A couple of words between students might bring about fifteen minutes of yelling from the teacher. . . . This morning Mr. Simmons the assistant principal made the crass remark: "You kids could stand through your whole lunch period or eat during the period, it doesn't matter to me. . . ." Yesterday all our teachers who screamed at us all year said we'd been lovely students—we'd brightened up their lives. What bull! They hate us, just as we hate them. . . . [From *High School,* ed. by Ronald Gross and Paul Osterman. New York: Simon and Schuster, 1971]

We had an opportunity to see at first hand what the authorities are up against while calling on the principal of an excellent school. He introduced us to a teacher and a 17-year-old student named Frank. "Well, what is it this time?" the principal asked.

The teacher said that Frank had been seen with two others stealing a $200-microscope from a lab. Frank denied it. "Who was there with you?" Vaguely the boy talked of a lot of kids. "Frank! You aren't answering my question! Okay!" cried the principal. "Frank, you are to go home and the matter will be looked into by the police unless the microscope is in my little hot hands by three o'clock this afternoon. I am not going to play judge here!"

After the teacher took Frank out, the principal explained that Frank has been on the carpet a dozen times, including times with his parents—a hysterical mother and a father who is a successful retail store operator. "We have lost a $5,000-typesetter, nine typewriters and ten cameras. We got the cameras back and while we were dealing with the thieves in another room, someone took the cameras from this office, and that's the last we've seen of them. They sell the stuff in half an hour. Frank, by the way, has drug problems. Did you notice his coat? Real leather. Two hundred dollars!"

Although his school is first class academically, the principal will not send his own children to it! "I don't like the values here." His secretary, a graduate of the high school, sighed: "Oh, how it has changed!"

A school can change for the worse rapidly. One suburban family sent four children to the local high school with satisfaction, but the fifth child, after three years of success, said the place was boring, and she was sent to a challenging boardingschool, which she loved.

The realization that public high schools, by mixing the few academically interested with the many academically unmotivated, can hurt some students is coming to the surface. The *Seattle Times* in the fall of 1973 ran an account of a mother whose son forced her to transfer him from high school to one of the few private schools in the Northwest, the excellent Lakeside School. The headline read: THE SAVING OF A BORED HONOR STUDENT. "At the end of his first day at Lakeside, he came home with an armload of books and a small secret smile. The second day the books increased and the smile enlarged." So wrote a mother in frankness about her boy who, she said, had been hostile, noncommittal, a cutter of high school classes and a TV viewer more than a reader.

Few can afford a Lakeside, yet more parents seem prepared to make the sacrifice. Galen Brewster, college counselor at Middlesex School in Massachusetts, a famous Harvard feeder in the old days, reports that applications rose in 1973 despite the threat of recession. School boards would do well to heed these signs if they wish their high schools to live up to reputations for excellence that may not in fact be deserved.

7

Private School: Tenuous Link

Until the sixties it was good insurance for a student applying to one or more selective colleges to attend a *good* private school. The cost of that insurance has risen, while the number of claims honored has sharply diminished. At Concord Academy in Massachusetts, considered to be one of the most academically demanding private schools, the tuition for boarders is $4,200, and most of the students hope to be admitted to a selective college. Half the 70 seniors do make it. This is well above the public school performance.

Burt Honea, the school's college counselor, believes that every parent secretly expects his or her child to get into one of the "better" colleges, despite warnings from the beginning that only the very best will enter the likes of Radcliffe or Yale or Princeton (in 1973 Concord Academy's acceptance score was 10, 5 and 4 out of 23, 21 and 12 applying to those three colleges).

From South Kent in Connecticut, where the academic level is not so high, about 10 percent get into highly selective colleges. Yet in both cases the schools have more applicants than they can accept. Private schools today are no longer just "prep" schools for prestigious colleges. Perhaps this is why so many students want to go to them; the despised preppy image has largely given way to an image of an exciting educational experience unavailable at public high schools.

And strong students in private schools can often improve their chances for selective college admissions. There are, of course, more strong students collectively in public schools, but they did not apply in such numbers to Vassar or Williams until recent years. On the other hand, private schools infrequently sent students to Stanford, Pomona or the University of Chicago in the old days.

"The general public has little interest in what it calls 'prep school,' " Theodore Sizer, headmaster of Andover, said in a speech in 1972, "perceiving them as being smug, outdated bastions of WASP society."

It might be thought that the general public is incapable of perceiving private schools at all without a microscope. Excluding parochial and denominational schools, there are 3,200 private schools with an enrollment of 200,000, one percent of U.S. secondary school students. Such a miniscule cluster is so small as to be invisible to most people. A Gallup International survey in 1969 showed that even in communities with private schools there was little knowledge of tuition, scholarships or philanthropic support of such institutions. Yet lacking specific knowledge about private schools, those surveyed expressed approval of them. Otto F. Kraushaar in *American Nonpublic Schools* (1972) concludes that private schools are "widely accepted as a natural expression of a pluralistic society."

The "nonpublic schools" include the 12,000 parochial schools, and they represent three-fourths of primary and secondary students not in public schools. Of the rest, most are denominational schools. The term "private school" refers to schools essentially secular in training, though some of the most famous are strongly Episcopal—St. Mark's, St. Paul's, Groton, St. George's, St. Andrews.

It is with the private, or independent, schools, as their administrations like to call them, that selective colleges have their strongest links, and it is these schools that have been attacked for their exclusiveness and supposed antidemocratic character. Kraushaar, who has taught philosophy at Smith, the University of Iowa and Harvard, wrote his study under the auspices of the National Association of Independent Schools, representing 800 private schools throughout the country. He points out that sociologists like C. Wright Mills and E. Digby Baltzell oversimplify when they describe elite boarding schools as transmission belts of upper-class tradition and regulators of those who will be allowed to join the wealthy establishment. He cites James McLachlan's study, *American Boarding Schools,* in describing the mission of such schools as the training of bourgeois gentlemen rather than an aristocratic elite.

Private Schools Not Declining

Many people assume private schools are on the way out, but the evidence is to the contrary. They have not kept apace of the baby boom of the fifties, but during the post-World War II period a number of new day schools opened. A few boarding schools have closed (military schools are all but extinct) and others have empty beds. But the better schools are experiencing no difficulty in attracting applicants; their greatest problem is inflation, which has required them to engage in tremendous fund-raising efforts that used to be limited to the colleges.

Robert Parsons, an educational consultant in Boston for 20 years, has as many clients as ever, and they come to him from Dallas and Grosse Point as well as from New York for his advice on the right New England schools for their children. The fact that some boarding schools are not hard to get into makes parents suspicious of cordial campus visits and they rely on Parsons for frank assessments. The renowned schools still can pick and choose among applicants, with Exeter and Andover leading as first choices. Overlapping applications are also a private school characteristic.

John Esty, former headmaster of Taft in Connecticut, has recently published a book, *Choosing a Private School* (1974), whose title suggests that the choice lies with the client. This is largely true with the exception of the most well-known schools. At Lawrenceville in New Jersey no one hides the fact that it is easier to be admitted there than it used to be, but it is still somewhat competitive. Middlesex in Massachusetts has noted a slight decline in the academic quality of its top students, but reports an increase in applicants in 1974 that is expected to show up in higher SAT average scores.

So the private schools are very much alive if not financially robust, and some like Exeter and Groton are in a stronger financial position than many colleges. Alumni of these schools often feel more loyal to them than to their colleges, and they are generous in their giving. Exeter has a larger endowment than Bowdoin, for example. At the same time, Exeter has cut its janitorial staff 20 percent and introduced a mountable vacuum cleaner to speed up sweeping the gym and other large areas.

Economy is so important that the modern headmaster cannot devote the time to education he once did. "The new headmaster," according to Howard L. Jones, president of the Northfield-Mount Hermon School in Massachusetts, "will be sympatico with young people but he won't be ever present and he certainly won't be unhurried or unharried."

The View from St. Mark's

A man having trouble converting to new ways is Edward T. Hall, headmaster of St. Mark's until the summer of 1974. This Episcopal school in Southboro, Massachusetts, was founded in 1865 and was at one time the quintessence of exclusiveness. This resulted from the simple procedure of registering male children with the school at birth. Parvenus wanting to send their children there could do so only if some of the places already spoken for were for some reason not taken up. It still caters to old families, but applicants are accepted on merit. There is an endowment of $14 million to ensure financial viability, but the administrative detail that faces Ned Hall is more than he wants to put up with in his mid-fifties. The headmaster still has his office in the school lounge where students come in for coffee or to read the papers, but this quaint intimacy is spoiled by endless demands on his time, much of which is spent on the telephone.

"I liked to put on goalie pads and get out on the ice with the boys," says this former Yale goalie. "But I seldom had the chance."

He probably knows as much about college admissions as any headmaster, for he was on the admissions staff at Yale in the forties and served the Hill School in Pottstown, Pennsylvania, as headmaster for 15 years before returning to St. Mark's, where he had studied and taught. He knew the college admissions directors on a first-name basis, and they were prepared to take his word on students. Hall's thoughts about private schools' difficulties in getting their students over the best ivy walls are worth paying attention to:

Several factors have seemed lately to militate against the admission of private school graduates. Among them are: 1. Increased participation in the admissions process by faculty members whose bias is in favor of high scores rather than "well-rounded" characters, minority students instead of "preppies." 2. The whole process of democratization and egalitarianism that began with the GI Bill. 3. The Ivy group's conscious effort to reach out more widely in schools throughout the country, many of which had seldom sent applicants to this group. 4. The improvement in quality of many high schools. 5. Public policy favoring equal opportunities for minority groups. 6. Women entering men's colleges, men entering women's colleges. This trend almost automatically does two things: increases overall interest in the college or university, and reduces the number of places available to the sex for which the college was originally founded.*

Hall believes the private school graduate's chances for admission to selective colleges will improve in the future. He cites the growing difficulty of all but a few colleges in providing financial aid to every accepted applicant; resentment of alumni over present admissions policies that seem to give insufficient favor to their children and to athletes, and resentment of alumni volunteers whose candidates are turned down; realization by the colleges that they need some affluent students who will be their future benefactors.

The decreased percentage of private school graduates in the colleges where they predominated is due to meritocratic policies that arose with the expansion of the middle classes and the mountains of applications from public high school students. Colleges such as MIT and Mount Holyoke have traditionally drawn three-fourths of their students from public schools and so no policy changes occurred in those and in others with a small private school clientele—Rutgers, Boston University, Stanford, Cal Tech, etc. Had the Ivy colleges not been more open to high school applicants, they would have found themselves increasingly isolated and provincial in a changing nation. They responded to criticism of their predominantly Protestant Anglo-Saxon character by a vigorous search for *worthy* high school candi-

*Princeton ended quotas on the number of women admitted in 1974. The 800/300 enrollment of men and women is expected to change to between 730 to 760 men, and 370 to 340 women in the Class of 1978. Before women enrolled in 1969 a class numbered 800. Yale has eliminated sex quotas, and Harvard has reduced its class size to allow Radcliffe to expand.

dates. But the response in some cases took the form of overkill. Inevitably the private schools suffered a neglect that may not always have been benign.

Exeter's Lament and Choate's Troubles

To be blunt, it is difficult not to perceive some "tilt" in favor of high school candidates as an unwritten limit on the private schools to quotas considerably smaller than in the past. This is vigorously denied by admissions officers, who reply that the high school candidates are so impressive that their merit commands their admission in most cases, save those of athletes, alumni children and minority groups. To take the instance of Harvard and Exeter, here is the 35-year record:

TABLE II

	NUMBER APPLYING FROM EXETER TO HARVARD	NUMBER ACCEPTED BY HARVARD FROM EXETER
1935	93	93
1940	72	72
1945	73	71
1950	76	72
1955	96	94
1960	108	60
1965	98	47
1970	95	38

Harvard acceptances are now stabilized at about one-third of the Exeter applicants.

Is it possible that the quality of Exeter students fell off sharply between 1955 and 1960, as the figures indicate, or that Exeter declined in its academic excellence during the sixties? The inference to be drawn is that Harvard and other colleges that were fed large numbers from a handful of prep schools—Lawrenceville used to send 80 a year to Princeton!—found that students from these schools were too socially dominant and invariably clubbed together, not necessarily excluding high school students, but certainly constituting cliques that no high school group could offset.

By rejecting so many Exeter students, Harvard in effect redistributed the wealth of talent. There is no need to feel very sorry for those who did not get in, for some of them went to: Brown (19), Dartmouth (21), Penn (14), Princeton (13), Yale (28), Radcliffe (4), Amherst (5) and so on. Overlapping applications allow Exeter to make an impressive record of acceptances by selective colleges. In fact the fraction of the upper third of the graduating class going to Princeton, Yale or Harvard has remained a constant two-thirds since the 1930s.

A famous instance of open hostility to a private school was the interview Inslee Clark, director of admissions at Yale, gave to the *Choate News* in 1968. At that time Yale's private school admissions had dropped to 38 percent, as against 63 percent 20 years earlier. Clark, a public school graduate, displayed no deep affection for Choate in the interview. Later Clark talked to Peter Prescott, a *Newsweek* staff writer on leave to do a book about Choate:

A school like Choate, [said Clark,] if it wants to be a truly national school, and wants to admit, say, one hundred new boys, might consider having two or three full-time men in the admissions department out beating the bushes throughout the fall term. Six to eight weeks' travel per man. The school has to decide what it wants to be. For example, is it going to be a school for the most talented boys in this country, in other words a great national high school? That's one approach. The other approach is to say: "We have a special kind of function as a boarding school—individual attention, special help, taking many of the sons of our alumni and helping them develop so they'll be better, stronger students than they would have been if they'd gone through public school." All of which may be justified. But this may not lead to great numbers getting into Yale.

In the long run, what's going to pay off in college admissions is the capacity and the motivation and the performance and the talent of the individual—not just the training. I don't see any way, frankly, for Choate to get great numbers into Yale, if that's an objective, unless they go out and find the most talented boys in the country. Just training those that they've got will not do it. [*A World of Our Own*, New York: Dell, 1972]

No Harvard admissions director ever talked that way about Exeter because Exeter *does* beat the bushes for talent and *is* a national high school. Clark's meritocratic enthusiasm was not appreciated by some Yale alumni. His indifference to an Andover athlete was bitterly remembered when Harvard took the boy, who was particularly successful in leading the Crimson to victory over old Eli. Clark is now headmaster of a New York private school, Horace Mann.

A Sense of Outrage

Every private school has an outrageous story to tell about selective college admissions, but the raconteurs speak off the record for the most part, or they confine their griping to those college admissions officers who are sympathetic and can always say that they wanted a particular candidate in question to be admitted, but were overruled by the admissions committee.

Headmasters have learned to live with the knowledge that only their top students will get into the top colleges, even though the second level is probably as strong or stronger than many high school applicants that are admitted. A Radcliffe girl who went to a rural high school says candidly, "I probably could not have been admitted from the private school where my mother teaches." From that same private school Princeton took six students. A seventh, whose father is a Princetonian, was rejected, although she had SAT scores in the low 600s. From the local high school she might well have made it, because Princeton just was not going to take another boy from that school. The Princeton admissions office doubts this possibility, but a Harvard admissions man agrees that this could happen at Harvard.

At least all this is far from the myth that anyone can get into these colleges with pull. It is the world turned upside down in some cases, where wealthy alumni are unable to help their privately educated children beat out others who have no pull whatever, but may be public school graduates. A Yale alumnus running into an old classmate for the first time in years at a hockey game asked him what he was doing in New Haven.

"I'm on the schools committee and I'm here talking to the admissions office." At which the other man burst out in anger, "Bringing in some high school kid to take my son's place!" His son was at a boarding school.

The only guarantee a private school student has for admission to Yale is to study like hell and aim to be as high in his class as he or she possibly can be. Yale has told Exeter they will not look at any student with less than a B minus average (an Exeter C plus is a B plus at a good high school). But failing to reach the top of the class, most private school students still are the beneficiaries of a special kind of experience, and they spend their time in an environment that is certainly different from public high school or the private school of the past.

What John Esty calls "shopworn Protestantism" has just about disappeared from private schools, and because they are on the defensive and feel put upon, they have had to discard their sense of natural superiority and justify their existence to a skeptical world. With their link to the selective colleges weakened, private schools are rethinking their *raison d'être,* and while doing so are providing extraordinary education for those few who can afford it or are lucky enough to win scholarships.

Sumner Rulon-Miller III, chairman of the board of trustees of Proctor Academy in New Hampshire, has his board actually looking into the question of whether the school should continue to exist, which is really a challenging way of asking its purposes to be defined. With almost no endowment, Proctor has discovered that its chief asset is its 800 acres of wilderness that provide a laboratory for ecological studies and a place where students can test their endurance. Other private schools have had to develop their own particular strengths in order to keep their enrollments.

Robert Parsons, the consultant, finds that private schools are leaner and have more muscle than they had a few years ago at the height of the go-go stock market (many tuitions at private schools are paid not out of earned income but from capital gains—of grandparents as well as of parents). And of course these schools started out lean. Look at the pictures of Taft when it was founded in 1890 in an old hotel in Watertown, Connecticut. The Protestant ethic, so much reviled now, required a spartanism that had no need for elegance. The private schools as we know them began to come into being after the Civil War, and most were founded in the twentieth century.

A Not Long History

Their forerunners were the academies, inspired greatly by Benjamin Franklin's *Proposals Relating to the Education of Youth in Pensilvania* and *Idea of the English School* (as opposed to the Latin school). Some 6,185 academies were in existence in 1850 in every section of the country. They were forerunners of the public high school as well as of the exclusive private schools. Kraushaar describes the academies as "either private or church-related schools serving a clearly public function, often in close partnership with states or counties which contributed to their support."

Academies were varied and unstructured, with students as young as six and as old as thirty. Some trained boys for college and others were in effect colleges, and became colleges later. Some were terminal. Boarders lived with local families, so the school was responsible for instruction but not for housing and feeding its charges. The level of academic preparation was by today's standards low, and as the colleges, really no more than glorified high schools by European standards, became more serious and demanding, they found it necessary to ensure themselves better prepared undergraduates by encouraging the foundation of "prep schools" like Hotchkiss for Yale and Lawrenceville for Princeton.

The academies gave way for the most part to the public high school. Some of the most famous retained the name *academy*: Phillips Exeter, Phillips Andover, Episcopal, Milton, Deerfield, as contrasted with St. Paul's School or the Hill School. The new model of the boarding school was based on a concept first developed at a school called Round Hill in Northampton, Massachusetts, operated briefly by Joseph Greer Cogswell and the historian George Bancroft in the early 1830s on the principles of the Italian educator, Pestallozi, and his Swiss disciple, Fellenberg. While not disciplinarian in character, Round Hill demanded that the entire life of the student be guided by the school according to Fellenberg doctrine:

The great art of educating consists in knowing how to occupy every moment of life in well-directed and useful activity of the youthful powers, in order that . . . nothing evil may find room to develop itself.

No more boarding off the premises. No more association with the local community. The new school would withdraw the student in order to strengthen him for the rigors of higher learning. St. Paul's, St. Mark's and Milton Academy were founded on the Round Hill model. Round Hill had attracted wealthy families, and the descendants of Round Hill alumni went to such schools generation after generation. Lawrenceville, founded in 1882, was a leader in creating a model for nonsectarian boarding schools that had both dormitories and smaller houses where boys lived with a master and his family.

These schools catered to the wealthy, and as the country grew larger, more private day schools and boarding schools were founded around the large cities of the East and Middle West. Most of them were not very exclusive and rarely very selective. During the Depression some closed their doors. In 1942 a young teacher reporting in September for the first time to Simms Adams, headmaster of Lakeside School in Seattle, found him in an exhilarated mood, holding up an adding-machine tape. "We made it!" he told the newcomer. "We just enrolled another boy and we'll break even."

Coeducation was all but nonexistent in the new private secondary schools, and as we now all realize, the education of women was somewhat neglected in the early days of the republic. Nonetheless, most Midwestern academies in the nineteenth century were co-ed. In the East three institutions set the pace among what were called in a highfalutin Latinized term, female seminaries: Troy Female Seminary, 1821 (now the Emma Willard School); Mount Holyoke Seminary, 1836 (which became the college); and Hartford Female Seminary founded in 1828 by Catherine Beecher, sister of Harriet Beecher Stowe, author of *Uncle Tom's Cabin*.

These schools went beyond the finishing-school purpose of creating gracious consorts for cultivated gentlemen, and taught a range of academic subjects that fitted many of their graduates to be school teachers. Latin was not in the curriculum and the emphasis fell on science and mathematics. Competitive athletics were not stressed, so the atmosphere at first was quite distinct from the boys' boarding school. As more women went to college, the female seminaries came to be more like their male counterparts, and today the two have come together as coeducational schools. Rosemary Hall in Greenwich, Connecticut, joined Choate in Wallingford, 69 miles away (Choate put up $3 million for the move), Andover absorbed Abbot Academy and also absorbed the $1,000 difference in tuition between the two schools.

Just as Belmont Hill in suburban Boston was a feeder to Harvard, Dana Hall in Wellesley was to Wellesley College, Baldwin outside Philadelphia was to Bryn Mawr, and Brearley in New York was to Radcliffe. There were girls' schools that remained fashionable finishing schools until after World War II, when they too became preparatory schools—Foxcroft, Ethel Walker, Miss Porter's, schools which still have enormous cachet for those in the Social Register and which also send their graduates in some numbers to the selective colleges.

The perpetuation of private schools seems assured after some serious doubts that arose in the turbulent sixties. John Esty, coming at the age of 30 from Amherst teaching and administration to the headmastership of Taft, predicted in 1966 that two-thirds of the private schools would not survive. Of more than 3,000 only some 30 or 40 have gone out of existence since then, and Esty now has revised his judgment, while still feeling that private schools have not been particularly inspiring in helping youth establish a strong set of new moral values.

World of Their Own

No private school has ever been more closely scrutinized than Choate by Peter S. Prescott in 1967–68. A graduate of Choate and Harvard, he was given permission to spend a school year on campus watching, listening, interviewing. He found himself at a troubled institution where masters sat up until two in the morning discussing the rigidity of the school's structure and the stultifying effect that four years of living in *A World of Our Own,* as Prescott called his book, can have on young minds and spirits.

In a poll of the seniors, only 53 percent said they would come to Choate if they had it to do over. A silent vigil of protest outside the chapel on National Student Protest Day, unfortunately reported in the *New York Times,* along with similar protests in Prague and Warsaw, caused the headmaster, Seymour St. John, to dress down the faculty members who encouraged dissidence among their students, and some 96 boys were punished. A poll of 536 students revealed *inter alia* not just pot smoking among 20 percent, but cheating among 50 percent. Forty percent boasted they would go to a prostitute, and 82.7 percent said they would sleep with their fiancées before marriage. All of this in a very *Episcopal* school with compulsory chapel!

A few days later St. John, usually a quiet sort of authoritarian, blew his stack before the whole school assembled, reading the riot act —which he had taken pains to write out:

> I am so fed up with human beings who expect to be happy without working for it—the sniveling, self-pitying, non-contributing crybabies— that I can't keep it to myself any longer. I refer to a few chronic gripers who have been given everything, for whom men and women at this school and elsewhere have worked their hearts out. . . . They know the kitchen staff will always be up at five A.M. so that their breakfast will be ready. But they're 'dissatisfied.' They are too young and too spoiled to realize that satisfaction and happiness cannot be served up on a silver platter.

It was something you would expect the *New York Daily News* to run as an editorial. College admission was not neglected.

> No one believes college admission is the major aim of education. But listen to this. A boy said a month ago that if he didn't get into the college of his choice he'd walk out of school—if you can imagine such an attitude. Well, through our joint efforts he did get in. And do you know what he then criticized? The fact that Choate is too concerned with college admission—that college admission really isn't that important— that he wishes he'd gone to a school where less emphasis was put on academic work and more on something else. How can you win?

He ended by inviting any boy who was dissatisfied to come to his office and withdraw from the school forthwith.

No student withdrew, but some teachers resigned. A strong hand had subdued what? A reasonable restlessness and dissatisfaction with the status quo. Next year Prescott's book, which St. John had vainly attempted to see in manuscript, was required reading in senior English. Choate, now co-ed and without St. John, who retired in 1972 after 25 years, is a happier and less-structured school, as most good private schools seem to be today.

Theodore Sizer as dean of the Harvard School of Education was outspokenly critical of private schools, but now as headmaster of Andover he has said: "There are few students who would not benefit in their high school careers for some period of months or years with experience in the intense learning community that a great boarding school can be." Which pretty well says that private schools are so good that everyone ought to be able to go to them.

But to what end? Frederick C. Calder, headmaster of Germantown Friends School in Philadelphia, has this to say:

> The fact is that most of the pressure to go to college originates in the students themselves and in their families, who are naturally influenced by a society that places an immense value on a college education. Much of the motivation for going to college probably has little to do with improving the mind and much more to do with placing one's self, or one's child, where power and prestige unite in a formidable promise of future success. This is especially true of the Ivy League and a few similarly established colleges and universities considered equally competitive.
>
> Of course, Germantown Friends School wants everyone to have the chance to go to college, if that is what he or she wishes, but we also want some people with or without a college education to have a chance to be a farmer, a carpenter, an athlete, a poet, or a prophet. What we really wish is for anyone who leaves our school to do whatever he wants as long as it strengthens him and in some small way improves the world instead of spoiling it.
>
> If college, *per se,* isn't our goal, then what is? Why struggle to keep this expensive, complex community going? The answer is that we have a lot of hopes for the young people who make it through here. We hope that when they leave they will be well on the way to becoming cultivated men and women; people with sharpened intellects, with developing good tastes and with a strong sense of civility. We hope that they will have a slightly better sense of humor than when they came; that they will be able to laugh at their own foibles and vulnerabilities with the rest of the world. We hope that the world and how it works will be a great deal

clearer and that reality will surprise them much less often than it did before. We hope that they will like themselves a little better, because until they do, they will never be free to love others. And finally, we hope that they will understand better that whatever happens to this planet and the creatures that live on it, they can never by themselves alone overcome the eternal obstacles to peace, freedom and happiness.

So how does college fit into all of this? By itself it doesn't. College is simply another place of experience in the journey we all take through life and if a student wants to go there, well and good; but that's not why GFS is here.

The last sentence may be true, but few parents would spend money for a private school that ignored its obligation to see that their children got into the best colleges they could. Sensible parents accept philosophically the risks of their children being rejected by some of the stiffer colleges, but they still expect that a private school can do a better job than a high school in preparing them for whatever college they can make. Moreover, they expect, and rightly, that the private school will be more knowledgeable about alternative colleges and will better help their children through that strained period when they are applying to colleges, visiting campuses, taking tests and being interviewed by alumni, coaches and admissions officers.

Inside Exeter

To see what a private school has to offer, let us spend a few moments at Exeter. The Harvard of private education was founded in 1781 and has 30,000 living alumni. It is the most heavily endowed of private schools ($79 million in 1973) but it does not have the aura of old family wealth found at a St. George's, and it has one of the lowest tuitions—$3,000 in 1973. Twenty-eight percent of the students are on scholarships ranging from $300 to $3,000, and this costs the school $550,000 a year. It is now co-ed.

Although its enrollment of 950 is twice that of some and thrice that of most private schools, an atmosphere of intimacy is achieved through residence in houses of 40 supervised by a faculty member, and in classrooms limited to 12 students. Competition for admission is severe and an applicant has one chance in four of being admitted. Competition within Exeter is also severe, and academic requirements are grueling.

An alumnus back for a football game observed how small the band was. "What's the matter? Not taking in enough musicians?" No, he was told, there were lots of musicians in the school, but most of them just did not have time for the band.

A member of the Class of 1957 described the rigors of Exeter's training: "After leaving a public high school as a sophomore, number one in my class with nothing but As, I entered Exeter in my upper middle year (junior). I immediately saw nothing but Cs and Ds. It took me two years at Exeter to pull myself up to High Honors. At Exeter I learned to think instead of memorize. I learned the value of a course was the experience involved and the thoughts and thought processes derived and not the grades. I learned that the striving for scholastic excellence is an involvement in life itself and not merely a classroom experience and means to a grade."

Since the early thirties, Exeter has taught on the Harkness Plan, which doubled the faculty and cut classes in half, thanks to a $5-million gift from E. S. Harkness, a Yale man best known for making possible by his philanthropy Harvard's house system. Sitting around oval tables day in, day out, the students have no place to hide and must recite daily. "They teach each other," says Charles Burdick of the English department.

Paul Sadler, director of publications, recalls his days as a student in the forties. "You could learn a lot by finding out how little you knew. You'd get wound up and the teacher would say, 'Go ahead, Sadler, you tell us.' Pretty soon you'd feel those eyes on you—not the teacher's, the rest of the class. They wouldn't even have to say anything sometimes to make you realize you hadn't thought it through."

Few private schools take students just for a year, but Exeter has always taken a number of one-year students, some who have already graduated from high school. A postgraduate in the Class of 1949 commented: "I was able to say that I learned more in one year at Exeter than I had in the entire three or four years of studying a particular subject in high school."

Needless to add that Exeter, set in a lovely old southern New Hampshire town, has one of the most beautiful campuses anywhere, and outstanding facilities for varsity and intramural athletics, drama, publications, music and other extracurricular activities. But of special interest is the attention devoted to a student's college admissions choices. David Thomas of the English department was assigned to supervise this work for a five-year period with the help of a part-time assistant. Thomas does not teach while holding this position, which is full time and involves getting to know 350 candidates and their chances of getting into the colleges of their choice. Here is Thomas describing his work:

> We begin with a meeting of the juniors in January, alerting them to the March SATs. In February I write the juniors' parents, explaining admissions procedures. I urge them to take their children to college campuses during spring vacation to begin laying the ground for deciding where they would like to go. Interviews are not given in early spring many places, but the visit can be profitable. We allow no time off at Exeter for campus visits—ever.
>
> Between April and June we interview the juniors to get their reactions. During this time some colleges will interview juniors on the Exeter campus, and arrangements will be made for interviews elsewhere during summer vacation. In June the parents receive their second letter, more personal this time, based on our talks with their children. Most parents do not get too deeply involved in the admissions process, but occasionally we have some intense telephone conversations when there is disappointment about a rating or an actual rejection. Some will say they sent their son here to get into Harvard and want value for their money.
>
> Each candidate is carried on a college choice card where we mark the grades as they come in. In a few instances only two applications are filed, but we want most students to have three choices, and some even apply to more. They generally are realistic about their chances. Exeter seniors get into about 70 different colleges. At least that many send representatives and more would like to, but we have to say no.
>
> Senior year we interview the candidates again and make sure that if there is any slippage in performance that the safety valve application has gone in. Our files on each student include reports from teachers, dormitory supervisors, coaches, advisors beginning in junior year. From this we compose a report that goes to every college every applicant has filed with, and no student sees these. Princeton has told us that ours are the most useful school reports they get. In addition, the applicants get their teachers to write reports. These are done with enormous care and

love. The record I know of was 87 reports by one teacher. It takes an hour to write a report, and of course no teacher would repeat what he has said or stoop to Xerox something and use it at more than one college.

This kind of college admissions guidance is done so confidently and without fanfare that students and parents scarcely realize what a burden has been lifted from them. All good boarding schools do something similar, although not many can afford a full-time college admissions counselor these days.

At Northfield–Mount Hermon, the biggest private school in the country, there are two full-time and two part-time people doing this work. So important is this to private schools, some now hire consultants who specialize in college admissions to take over this function. Parents choosing a private school when a child is only 14 may neglect to inquire what kind of college admissions counseling can be expected in junior and senior years, and then find this service is inadequate when it is too late to do anything about it. At that point parents generally turn to a consultant to whom they must pay a fee that rightfully should be part of private school tuition.

We believe that most parents ultimately consider the private school's chief function to be good preparation for higher education. For them the payoff is college admission. But if some private school graduates never get to college they have already had a superb education. Exeter has four courses in anthropology, something many *colleges* do not offer. Concord Academy has 41 course in media arts, particularly in film. South Kent students still must go to daily chapel. At Putney cross-country skiing is taught by the coach of the U.S. Olympic team. The new library at Middlesex is something any community would treasure.

Newspapers like the *Choate News* provide journalism training. Taft is well known for its theater and music programs. Thatcher students become accomplished equestrians. And although discipline is not as rigid as it once was, there are private schools that still have dress codes—Exeter, South Kent, Avon–Old Farms, for example. Pot smoking may be widespread, but it brings instant expulsion if found out at most private schools. Four Exeter seniors were expelled in 1973 because they were found off limits with a six-pack of beer. One school that has few rules is finding that long hair and indifference to appearance leads to sloppy academic work.

The largest growth in private education has come in day schools. The lower tuition appeals to parents, and living at home is preferred by some students. Remaining in their community the students still keep in touch with their friends, while profiting from the stiffer competition and general excellence of the private school (not all, of course, are excellent, but it is difficult for a weak school to survive now).

In determining between a boarding school and a day school for their children, parents have to evaluate the talents, interests and needs of the individual child. This is not easy for parents, and professional counsel can be helpful. The important thing is to examine a number of schools. Private school selection is just as important as college selection. A student who is unhappy in school is less likely to get into the college of his choice.

Small as private schools are by comparison with the massiveness of American high schools, they appear in their present scope here to stay, because alumni and trustees and others with a vested interest are persuaded that the good ones offer the best secondary education and a better chance of getting into selective colleges. The record is persuasive. Lucky are the students who get the chance to go to them. Challenged by the improvement in the best high schools and by the search for the best students for selective colleges no matter where they get their secondary training, the independent schools are developing a diversified and well-prepared student body.

8

Testing, Testing

Not long ago Ralph Nader, a Princeton graduate, called on Tim Callard, Princeton's director of admission, to discuss the College Entrance Examination Board.* Callard got the impression that Nader was uneasy about the enormous influence this one organization has over the admission to college of so many applicants. But Nader has made no public statements about the College Board, and apparently he has no plans to, although an undergraduate at Princeton who worked for Nader one summer is doing a study of the Board on his own. Not to be worthy of investigation by Ralph Nader these days is a high compliment indeed, for the College Board would seem a natural target, given some of the hostility it arouses among students, teachers, parents, counselors—and among some admissions officers who would be lost without it. The press has suggested more than once that the Board's influence may be waning, but in fact it is waxing.

Before we go any further, how about a little test?

Directions: In each of the following questions, a related pair of words or phrases is followed by five lettered pairs of words or phrases. Select

*The College Board is often referred to now by its initials C.E.E.B. We believe "College Board" is clearer and more graceful than C.E.E.B.

the lettered pair which best expresses a relationship similar to that expressed in the original pair.

CISTERN: WATER:: (A) shower: cloud (B) official: power (C) science: matter (D) museum: antiques (E) vault: valuables

CRUTCH: LOCOMOTION:: (A) paddle: canoe (B) hero: worship (C) horse: carriage (D) spectacles: vision (E) statement: contention

WANDER: TRESPASS:: (A) eat: gorge (B) recline: sprawl (C) mar: destroy (D) narrate: perjure (E) glance: examine

The correct answers are: (E), (D) and (D). These are actual questions appearing in an SAT verbal test. The first was answered correctly by 84 percent of the students, the second by 61 percent and the third by only 29 percent. They appear in a pamphlet distributed to those taking the tests as samples of what to expect. They are also "freebies," inasmuch as they appeared in the upcoming test and the students were advised to study them so that they could get them right.

If you did not tighten up a bit at the sight of these questions, you are indeed unusual. Imagine then the apprehension that some students feel when faced with three hours of this sort of thing. Now try just one math question. You need only a ninth-grade math background:

$$\text{If } 16 \times 16 \times 16 = 8 \times 8 \times P,$$
$$\text{then } P = \text{(A) } 4 \text{ (B) } 8 \text{ (C) } 32 \text{ (D) } 48 \text{ (E) } 64$$

On this one 70 percent got the correct answer, (E). The "insightful approach," the pamphlet notes, is not to work out the multiplication of 16^3 and divide by 8^2, but "to find what additional factors are needed by the right member to match those in the left member."

A teacher at Kent School once wrote a book called *Study Is Hard Work.* Those of us who have been out of school for some time tend to forget just how hard studying really is. The purpose of the College Board tests is not to torture but to test, to determine just what level of *hard* studying a student is capable of. Complaints that the tests are unfair would be better directed to the Almighty who failed to give everyone instant Omniscience, than to the mere mortals who concocted this means of discovering capacity for college work. They might find it easier to storm the heavens than to penetrate the formidable pedagogy that underlies the College Board.

Origin of the College Board

Just what is the College Board, anyway, and where did it come from? What is its writ and whence its authority? Originally the College Entrance Examination Board was literally a board of teachers drawn from high schools, private schools and colleges who made up examinations for a handful of Eastern colleges desiring some uniformity in entrance requirements. They were only testing a few thousand candidates and it was a very clubby affair carried on in the library at Columbia, whose president, Nicholas Murray Butler, was the driving force behind the Board's establishment in 1900. Pen-and-ink corrections sufficed and grades were naturally computed by hand.

The need for such a board was cited as early as 1885 by the principal of Andover, Dr. Bancroft, who said: ". . . out of forty boys for college next year, we have *over twenty senior classes.*" Meaning that 20 colleges had different requirements to be met by the secondary school.

The idea of creating a board designated to bring some sensible common standards for college admission into being was misunderstood by the president of Lafayette, Ethelbert D. Warfield, who said:

> Lafayette College does not intend to be told by any Board whom to admit and whom not to admit. If we wish to admit the son of a benefactor, or of a Trustee, or of a member of the Faculty, and such action will benefit the institution, we are not going to be prevented from taking it.

To which objection President Eliot of Harvard replied:

> The President of Lafayette College has misunderstood Mr. Butler's proposal. The College Entrance Examination Board, if constituted, is not to admit students to any college, but so to define the subjects of admission that they will be uniform, to conduct examinations in these subjects at uniform times throughout the world, and to issue to those who take the examination certificates of performance—good, bad, or

indifferent. And, President Warfield, it will be perfectly practicable under this plan for Lafayette College to say, if it chooses, that it will admit only such students as cannot pass these examinations. No one proposes to deprive Lafayette College of that privilege.*

Charter members of the Board were Barnard, Bryn Mawr, Columbia, Cornell, Johns Hopkins, NYU, Rutgers, Swarthmore, Union, Penn, Vassar and Woman's College of Baltimore. For all his put-down of Lafayette, Eliot did not see fit to bring Harvard into the Board for four years. Yale came on in 1909 and Princeton in 1910, but until 1915 the Big Three also administered their own entrance examinations (it was these that F. Scott Fitzgerald flunked the first time as a senior at Newman School).

The earliest exams were simply the usual written examinations in given subjects. They were not necessarily "objective," as the SAT and Achievement tests today must of necessity be. The examiners judged essay responses just as they did in the classroom, according to their own lights. Thus preparation for the College Boards, as the exams came to be known, meant learning the subject matter on which you were to be examined, and in this respect they differed little from the usual school examinations. But the degree of learning required was higher than what you might expect in the average high school, so the College Boards represented something of a challenge. Nonetheless, from the very beginning 30 percent of the candidates came from high schools.

The first tests on June 17 were held in 67 centers in the United States and two in Europe for 973 candidates, to be graded by 39 men and women who perused a total of 7,889 papers. Forty percent received grades below 60, which was passing.

Gradually the number of colleges on the Board increased, as did the candidates tested, but it remained an Eastern affair. "The Middle West and its great state universities were indifferent to the Board and its work," wrote Claude M. Fuess in his history of the Board's first 50 years (1967), "and the Far West and Deep South, still committed to admission by certificate (diploma) ignored it." In the twenties, the number of candidates hit a high point of 25,000, dropping to 15,000 during the depth of the Depression. Remember that today about a

---

*Claude M. Fuess, *The College Board, Its First Fifty Years,* College Board, 1967.

million candidates take the tests for undergraduate college entrance. By 1930, the Board had established a laboratory in Princeton, New Jersey, to study its own work. It was discovered, for example, that the tests lacked uniformity. In 1926, only 52.8 percent passed physics; two years later the percentage who passed jumped to 81.9. The tests were available to teachers and students in bound volumes, so that preparing for the Boards became something of an art. At Haverford School in Philadelphia moments before the Latin College Board, the teacher held a session in which all the essential rules of grammar were shown to the candidates on a blackboard. "First thing you do in that exam room is write these rules down on the back of the test," he told the boys. It was hard to flunk after that.

Cramming had been deplored from the start, but it was necessary to cross up the cramsters to nullify their efforts. In 1935, after generations of multiple-choice essay questions in American history (that is, not the choice of checking off one out of five boxes, but a choice perhaps of whether you would write an essay on the Federalist Papers, Tom Paine's *Common Sense* or the Declaration of Independence), the exam appeared with just six essay questions without any choice, to be answered in three hours! Incidentally, by 1935, many of the candidates were taking only four comprehensive three-hour exams, while others took several exams each year for three or four years! They were held in June and results were announced late in July.

By this time the actual number of examiners had risen to almost 500. For them the work meant some extra money after the spring term was over and agreeable company in a genial atmosphere. They liked to exchange candidates' boners with each other:

"Macbeth is a typical husband, courageous and strong when away from home."

"He sees everything at once and writes them down in that order."

"The hound rushed over the moor, emitting whelps at every leap."

"He had reached the zenith of his apathy."

"Let us call this boy Bill, for that was his name."

Today the *tests* present the candidate with boners and ask that they be corrected: "Hamilton told Jefferson that the reasons were not obvious to Franklin and he." The candidate must blacken a space on this answer sheet corresponding with a letter, D in this case, if the sentence contains faulty grammar or sentence structure.

Until World War II the Scholastic Aptitude Test, first developed by the Board in 1926, was a supplement a candidate took without much concern. It was in effect an intelligence test. But psychological testing of American soldiers in 1917–18 to distinguish morons from "officer material" had come under attack by certain New England headmasters as crackpot. Giving an intelligence test the name of Scholastic Aptitude Test not only took the sting out, it also defined the purpose of such a test: to determine a student's aptitude for college-level work.

Professor Carl C. Brigham of the Princeton psychology department was responsible for introducing the multiple-choice SATs with such modest claims that no serious objections were raised. No candidate ever was told what his SAT scores or his examination marks were. The Board reported results exclusively to the requisite college admissions office. Even at Harvard the most brilliant student was simply told that he was admitted, and was indistinguishable to his classmates from a mediocrity at entrance. So far as Board results went, they were invisible. By 1937, objective Achievement Tests were introduced.

World War II was the watershed for the College Board. Having the expertise in testing and being dominated by Harvard, Yale and Princeton, the government naturally turned to the Board for testing services. It so happened that on the very day of Pearl Harbor, December 7, 1941, the admissions directors of the Big Three were meeting at Princeton. By December 18, it was announced: "The three universities will move together to a war-time footing." This involved year-round classes, and for the first time the College Board tests would consist of the SATs and Achievements given in April instead of June. Significantly, the essay-type examinations were abolished, a radical departure impossible according to Dean Heermance of Princeton "had they not been done away with as a war-time measure." The age of machine-corrected tests had begun.

In 1943, the College Board conducted tests for the Navy's V–12 and the Army's A–12 programs for 316,000 candidates, more than 12 times the number ever tested before. Such a mass could be tested only by objective tests marked automatically. The services performed for the government expanded to the State Department, and the Coast Guard. Clearly the College Board had gone beyond its original purpose and had become a national testing center. One job for the Bureau of Naval Personnel required the printing of 36 million pages of tests, answer sheets and bulletins. Actuarial societies were clients of the Board.

It became necessary to separate the College Entrance Examination Board from all this extraneous new business. In 1947, the Educational Testing Service was created with headquarters in Princeton, while the Board opened offices in New York. It is still believed that the Board is in Princeton because all the materials of their tests come from ETS there. There is a post office box in the Board's name in Princeton, but ETS opens it. ETS is a service organization, and the Board is its client, responsible for policy and for bringing in the business. For although the Board is a nonprofit organization, as is ETS, it depends for its existence on revenues from test fees. For a time in the late sixties and early seventies revenues were threatened by competition from a new Midwestern organization, the American College Testing Program, known as ACT, which gained a clientele among state colleges. This challenge has forced the Board to expand its services and develop new programs like CLEP, the College Level Examination Program that allows a person to get college credit after passing a CLEP test in a particular subject. Today, one of the most valuable services of the Board is the College Scholarship Service which channels information on financial need of college applicants to hundreds of colleges.

The Board Today

"The entire country is gradually becoming the Board's stage," said its director, Frank Bowles, in 1947. No longer limited to Eastern private colleges, its membership includes 2,000 colleges, universities and secondary schools. Annual meetings once small enough to fit into the trustees' room in the Columbia library are now held in the grand ballroom of the Waldorf-Astoria, and include as many as 10 discussion sessions on issues like "Recruitment for Survival" and "The Nontraditional Student."

In 1971, the Board for the first time went outside the Ivy League for its president and named Arland F. Christ-Janer, a Midwesterner who had been president of Cornell College in Iowa and Boston University. Under his direction, the Board was restructured to allow more regional participation in its policies. Of its 25 trustees, less than half are from highly selective colleges. Christ-Janer is now president of New College in Sarasota, Florida, and the Board is being run by Sidney P. Marland, former U.S. Commissioner of Education.

The Board's services include Guidance and Planning, College Entrance, Credit and Placement, Financial Aid and Research. In addition to the SATs and Achievements, the Board offers the Preliminary Scholastic Aptitude Test, National Merit Scholarship Qualifying Test, Test of English as a Foreign Language (TOEFL) and the College Level Examination Program (CLEP). It also administers the Advanced Placement Program and is responsible for the financial-aid programs of the College Scholarship Service. Its publications list fills a 70-page pamphlet and it publishes the *College Board Review* quarterly and the huge *College Handbook* annually. All of the Board's work can be done on two floors of a New York office building and in four small regional offices. Educational Testing Service requires an extensive campus with buildings for 2,000 employees.

Most of the financial support for the Board is derived from a fee of $6.50 for the SAT and $11.00 for one, two or three Achievement Tests taken the same day. Colleges pay nothing for the reports the Board sends them on candidates' results. Membership fees are $200 a year for a college and $100 for a secondary school. Research grants have come to the Board from several foundations, the federal government and certain state agencies.

The Board is an example of the leadership role the selective colleges play. A creature of the Ivies at the turn of the century, scorned by the public institutions, it became an all-embracing national service by the sheer weight of its excellence in setting standards and developing a sound and fair testing procedure. It has not only become indispensable to colleges with long lines of applicants, but colleges trying to fill their enrollment also turn to the Board for counsel and technical assistance through its College Locater Service. When Lawrenceville School is told by Berkeley that all the applicant need send in are Board scores, then the enormous faith placed in these tests becomes evident. Half of the colleges receiving Board reports are public colleges. In all, 3,400 institutions beyond secondary school receive the reports.

An example of the College Board's authority is its influence on secondary school math curricula. In 1955, the Board created a Commission on Mathematics "to review the existing secondary-school mathematics curriculum, and to make recommendations for its modernization, modification and improvement." Frank Kendig, writing in the *New York Times Magazine* ("Does New Math Add Up?," January 6, 1974), quotes a critic of the new math, Morris Kline, as blaming the College Board for its content. But the Board points out that the SAT math test is traditional in the questions it poses, and is based on arithmetic, algebra and plane geometry and not on set theory, binary numbers or symbolic logic, characteristics of the new math. Nonetheless, the Board did support math curricular reform, and the Achievement Tests reflect the new math, which though under fire is still being taught almost universally in American grade and secondary schools.

The College Board does not have a lovable public image. It is in the position of a public utility, which is seldom praised for its service and always damned when ice brings the wires down. Rightly or wrongly the Board scores are often blamed when a candidate is rejected. The SATs are a hanging judge in the eyes of students and counselors. Those who get good scores never write thank-you letters to the Board. To try to answer questions (some hostile) on the minds of students and teachers, the Board issues a 28-page guide carrying 54 questions and answers to them: "How much different must a repeat score be to indicate a true difference in performance? . . . What can you do if a student's senior-year SAT scores are not what you expected from his earlier scores?" At the end of the list is the question: "Still in a quandary?" with suggestions where to get further information.

The Tests

The enormous professionalism that goes into the testing program is not widely appreciated. The experience of testing so many students over so many years has developed an expertise that only the bold will question. In the first 13 years of the SAT, 363,111 were tested; in the next 15 years, over 19.5 million were tested! About a million students take the SAT currently.

The SAT is given five times a year. Every test is different. An SAT is made up by 15 members of the Educational Testing Service in

Princeton and 10 outside teachers who send in "items" for consideration. A typical SAT verbal has 90 items and the math 60. The items
vary in difficulty. To avoid ambiguity of interpretation, no item is used
that the staff does not unanimously get right without looking at the
key. But as a further insurance, the items for each new test are
pretested by the candidates themselves, for in every SAT test there are
25 new items that do not count! The students do not know which
items these are. The results of these 25 items are studied and some of
the items are discarded because they do not correlate properly with
the rest of the candidates' performances.

ETS recognizes that the results of the six tests vary because it is
impossible to make every test equal in difficulty, and there is a tendency for brighter students to take tests earlier in a school year than
the less bright. The raw scores of each test are then adjusted by a
formula worked out in Princeton by mathematicians to weight them,
and thus eliminate any advantages or disadvantages arising from these
variations. The scoring is done in a series of steps.

An optical scanner going at the rate of 10,000 answer sheets an
hour transcribes the answers onto a magnetic tape, which is then
compared with the correct answers in a computer's memory to obtain
the raw scores. The statistical staff of the Test Development Division
of ETS then feeds its adjustments into the computer, which converts
raw scores into the final scores. Thus all scores over the years are
related by this system of weighted adjustment so that it is possible to
compare scores from one decade to the next and see that they rose on
the average during the sixties, peaked and are on the decline now.

The purpose of *Achievement Tests* is straightforward, and many
colleges use them to determine a freshman's capability in certain
subjects (there are 18 Achievement Tests given, nine of them in languages, the rest in math, science and humanities). Except for the
English Composition test the Achievements, given three times a year,
are objective and are scored by computer.

The purpose of the SAT is more subtle. Here is how Thomas F.
Donlon and William H. Angoff describe it in a technical report issued
by the Board in 1971:

> The Scholastic Aptitude Test (SAT) is a measure of basic reasoning
> abilities in two areas: Verbal and mathematical. It provides a separate

score for each of these areas, and is intended to supplement the school record and other information about the student in assessing his competence for college work. It is a broad-gauge instrument, providing effective discrimination over most of the range of academic ability of college-bound students. It is aimed not only at serving the decisions of institutions that have high-scoring candidates but also at describing levels of ability among lower-scoring candidates for admission to college.

The utility of this kind of supplementary measure arises in part from the fact that it can provide unique information about the student, and in part from its ability to confirm or to question the assessment based on subject-matter achievement. It is, therefore, a supplement that will normally help establish candidate ability when it is consistent with other information, but that will be perhaps most useful when it is in disagreement with other data. When properly used in the context of other information with which it is inconsistent, it effectively sounds a warning bell and leads to the search for more data to clarify the assessment in question.*

Abe Lass, an authority on testing, uses the word "value" rather than "purpose" in discussing the SAT in basic terms: "The chief value of the SAT is that it provides one standard measure of how you reason verbally and mathematically in relation to others who take the test no matter what high school they come from. If every student applying to college attended the same high school, there would be less need for college admissions tests."

A uniform measure of the ability to reason in words and mathematical symbols, that is what the SAT comes down to. Providing the measurement is sound, this should present no problems in assessing a candidate's expected performance in college according to his scores. But the Board itself defines the SAT as having "an inherently supplemental nature." *To admit into college a candidate with high SAT scores and expect a high college record is an unsound procedure unless the secondary grades have been consistently high too.* A student with a C average who gets high SAT scores sounds for a selective college admissions officer that warning bell Donlon and Angoff refer to.

* Thomas F. Donlon and William H. Angoff, "The Scholastic Aptitude Test," in William Angoff, ed., *The College Board Admissions Testing Program,* College Board, 1971.

Seldom will such a candidate be admitted by the most selective colleges because he or she is identified as an underachiever, someone who has not been able to harness his mental ability. Lacking the study habits that would have allowed such a person to be an A or B student in high school, it is highly unlikely that such habits will suddenly be acquired in a selective college where the demands are considerably stiffer.

But what of the opposite inconsistency, the A student who scores in the low 500s rather than the high 600s? In this case the SAT is operating, in Donlon and Angoff's words, "as a 'leveling agent,' cutting across differences in local customs and conditions and affording the admissions officer a single metric for considering the records of all applicants." This is why admissions offices universally refer to SAT scores rather than grades in class profiles. A boy who was an A student at a good suburban school in Illinois found out just how bright he was when he took his senior year at Exeter and wound up with Cs and Bs. He did not get into his first Ivy choice. Exeter did not change his SAT scores by very much—he was in the low 600s in both junior and senior years.

A student with a good high school record and good SAT scores will generally do well in college unless some personality disorder arises. But what gives admissions directors pause about the SAT as a predictor is that students with *mediocre* scores can do *well* in highly selective colleges! This is true of minority students and of athletes as well as of others on whom the college decided to "take a chance," high-risk candidates they are called in committee sessions.

Fred Glimp, when he was Harvard's dean of admissions, had no trouble admitting certain candidates with mediocre grades and SAT scores because he picked boys with some other excellence, particularly athletic, and they seldom disappointed him in their ability to meet Harvard's academic standards because their characters were disciplined sufficiently to enable them to meet new demands. Now admissions officers are doing this with minority candidates who to the experienced eye look doubtful as prospects yet have the determination to make it, and they generally do.

To be sure, the numbers of candidates in selective colleges admitted below the 600 SAT level are few, but the fact that those who are admitted almost never flunk out makes the SAT relatively less useful to the admissions officer as a predictor at its lower levels. The Board itself is very much aware of the problem of predictive validity of the SAT and has been making highly sophisticated studies of it since 1927. *The College Board Guide for High Schools and Colleges* states that for "particular colleges" the predictive validity of SAT and Achievement scores "varies, but usually does not predict as well as the student's high school record. Neither test scores nor high school record alone are as accurate as some combination of the two. For some colleges the most accurate predictor is a combination of a student's SAT scores, his high school grades or rank, and the average of his Achievement Test scores."

The Board makes no exaggerated claims. Using 1 as the highest validity coefficient they report that in liberal arts colleges for men (the study predates the Ivy turn to coeducation) combining SAT scores and school records the predictive validity for those in the 90th percentile, (the upper 10 percent) was .68, and for women's liberal arts colleges .74. For the median the figures were .55 and .62, and for the bottom 10 percent .40 and .43.

The Significance

All of this only goes to show that it is difficult sometimes to predict the future in education, as in other spheres of human endeavor. The candor of the College Board in this respect is one of the reasons why its integrity is so widely acknowledged. Even admissions directors who are not altogether satisfied with the SAT are loathe to dismiss its usefulness.

One Ivy League admissions director says frankly, "I have heard it explained to me a dozen times and I still don't know just what it is the verbal SAT is measuring with its antonyms, sentence completions, analogies and reading comprehension." The truth is that only the student of psychometrics can follow the methodology that lies behind the tests and their validation. Here is the opening sentence on *Reliability* in the Board's technical report, in an article by Angoff and Henry S. Dyer: "The reliability of each form of each test in the Admissions Testing Program is routinely estimated after its first formal administration, ordinarily by means of the Kuder-Richardson formula #20, adapted for use with the formula (R-kW) scores."

Admissions officers are no more in a position to challenge the studies made by the Board's statisticians and social scientists trained in psychology and education than is the owner of a vineyard when confronted with technical soil reports by chemists and agronomists. The SAT is a technical report to be used with care. The SAT scores are accepted as about 90 percent reliable. They are accepted, too, as fair measurements of reasoning power even though it is not entirely clear to everyone what the nature of reasoning power is or how it can be stronger in college than it was in high school. What makes a student "catch fire"? No one knows.

Over the years the average scores on the SAT nationally have been dropping. In 1962–63 the verbal was 478 and the math 502. Ten years later it stood at 445 and 481. This is far below the competitive level of the 600s most students at selective colleges reach.

Why the drop? One theory is that secondary education weakened. Another is that because fewer students dropped out, there were more weak students taking tests—presumably those who failed to drop out were poor students. The College Board has no simple explanation to offer. For one thing, the Board refuses to indict secondary education as a whole when only one-third of the nation's seniors take the SATs. But is not this presumably the brightest third? Not necessarily.

"There are several factors that may have contributed to a change in the SAT population in recent years," said Dr. T. Anne Cleary, the Board's chief of Program Services in a press release December 20, 1973, "but we can only speculate about them at the present time. It is possible, for example, that substantial and progressively larger numbers of students who would earn high scores are not going directly to college and therefore are not taking the SAT."

The Board, in the absence of any hard evidence to explain the decline in SAT scores, must wait for new research before it can put an end to the puzzlement of educators. Meantime, its research is taking into consideration "the perplexing phenomenon" that the PSAT/NMSQT (Preliminary Scholastic Aptitude Test/National Merit Scholarship Qualifying Test) essentially a shorter version of the SAT taken early in junior year has produced *stable* test scores over a five-year period. Presumably the students taking both PSAT/NMSQT and SAT tests are largely the same. And the Board is certain that the difficulty of the tests has not increased.

While reluctant to blame the schools, Dr. Cleary is not averse to suggesting that cultural regression may be a cause. "It is evident that many factors, including family and home life, exposure to the mass media and other cultural and environmental factors are associated with students' performance," she said. At any rate, the dimensions of the decline are hardly Spenglerian, but it might not be a bad idea for parents to make sure that their children read more and view TV less.

More significant for our concerns is that the SAT scores in the top range fell considerably between 1972 and 1973: only 987 males reached the 750–800 range in 1973, while 1,573 reached it the previous year. No explanation for this change has been arrived at, but it does reduce the pool of very top men the selective colleges compete for. The pool of applicants above 600 appears to be about 98,000, a little less than 10 percent of those taking the SAT. In 1972, 80,203 student applications were filed with the eight Ivy League and Seven Sisters colleges (for about 12,000 places). The overlapping applications suggest that no more than 40,000 students are seeking places in these colleges out of the million who take the SAT.

Cramming Not Advisable

Since so much is riding on the outcome of the SAT, how can a student prepare for it? By being a good student in grammar school and high school, which means reading a good deal and doing work assigned. *Cramming or even studying for the SAT is believed to be a waste of time.* Four controlled studies of students who were coached and not coached showed no improvements in SAT scores among coached students that could not be attributable to chance or to the normal tendency for scores to improve somewhat between junior and senior years. The Board has issued a booklet summarizing these studies in an attempt to discourage those who cannot afford it from wasting money on tutoring. In a strong statement condemning tutoring the Board concludes: "But we are concerned most, and have been moved to make this statement, because we see the educational process unwillingly corrupted in some schools to gain ends which we believe to be not only unworthy but, ironically, unattainable."

A parental concern is that a low score may be caused by fatigue or emotional strain, but this is rarely the case and a student can always take the SAT again. Standard error of measurement accounts in part for changes from one test to the next. On the average the increase is 15 points, and while 65 percent of those tested get higher scores the second time, *35 percent get lower scores.* Likewise, 1 in 20 gains 100 points, while 1 in 100 loses 100 points or more the second time. *The higher the first score the greater the likelihood of a drop the second time round.*

One thing a student should do is to familiarize himself with the nature of objective tests, so that he is not forced to waste time trying to figure out what the test is asking of him. No one is expected to complete a test, so haste will only lead to mistakes. It is conceivable that a student will mismark a series of answers in the answer book if he skips one or more questions and gets mixed up about the number he skipped. Extreme carelessness like that will result in such a low score that it will appear obvious that it is unrepresentative and, one hopes, he will be advised to take the test again.

The matter of skipping questions you don't know leads to the question of whether to guess, because each wrong answer affects the raw score by ¼ of a point. The rule about guessing is not to guess if you know nothing, but to take a chance if you can eliminate one or more of the five choices offered. The Board advises the student not to spend too much time on any question, and to remember that high scores can be obtained even with omissions.

The formula for a test in which 50 of 90 questions are right, 32 wrong and 8 omitted is 50 rights $- \frac{32 \text{ wrongs}}{4} = 42$. The 42 is then converted to the SAT scale of 200–800. This scale is arbitrary and it involves some complicated mathematics to convert raw scores to the scale because some tests are easier than others and some groups of candidates are brighter than others.

A score of 800 is not necessarily a perfect score! It may mean getting all the answers right or almost all of them right. The conversion formula can give a score as high as 840, but only 800 is reported because this represents the soundest measure of excellence among large numbers over a period of time. Likewise, there is no such thing as a failing score in the conventional sense of a failing grade, but of course very low test scores are a handicap in getting into colleges with any degree of selectivity.

The *College Handbook* published by the Board is generally available in all secondary schools and most colleges submit their freshmen profiles in SAT score terms—most but not all, especially the most selective. For a college profile not listed it is necessary to write to or phone the admissions office. This information is not secret. The reason why some colleges do not publish it in the *Handbook* is to de-emphasize the importance of SAT scores. It stands to reason that if large numbers of high SAT score candidates are rejected it would be misleading to publish them in the *Handbook* context when most colleges are eager to admit high-scoring candidates. Harvard blandly states that it accepts students whose scores range from 400–800, thus making the SAT meaningless as a guide to a student wondering whether to apply to Harvard.

The Achievement Tests of one hour require little comment. Most selective colleges require the candidate to take three of them. They are a vestige of the old system that tested for specific knowledge and their purpose is: (1) to certify competence in a subject, (2) to provide placement information, (3) to improve prediction of college performance. The Achievements appear to be meeting these objectives. As for the students, if they know their subjects they will do well, and if not they will do poorly. Practicing multiple-choice tests, the Board points out, is no substitute for studying what you will be examined on.

The Bowdoin Option

In 1969, Bowdoin announced that candidates for admission would not be required to submit College Board test scores, and that other criteria would be used to judge their admissibility. This widely publicized move shook up the Board, which feared that it might be the beginning of the end. But Bowdoin alone of the selective colleges presents the candidate with the option of not submitting his Board scores. In 1973, 58.5 percent of Bowdoin's candidates withheld their test scores.

This option really does not help candidates avoid the tests, since they must submit their scores (actually the scores are transmitted by the Board) to other colleges they apply to, including many public colleges. But the option does help Bowdoin attract the kinds of candidates it wants, and it certainly has enhanced this small and remote college's reputation and greatly increased its visibility. Some admissions directors consider the move a ploy to put Bowdoin one up on its rivals, which are chiefly Amherst, Williams, Wesleyan, Trinity, Tufts and Middlebury.

An Amherst student paper reporting on admission statistics seized on Bowdoin's high candidates-to-places ratio and named Bowdoin the most difficult of all colleges to get into. Like most colleges not called Harvard, Yale or Princeton, Bowdoin still does not draw large numbers of applicants in the 750–800 SAT score category, and it must be satisfied like other selective colleges with a certain number of candidates rejected by some Ivy League and Seven Sisters colleges. But it does sometimes reject those accepted by Princeton and others.

Behind Bowdoin's decision to rely less on the Boards was a realization that this kind of college, located in Brunswick beyond Portland near the Maine Coast, "is not necessarily right for every good student," according to a report on the profile of the Class of 1977. After polling the faculty, the admissions office found that 50 percent of the students who, faculty members said, were models of what Bowdoin "could do without" had SAT verbals above the class average and 65 percent had higher SAT math scores than the average. Studying the honors graduates, the admissions office found that only 31 percent had come in with both SATs above the average and 24 had come in below the average of their classmates.

Bowdoin has not abandoned the Boards and still gives a profile showing that only 4.8 percent of those submitting SAT scores had less than 500 verbal and only 1.5 per cent had less than 500 math scores. Anyone wanting advanced placement credit at Bowdoin must take the Board's Advanced Placement tests.

Richard Moll, Bowdoin's director of admissions and a former member of the Yale admissions office, has written of Bowdoin's experience with candidates not submitting SAT scores in the *College Board Review* (Winter 1972–73):

> At the moment we feel the positive factors outweigh the negative ones. . . . Our applicant pool has grown considerably—162 per cent in four years. . . . we feel comfortable with a changed emphasis on admissions processing that attempts to preserve a humanistic philosophy in an increasingly computerized culture.

Apprehensive Bowdoin faculty members have been reassured by incidents like the senior entering with SATs of 555 verbal and 473 math winning a Rhodes Scholarship.

ACT—The Other Test

Although the American College Testing Program (ACT), which began in 1959, is not used by most selective colleges, it is noteworthy that the office of the dean of engineering at the University of Pennsylvania wrote ACT in 1973 asking why there were two testing programs and had any thought been given to amalgamating ACT with the College Board. ACT is the Western-based competitor to the Board, headquartered in Iowa City, created to satisfy "an increasing need for a much more guidance-oriented assessment program that would broaden, rather than narrow, the college admissions spectrum," according to the ACT reply to Penn. The two testing organizations have cooperated in developing common code numbers identifying secondary schools. ACT broadly suggests that its philosophy of opening rather than closing doors to students has been copied by the College Board. But of course ACT imitates the Board in many of its formats. ACT is testing more students than the Board tests, but there is probably little overlapping. ACT has carved out a market of its own. Incidentally, almost every college that requires ACT's will accept the College Board Test results. The reverse is not true.

Open Admissions

Open Admissions, in an unofficial way, has come into being at a great number of less selective private colleges in order to attract students desirous of an education in a small-college setting but who possess modest abilities and academic record. The largest official program of Open Admissions, however, has occurred within the City University of New York.

When one of the most selective public colleges in the country, CCNY, the "Harvard of the proletariat," adopted an Open Admissions policy in 1970, it startled the academic world, and the reaction of many CCNY alumni was that their degrees would have little in common with degrees granted thereafter. The specter of *lowered standards* seemed to be floating over Upper Manhattan, and the chaos that came from overcrowding the campus initially brought this liberal institution much bad publicity. It did not occur to meritocratic minds that a rather wonderful thing was happening in a city better known for its violence than its culture.

The impression that the poor children of New York tend to belong to gangs engaged in counterproductive activities has to be altered when 10,000 "disadvantaged" high school graduates a year apply for admission to their free city university—CCNY is one of 17 colleges in the City University of New York. Open Admissions was a response to a hunger for higher education among those least likely to "qualify." All very humanitarian, to be sure, but whose ox was to be gored? Presumably that of the traditional clientele, the poor but ambitious high achievers. The mob, it was claimed, would be so much cold water in the comfortably warm academic bath. As Timothy Healy, vice chancellor of CUNY, put it in an article in the 1973 summer issue of *Change* magazine: "Prophets of doom will argue that this means the end of quality education, but the link between the two results is emotional, not rational."

What Open Admissions means in New York is that every high school graduate is guaranteed a place *in the university system.* Already that is a qualification! Furthermore, CCNY limits acceptance to the upper half of these graduates, a further qualification. It should be remembered that in Ivy League colleges today there are some students with no better records than being in the upper half of their senior class in high school.

Healy reminds us that "the pieties of meritocratic admissions" were such that "merit could be variously defined: Size, speed and dexterity were upon occasion as useful as brains. So the athletic entry tunnel was dug and dignified. If the injunction 'Feed my goats' was ignored in practice, another, 'Amuse my goats' was generously honored."

If an athlete with 400 SAT scores can get through Harvard, a graduate of a New York high school who has done better than half his classmates can get through CCNY, although it will probably take longer—5 years is the average for the B.A. The much publicized dropout rate at CUNY is just about the same as the national average for both the senior and junior colleges in the system.

Middle-class parents who are disappointed that their children were not admitted to a highly selective college can take some comfort from the observation of Edward Quinn, chairman of English at CCNY and a Shakespeare specialist. In teaching a class at a remedial level he was approached by a delegation complaining that he had not given them any Shakespeare, although he had taught it in the same course the previous term. "My failure to include these [plays] this term—the result of a misguided experiment on my part—had been interpreted by them, quite correctly it now seems to me, as patronizing. They had arrived at a point where they could trust themselves and care enough to express that concern. They wanted the best I had to offer and wouldn't settle for less." What makes a student catch fire? It can happen to anyone, but it is apparently impossible to predict to whom and when.

Advocates of Open Admissions are cautious about evaluating its results in so brief a time and they rest their case for the present on the moral right of high school graduates to higher education. Alexander W. Astin, director of research for the American Council on Education, and Jack E. Rossmann, professor of psychology and director of educational research at Macalester College, in a study of the first year of Open Admissions at CUNY, found encouraging evidence that Open Admissions worked for those admitted and did not adversely affect academic standards. They conclude that students once considered "bad risks . . . are quietly achieving objectives that will help them lead more meaningful and productive lives" (*Change,* Summer 1973).

Open Admissions is by no means limited to CUNY. Most public systems of higher education must admit applicants into some institution if they hold a high school diploma. And most private colleges desperate for students to fill their enrollment waive academic requirements for applicants prepared to pay their way. They do not call it Open Admissions. Rolling Admissions is the term used because you can apply any time and be accepted within days or a few weeks.

Probably few Open Admissions students take College Board tests and most Rolling Admissions students do take them or ACT. The difference is one of class. Open Admissions opens higher education to the poor, while Rolling Admissions opens it to the middle class.

That Open Admissions advocates should be hostile to selective admissions is not surprising. Here is how Timothy Healy of CUNY describes selective admissions:

> In the first quarter of this century parents negotiated their children's entrance into the most prestigious colleges on the basis of money, blood lines and influence. While these young people, when they graduated, certainly formed an aristocracy, no one presumed to call them an aristocracy of brains. History, however, was at work. Seats in classes, the buildings that enclosed them and the budgets that paid for them could not keep up with the population. When demand rose beyond capacity, American colleges backed into objective testing and developed all the repulsive apparatus by which the admissions office is allowed to specify the "quality" of the college. Colleges found that their protective reaction was indeed the exercise of high virtue, and the pieties of meritocratic admissions were upon us.

A Critique of Objective Testing

It may be that some readers share Dr. Healy's dislike of objective testing, so let us conclude this subject with a reasoned attack by Dr. Banesh Hoffman, professor of mathematics at Queens College, CUNY. At a conference on Open Admissions at CUNY in 1971 he, as keynote speaker, took his audience over the hurdles he finds in multiple-choice tests:

> My purpose is to instill a healthy distrust of mechanized evaluation that parades as something scientific, and I shall start with one of my favorite multiple-choice items. You are given a sentence and asked to say which word if any should be changed. If the sentence is good as it stands, you pick the choice "no change." Here is the sentence:
> "Among them Tom and Dick could not find enough money."

If you substituted *between* for *among* you were right—according to the testers, because that is the grammatically correct preposition involving two people; *among* is used for more than two. But a clever mind like Professor Hoffman's discerns the ambiguity of *them*. To whom does it refer? Not necessarily to Tom and Dick. They could be holding up a group of poor people at gunpoint and among *them* could not find the money they needed. Another possibility is that the very use of *among* confirms that *them* cannot refer to only two people, and therefore the sentence stands correct as it is. Thus a subtle, thoughtful mind would be penalized for super-reasoning power, the very thing objective tests measure.

To drive the point home in an embarrassing way, Professor Hoffman then offered the now skeptical listeners this sentence:

> "Under persecution both Baptist and Quaker faiths flourished, whereas had they been ignored they might well have remained but a small handful of believers."

Urging calm, he finds the sentence defective because the second *they* referring to *faiths* cannot possibly make sense: faiths cannot remain a small handful of anything—grammatically that is. Now comes something of a trick: The sentence in all its clumsiness was not intended to be discerned as defective and appeared in a *reading test* in the "CUNY 1970 Open Admissions Testing Program," which "is part of a nationally-used test and was made by one of the leading test-making organizations. Moreover, it was selected by CUNY from a group of competing tests after an elaborate statistical study of their respective merits as placement aids in actual Open Admissions use."

Finally we close with an example Professor Hoffman took from a 1966 Selective Service College Qualification Test concerning a well-known poem by A. E. Housman:

> Loveliest of trees, the cherry now
> Is hung with bloom along the bough,
> And stands about the woodland ride
> Wearing white for Eastertide.
>
> Now of my threescore years and ten,
> Twenty will not come again,
> And take from seventy springs a score,
> It only leaves me fifty more.

And since to look at things in bloom
Fifty springs are little room,
About the woodlands I will go
To see the cherry hung with snow.

How old was the poet when he wrote the poem? (A) 20 (B) 40 (C) 50 (D) 70 (E) One cannot tell.

Professor Hoffman comments:

The second stanza of the poem tells us that the person therein is twenty years old. Do we, then, pick (A)? Look at the wording of the question: "How old was the poet when he wrote this poem?" Clearly we cannot tell from the poem itself. That tells us only about the person in the poem. Therefore we choose (E)—"One cannot tell." And we feel rather pleased with ourselves for having avoided a neat trap.

Unfortunately the wanted answer is not (E) but (A). Do we not feel a sense of outrage? Suppose the testmaker was not as competent as he should have been, and we would therefore make allowance for his incompetence and pick the answer "20." But when the testmaker gives us as one of the choices "One cannot tell," and carefully—if that is the word—asks how old *the poet* was, we are trapped into giving the only valid answer and thereby scoring an objective zero on the question.

It is noteworthy that the College Board is not mentioned in this critique. The Board freely acknowledges a small margin of error in its measurement, and is not threatened by such an analysis. Statistically there is no evidence that very clever students are tripped up by their probing intelligence. Still the analysis is not only amusing, it is a refreshing challenge to educational psychologists. Objective tests are little more than half a century old. It is not inconceivable that by the year 2000 some new way of measuring scholastic aptitude will be developed—or it just might come about that such measurement could be altogether abandoned. That would mean the end of meritocratic selectivity.

For no one can doubt that the greatest value of objective testing is the elimination of preference for students from schools well known to the colleges. Without some system for fairly measuring *all* the good students in the country, selective admissions offices would be forced to revert to a dependence on recommendations from a few hundred private and outstanding public high schools.

9

Visiting a Selective Campus

Visiting several campuses is not a ritual, it is a basic element in the whole admissions process. Colleges welcome visits in order to encourage applications and dispel the stereotypical images that hang on. But why should colleges that already have thousands more applicants than they can take want still more? *Because the larger the applicant pool, the greater the chance for enrolling a talented and diversified student body.*

Guidance counselors and headmasters are constantly amazed by the width of the net the selective colleges spread. There may be some callousness in admissions offices which invite many applications so that they can pick out the most promising ones in the interests of creating an exciting freshman class. But the other side of this coin is the assurance to the student who enrolls that the selection process allows him to live and study among the most outstanding young people the college can attract. And the presence of such students tends to determine more of them to enroll at a particular college. A visit to the campus will quickly give a true picture of its diversity of people and activities.

For example, Princeton enrolls only 55 percent of the freshmen it admits. Almost all the rest choose to go to one of the other selective colleges. In 1973, a determined alumnus in the Camden, New Jersey, region took a busload of candidates to the campus, introduced them to undergraduates, and later after 30 candidates had been admitted, he invited 30 undergraduates to a dinner outside Camden. Each candidate found himself flanked by an undergraduate. After such exposure, of the 30 admitted, only two turned Princeton down.

The moral is clear. In visiting a college campus a high school junior or senior should spend as much time as he can with undergraduates. We have found from talking to hundreds of students that they react much more strongly to the undergraduates than to the facilities or even to the faculty. Faculty contact can actually be misleading. To drop in on a dull lecture or on a math class that repeats material already studied in high school may give the impression that a great college has no right to its reputation.

Selective colleges want visitors, but they avoid the direct-mail solicitation that many very good colleges now engage in to attract top students. National Merit winners may receive as many as a dozen brochures, sent first-class mail at 20 cents or more. "What was that name again?" begins a brochure describing Rockford College in Illinois. Swarthmore hardly needs to advertise. It and other hard-to-get into colleges seek visitors to their campuses through personal invitations from admissions staff visiting high schools or alumni committees.

The campus visit gives candidates or potential candidates the chance to verify impressions already received from adults or other students. It is amazing how many students will not apply to colleges they would be very happy in because they think one is snobbish, another too full of athletes, and another overintellectual. Any of these notions might have had some validity at one time, but they have lost their force because of changing conditions. Negative ideas about a place never seen need to be challenged by the student.

Another reason to look over some campuses is because a student spends four extremely important years of his life in college taking part in what is akin to a religious experience. Daniel Boorstin, looking at the history of higher education, calls it "a new American religion" characterized by Gothic architecture associated with the medieval church, "less a place of instruction than a place of worship—worship of the growing individual" (The Democratic Experience). Each campus supposedly remakes its students into something new, turns on some inner light that illuminates "a Williams man," "a Cliffie."

It were well to have some notion of what transformation you will undergo at one place or another, and certainly the way *not* to reach judgments is to accept without question vague images and ideas about colleges. "Harvard is cold and impersonal." Is it really? If you spent a night with a student in one of the Harvard houses you could not agree to that idea, and not only would you find students who are warm and personal, but you would meet faculty and administrators who have time for undergraduates (it is possible to take a course at Harvard in which you are the only student!).

Girls are flocking to what were once men's colleges. Brown by dropping the name of the girls' college, Pembroke, has seen its female enrollment rise sharply. But a girl ought still to look at Wellesley, Smith, Bryn Mawr or Mount Holyoke to see why these colleges believe they should remain female. There is an interesting story behind their decision. In the sixties when the potential pool of applicants to private colleges began to shrink, many men's colleges went co-ed simply to enlarge their number of good candidates. For the same reason, by 1972, 119 women's colleges had become co-ed or coordinated with a men's college. Of the top colleges only Vassar, Bennington, Sarah Lawrence, Pitzer, Radcliffe, Pembroke and Connecticut College became co-ed.

The reasons for a college remaining female have been stated by Edward D. Eddy, president of Chatham College:

> One need not embrace the Women's Liberation Movement to subscribe to the notion that there is indeed a barrier against women in many channels of opportunity. Women still have a long way to go before we can say in all honesty that they are free to compete as individuals. This fact alone affects the continuing possibilities of single-sex women's colleges.

We feel that a strong student should choose a quality girls' college over a mediocre coeducational college. Wellesley's new president, Barbara Newell, has observed:

> Women coeds receive conflicting signals on the "femininity" of intellectual vigor and do not take full advantage of college. . . . The current trend toward coeducation has increased rather than lessened male domination of American higher education. I fear it is naive to believe that

any movement for educational equity for women can come out of such colleges and universities.

The Southern Association of Colleges for Women has declared:

Society's double standard has probably taught you to defer to men— particularly if you wish to be socially attractive. Thus you may never have realized your potential because you were not expected to excel. At a women's college you are free from artificial restraints. You can speak out, probe, pry, challenge, debate.

The attractiveness of co-ed colleges and the limitations on the number of applicants available mentioned above has made it less difficult to get into a women's selective college now, but the competition is still stiff nonetheless.

Misconceptions abound and they can best be dispelled by campus visits. MIT is thought of strictly as a men's engineering college, but it has always enrolled women and *only a third* of the students are studying for engineering degrees. Another third are science majors and another third are humanities students, and not just social sciences but English and history are their majors. The flavors of the smorgasbord of higher education cannot be sensed from pictures or reading catalogues and brochures.

For that truly living color one needs to walk the streets of Brunswick, Maine, and see how Longfellow's Bowdoin has been changed by coeducation, liberalization and diversity of the student body. Is an urban college exciting and socially involving? Until he actually spends a day at Columbia or Penn, the student is liable to fantacize about the glamour of the city. Or he may revise his feelings about going to a small-town college.

Campus visits can be an education in themselves. He who does not get into the college of his choice will have seen that thousands of students are happily studying elsewhere. It would not be the end of the world to join them instead of, say, the Yalies he so much admires. The student who has looked at Chapel Hill and says, "If I can't make Duke, this is for me," is in a much better psychological position to reach his goals than if he has not seen the place and says, "I'll have to settle for Chapel Hill. It's got a darn good name." There are students who look over the Ivy League and turn down acceptances and go to Michigan State, Boston University or UCLA.

"All too often students settle for a routine and unprobing exposure to a college campus," John Hoy wrote in *Choosing a College*. "Most give it very little thought and aimlessly wander across campus lawns and in and out of buildings, timidly taking a meal in the commons and perhaps greeting one or two of the students. . . ." A candidate for a selective college should have a spirit of inquiry that will make a visit profitable.

The best visit is one that is overnight in an undergraduate's room. Most colleges can help make this arrangement if the candidate has no contact of his own on campus. On such a visit the candidate gets an unvarnished look at what he can expect if he enrolls. He will be talking and listening to many students, eating with them, perhaps attending a campus event or two—a basketball game, a play, a debate. He can also attend a few classes and even talk to some professors if he is lucky.

Official visits arranged by alumni and the admissions office are extremely worthwhile because there will be some meetings with administrators and faculty, to whom questions can be put. These include visits arranged by coaches. Naturally, athletes are going to be exposed more to athletics than to art history, but the athlete who has strong academic interests will be encouraged to visit academic departments. For instance, part of Penn's attraction to athletes is that college's renowned Wharton School, tops in undergraduate business training. A wise student visiting any campus will put in some time exploring the activity he expects to become most deeply involved in, whether it be astro-physics or the daily paper. That way he will be able to make intelligent comparisons at each successive campus. A radio buff may decide on Columbia because its campus FM station is a highly professional broadcasting operation listened to by a large number of people in New York and northern New Jersey, and he would like to work for that station.

Many visits are made by candidates with their parents, and the parental interest and encouragement can be most helpful. Unfortunately, not every parent stops to think that it is the child and not the parent who is going to college. For this reason the reception of parents by the admissions office is generally courteous but brief. At Middlebury the parents are called in after the candidate has been interviewed.

"When people come all the way to Vermont, we owe them the chance to ask us as many questions as they like," Fred Newberger, dean of admissions, believes. They do not have so many questions, but they do appreciate the attention. There is little parents can do at this point to help their children. To point out to the college that "Jim has been varsity goalie for three years," is of no help when the college may already have *five* goalies to choose among.

During the campus visit, parents should try to be seen and not heard.

And afterward they must be careful in how they voice their opinions and reactions, especially their enthusiasms, lest they incite a negative feeling for the place in the mind of an adolescent who may at this time of life have the habit of opposing whatever his parents like.

The Interview

More and more the interview is considered to be a service to the student as much as an evaluative tool of the admissions office. "We can't make definitive judgments on the basis of twenty minutes or half an hour with a student," we were told at Dartmouth. The most important use of the interview by the admissions office is to confirm what is already on the record and to clarify the student's interest, goals and motivations, some of which are not always stated as clearly by secondary schools as they might be. A good interviewer can spot in a qualified applicant the lack of some critical characteristic that makes for success on his campus. A student should keep in mind that academic performance, quality of curriculum, school and other recommendations, plus test scores, will be the significant determinants of admission to a selective college, not a brief meeting under sometimes strained circumstances. The accompanying form used by one secondary school shows how much more a single report can mean than an interview.

Many students come to the campus interview uptight. A girl visiting Bowdoin simply avoided an interview because she said she was not ready for it. To ease the tension a student should have a goal, to learn something about the college. The interview, to be profitable

TABLE III
GERMANTOWN FRIENDS SCHOOL
GERMANTOWN, PENNSYLVANIA

We trust that the admission officer, in reading this evaluation, will keep in mind that the check-list on the individual student is based upon a comparison with his fellow students in a highly selective academic setting.

Name of Candidate ....

ACADEMIC RATINGS

Below average	Average	Good	Excellent (top 10% but not 2 or 3%)	Truly outstanding (top 2 or 3%)		No basis for judgment
a.					Motivation	
b.					Creative Qualities	
c.					Self-discipline	
d.					Growth Potential	

B. Character and Personality

1.

CHARACTER AND PERSONALITY RATINGS

Below average	Average	Good	Excellent (top 10% but not 2 or 3%)	Truly outstanding (top 2 or 3%)		No basis for judgment
a.					Leadership	
b.					Self-confidence	
c.					Warmth of Personality	
d.					Sense of Humor	
e.					Concern for Others	
f.					Energy	
g.					Emotional Maturity	
h.					Personal Initiative	
i.					Reaction to Setbacks	
j.					Respect Accorded by Faculty	

2. The main factors contributing to the respect accorded the applicant seem to be:

- ☐ Superiority in studies
- ☐ Accomplishment in activities
- ☐ Success in athletics
- ☐ Interest in other students
- ☐ Leadership in activities
- ☐ Personality

The main factors contributing to his *not* being respected seem to be:

- ☐ Superiority in studies
- ☐ Conceit
- ☐ Lack of interest in other people
- ☐ Not well known
- ☐ Manners and personal habits
- ☐ Other (please specify)

3. Has the candidate experienced any apparent emotional or physical disability which affected his performance in school or is likely to do so in college? If yes, explain in C-1.

4. Do you have any reason to question the personal integrity of this student? If so, please explain.

5. I recommend this candidate for admission:

	not recommended	without enthusiasm	fairly strongly	strongly	enthusiastically
For academic promise:	☐	☐	☐	☐	☐
for character and personal promise:	☐	☐	☐	☐	☐
Overall recommendation:	☐	☐	☐	☐	☐

Signed..Length of time acquainted with candidate.................................

Please Print Name...Position..................................Date.........................

to the student, should be an information-gathering time. The college will get most of the information it needs to make a decision on admission elsewhere. It will rely far more on what teachers who have known a student for several years say about him, than on how he appears to them on a spring day. Of course, if a student comes in and asks obvious questions that could be answered by glancing at the catalogue, the admissions officers may put a report in the folder, "Not very interesting to talk to." But this will probably only confirm what the rest of the record shows and have slight bearing on the decision to admit or reject.

Some of the most brilliant students can be the most silent and least forthcoming in an interview. It should be remembered, too, that the college through the interview may be subtly selling a candidate who has already been accepted, unbeknown to him. Some selling jobs are not subtle at all. Harvard and Princeton both arranged a meeting of faculty with a genius of 14 who had only finished grade school but had perfect College Board test scores achieved by self-instruction! Harvard won that contest, apparently by convincing the boy and his family that at his age Harvard was in a better position to protect him from the possibly bad impact of older students.

The golden rule for the candidate in an interview is: BE YOURSELF!

"Do I have to engage in social-service work?" a high school junior asked Ed Wall of Amherst. The answer is, of course not! The whole idea of diversity is that you do not have to conform to any type at all these days. If you deliberately undertake activities or studies because you think they will help your chances of admission, you are shortchanging yourself. Admissions offices can spot this kind of attitude because the performance generally shows a lack of heart. By the time you are interviewed, the die has been cast: you are what you are, and the prouder of this you seem, the better.

It is a good idea for a candidate to inform himself in depth about a college before the interview so that he will have some serious questions to put to the admissions officer, or to the alumnus if the interview is off-campus. We have interviewed many candidates and those we appreciated most asked the most searching questions. A question like, "Isn't your campus pretty homogeneous?" can lead to a discussion of the virtues or disadvantages of homogeneity. At Dartmouth a girl asked some questions about dormitory arrangements. When told that there are both single-sex and co-ed dorms, she asked: "Would I have to room with a boy I didn't know?"

The more interviews a student has, the more useful each one becomes, and no one should be afraid to embarrass an admissions interviewer by pointing to the advantages of another place. Selective college admissions officers have nothing to hide and will not deceive a prospect. Fred Copeland of Williams frankly tells visitors that his college offers as fine a liberal arts education as any but it does not have specialized areas like oriental studies or nuclear physics. He can afford to counsel candidates to advise them to look over certain colleges that offer what they are looking for, because he does not need to admit a student who will not be happy at Williams.

Is there a preferred time to visit a campus? Spring and fall are better than summer when the campus is liable to be empty. Winter visitors are not likely to get an interview at many selective campuses because of the work load in the admissions office, but the more remote the college is, the more flexible it becomes. Dartmouth even has people on duty on Saturday during Winter Carnival weekend. "How can we not see someone who comes all the way to Hanover?" they ask.

The sensible and polite thing to do is to make an appointment for an interview in advance, but campus tours are held daily for all visitors by student hospitality groups like Dartmouth's Green Key or Wesleyan's Cardinal Key.

For students making comparisons of campuses, it is helpful to keep a notebook of impressions. A sheet can be filled in in a few minutes. It is surprising how rapidly feelings about a place are forgotten or distorted. Notes can be helpful later in talking with parents, counselors, alumni and others before making a decision to accept a particular college. As we said, parents' impressions should be reserved.

A father, after visiting what appeared to be a quiet, small-town selective college, advised his son who was in boarding school in Switzerland, to apply there because it seemed an ideal place for reflective study with a minimum of distraction. "I'm glad he picked it," the son, now a prominent businessman, recalls, "because between the booze and the babes, I had a ball!"

Howard Greene Associates have developed a guide to the college visit, which should help students clarify the reasons for their visit, and how they felt about it.

A GUIDE TO VISITING COLLEGES AND THE INTERVIEW

Why Visit the College Campus

If you were at this moment to be asked on the spot what you felt about a certain college or which you would like to attend, you would most likely be responding on the basis of very general impressions gained second-hand from other people or, at best, from a reading of a catalogue. A visit to a campus, wisely spent, can help you gain a firmer awareness not only of that particular school but also of your personal likes, dislikes, and needs, of the climate that would be most conducive for you to grow in socially and academically.

Students often state they want a certain size or location or type of campus, but very often they will change their minds after an *in-depth* visit to a college. It has to be your feelings and observations, not another student's, that will best tell you what kind of college you want. College catalogues will prove helpful in describing the ideals of the college, its size, programs, requirements and the like, but since it is written for a broad, highly diverse audience it will not tell you if it is the proper home for you as an individual.

Seeing several different types of schools (for example, any big state university or small rural college or urban commuter school) will tell you much about the majority of colleges in a similar category. So you do not have to visit every college or university to decide if it is the kind that is best suited to you. Careful planning and execution of college visits and interviews can be one of the most critical factors in finding the college that is best for you.

When to Visit

Select those colleges to which you will make a visit only after you have read a number of catalogues carefully, talked to your counselor or professional adviser and to students who are attending colleges of possible interest to you. You must develop some form of "game plan" to hit the college circuit with. Doing the research by the above methods will help you to decide which types of schools you prefer, and thus help you in your choice of which specific ones you wish to visit. Obviously, if the catalogue and the counselor tell you that College X does not have the location or the programs you want or is too far beyond your reach academically, it makes little sense to visit it with the futile hope of changing it to your liking.

The best time to visit is during the normal school session, either in the spring of your junior year or late September, October or November of your senior year. An academic calendar in the catalogue will tell you when school is in session and when major events are in effect. Do not visit on a big football weekend or during final exam time, for example; you will gain a very one-sided view of the campus and its students. How would you know if that was what the school environment was like most of the time, either glum and tense during exam periods or wild and alcoholic during houseparties?

Start a notebook on every college so that you can write down: the questions you wish to ask the admissions officer or the students or the faculty; the impressions you wish to have confirmed or denied from your visit.

Many catalogues include a list of students in attendance and their hometown. You may want to contact someone from your home area by letter, asking him to meet you during your campus visit.

Do not make your first visit and interview to a college that you feel may well be your first or second choice. Gain some experience and self-confidence by visiting several others first. You will develop a keener eye and greater ability to ask the questions you really want to ask and be better able to make comparisons among several schools.

How to Arrange Your Visit

Pick out several dates on which you (and your parents if they are providing transportation) can get away from school and other commitments to visit the college. *Telephone* the Office of Admissions two to three weeks prior to that time to request an appointment for an interview and tour of the campus. You will find that writing to set up an appointment is an inefficient method: too often the secretary writes back two weeks after receiving your letter that there are no openings for interviews on the day requested. Telephone calls are easier on the Admissions Office as well as on you.

Plan to spend the entire day. Ideally, spend a night as well with an acquaintance in a dormitory if that is possible and if it is a school about which you are reasonably serious.

What to do about parents? Leave them home if you feel that embarrassed about their tagging along. If you need a free chauffeur, take them along and let them explore the school on their own. They are not expected (and usually not of help to you) to go into the Admissions Office with you. My own experience as an admissions dean has been that parents' presence tend to make for a poorer interview because of the greater degree of self-consciousness the student experiences. The admissions officer is always more impressed, as well, with the student who has been able to make his own arrangements and move about on his own.

A note to the wise parent: all too often a student will balk at considering a college that may be excellent for him simply because the parents reacted too positively toward it during a visit. Says the high school senior, "There must be something really bad about it if my mother liked it so much." Let the student see the place on his own terms, for it is the only way he will feel comfortable with a consideration of it.

The Interview

Golden Rules for Students: (1) Do not "be" what you think the admissions officer wants or expects of all applicants to his college. State frankly your interests, thoughts on schooling, hopes for a college experience, and concerns so that he can see you as an individual, not a mannequin. This is the only way he can help you to know if his college is appropriate for you.

(2) Remember that the interview is a 50–50 proposition. On the one hand, the interviewer wants to learn more about you as a person and an intellect than is learned from a batch of papers and test reports he will see later on. On the other hand, you want to know all that you can about the college. Make the interviewer work! Ask him some or all of the questions outlined below if it means you will come away with a deeper insight into the institution. At Princeton, I would see eight to 10 applicants in a single day of interviewing. The boys who always made my day and whom I remembered positively were those who challenged me to think because of their concerns, their questions and their opinions.

(3) Any question is legitimate if it helps you to gain a fuller knowledge of the college and it is not answered in the literature you have been provided with. You should not waste the interviewer's or the student-tour guide's time by asking questions that can easily be answered by a

careful reading of the catalogue. There is no easier way to "turn off" an admissions dean.

The Questions

This is a suggested list of questions, the answers to which will help you to flesh out the college, to see if it is what you thought it would be, if it has all or most of what you are seeking. Many of these will be answered partially in the catalogue or in conversation with advisers, but many will need to be asked in an interview and during careful inspection of the campus.

I start with a consideration of social concerns for two reasons: you will know from the preliminary investigation whether the college is academically strong and, second, few students are ever happy at a college of even the highest academic caliber if they are unhappy for a myriad of personal and social reasons. There is no reason for the order of the questions—you decide which matter most concerns you, personally. All are important, however.

The Social Concerns

(1) What type of housing is available? What options for choosing roommates? Is off-campus housing available, popular or not?

(2) If a school with fraternities, what percentage of the student body belong and what percentage live in the fraternity houses? Is there freshman rushing? What is the college's official attitude toward them? Is there a stated policy on possible fraternity discrimination? What are the arrangements if you do or do not belong to a club or fraternity? (Apply the concept of sororities as the case may be.)

(3) What are the social opportunities if you choose not to join a fraternity or club? What facilities are available for parties, dances and intramural athletics?

(4) What activities, such as dances, concerts, speakers, informal athletics and the like does the college sponsor? Do a majority of students remain on campus on weekends for such activities or is it a "suitcase college" atmosphere?

(5) What types of students are found in the student body? Does any one group or type dominate the campus atmosphere? Some clues that will help you to find the answer to this vital issue: where are the students from—national, regional or only local representation? What are the most popular majors in the college? What percentage of each freshman

class graduates four years later? What percentage goes on to graduate training? What do the majority of students do in the afternoons or evenings?

(6) How much freedom is there in social rules and dormitory regulations? How much political activism do you hear from talking to students and looking at posters? How much of a drug-culture is there? Does it dominate the campus? Is it the major or only social activity? How much pressure to conform to either political activism or drugs, or both if they are very much in evidence?

(7) What role are students able to play in the college's social and academic life? Do they sit on judicial committees, or help effect policies at any level?

(8) What kind of religious diversity is there? Are all religious and ethnic groups adequately represented in each class? Are religious facilities available for you if you so desire? If the school is church related, how much stress is there on this religion? Is Chapel or are religion courses required?

(9) Are counseling services available to get on-campus jobs, summer employment, or decide (with its help) on graduate or career plans?

For Girls: If coeducational, what is the ratio of girls to boys? (While few girls to many boys may sound great, it oftentimes creates a very one-sided atmosphere that can make a girl uncomfortable socially and academically.) If not coeducational, what colleges are nearby? What programs does the college, the Student Government, or the clubs sponsor?

The Academic Concerns

(1) What departments are considered to be outstanding? Which are considered to be average or weak? (You will be surprised by the honesty of most admissions officers.) What is available beyond the courses listed in your fields of interest.

(2) How much opportunity for self-selection of courses? What is required in terms of specific courses? Is it possible to move across departmental lines into other related fields to build your own concentration?

(3) Opportunities for independent study or honors programs: do you *have* to take independent work? Are work periods away from campus available?

(4) What is the student-faculty ratio? Be careful of the college that includes every living person in their faculty roster. Your concern is with teaching faculty available to students.

(5) What teaching methods are used? All large lectures, or are there seminars or discussion classes? How many in a typical course? How many courses have enrollments over 50, or 100 or 200 students?

(6) How do the faculty view the student? (Ask students on this one.) Are they available beyond the classroom? Are they turned off on students, seeing them only as bodies to be lectured to? Where do the faculty come from in terms of geographic and educational background—is there diversity here?

(7) Are most courses cut-and-dried schedules of two hour exams, one paper, and a final? How much individuality to each course and teacher and department can you see?

(8) Who teaches the introductory courses—professors of all ranks or graduate assistants? What kind of tradition, if any, has the top faculty toward teaching of undergraduates, particularly freshmen?

(9) What is the policy regarding recognition of advanced courses in high school, especially advanced placement work?

(10) What kind of counseling services are available if you run into problems academically? Are remedial or tutorial services available?

Talking to Faculty

If you are especially concerned about the course offerings and program of a particular department, you should feel free to ask the admissions officer to help you contact the departmental chairman or representative. Faculty are excruciatingly honest in most cases, not only about their departments but also about the caliber of students and facilities in their field. In the area of the creative or performing arts, a discussion with a faculty member can help you to evaluate your level of attainment relative to students at that school and to learn if you wish to be as involved or uninvolved in the area as that school requires.

Talking to Coaches

Athletic coaches are always eager to talk to prospective participants. Write to them beforehand or ask the interviewer to help you contact them.

The Library

The library is a critical facet of every school. You should both ask questions about its facilities and see it with your own eyes. Some key factors to consider: (1) The size of the library in proportion to the number of students (some small schools have fewer books but superior libraries for their enrollment than do larger universities). (2) hours accessible to students. (3) Open or closed stacks. (4) Convenience of reserve rooms. (5) Facilities for reading and doing homework. (6) Special collections or general coverage in the areas of your interest. (7) Periodical and reading-room facilities for reference resources and magazines.

This is important to you because, unlike high school, you will sorely need many books for papers and independent study and because you will need a place to study away from the noise and distractions of the dormitory.

Also, you can be sure that a school with mediocre or downright poor library facilities has great difficulty attracting a decent faculty. It can be a real tip-off in many instances.

FINALLY, be sure to write down your reactions to the many things seen and learned at the school. General impressions will be helpful to you as you see more schools and can begin to evaluate them in comparison to one another. Your notes will help you avoid confusing one college with another while at the same time serving to refresh your memory. Lastly, you will most likely want to speak to your counselor to review your impressions and to discuss their validity and to decide if you definitely wish to apply to that particular college.

COLLEGE VISIT SUMMARY SHEET

Upon completion of your visit, write in your responses to the issues contained here. Do this for each college visited and then compare your summaries for each.

Name of College: Location:
Date of Visit:
Interviewer:

STUDENT BODY
(Impression of student body in terms of appearance, style, degree of interest and enthusiasm, diversity of their social, religious, ethnic background.)

ACADEMIC FACTORS

(How serious about academics is the school and its students? How good are the facilities for academic pursuits? How varied is the curriculum? How strict or flexible the requirements?)

CAMPUS FACILITIES AND SOCIAL LIFE

(How complete and modern are the facilities such as dorms, dining room, student center, cultural center, athletic facilities? How active is the social life? How diverse is it? What are the parietal rules for students? Is it a suitcase or commuter campus?)

OVERALL IMPRESSIONS

(What you liked least and most; what seemed different or special about it. What type of student do you feel would be happiest here? Are you the type?)

RATING

On a scale of 1 to 5 (with 1 being the top grade) rate the college on the basis of your interest in it.

10

Jocks Vault Over the Ivy Wall

A professor in a state university who heard we were writing this book said: "I'm dying to read the chapter on athletes and admissions." At the time we had not intended to include a separate chapter on the subject. "Oh, you must!" he said. He then launched into a tale of his struggle in a faculty committee with the director of athletics over the disposition of money intended for physical education courses. It was finding its way into the athlete recruitment budget.

And then the *New York Times* came out with a series of six articles in March 1974, calling sports recruiting "a college crisis . . . a costly business . . . a public scandal." They cited the case of 17-year-old Butch Lee of Dewitt Clinton High School in New York receiving 300 offers, and the Petersburg, Virginia, post office sending out Christmas greetings "from Petersburg, the Home of Moses Malone." Both Butch and Moses are fantastic high school basketball players.

So what else is new? The problem of overemphasis of college athletics has been with us since the advent of the stadium. The eight Ivy League colleges have football stadiums with a total capacity of 320,000! The crucial question is: Why should higher education foot the bill for a farm-club system for professional football, basketball, and even hockey (only occasionally baseball)?

Faculty members would prefer a British or European system in which sports are informal and independent of the institution's administration. But as Shakespeare said, "There is comfort in heaven and we are on earth." The reality is that sports in America is now big business, bigger than ever. For those who are good enough athletes it is one of the more rapidly moving escalators of upward mobility. It is also a force for civil rights. Would Jackie Robinson have reached the major leagues if he had not starred at UCLA?

The prestige colleges have traditionally maintained a somewhat holier-than-thou attitude. They offer no athletic scholarships—as such. They recruit athletes nonetheless. There are no "full rides" with all expenses paid plus, in some cases, a car, an apartment, credit cards, girls. But alumni may subsidize an occasional fifth year in prep school, or even better, they may give the assurance of being looked after in business upon graduating from a prestige college.

Make no mistake, *the Ivy League and other hard-to-get-into colleges are easier to get into if you are a standout athlete.* At some prestige places the compromises with academic standards gall admissions officers. One director of admissions complained to us about the "jock ghetto," a subculture of male students clearly outclassed by other students academically and being exploited by coaches. It is reminiscent of the phrase coined in the thirties by Yale's great and flamboyant end, Larry Kelly: Poison Ivy League.

Still, there is a distinct difference in the selective college approach from that of some of the big-time state colleges or Catholic colleges. The *New York Times* series could cite but a few minor instances of questionable practices by selective colleges.

How Do Selective Colleges Differ?

In the first place the selective colleges love *all* athletes, not just the superjocks, so that anyone who has played a varsity sport in high school, who has won a letter, has an increased chance of being admitted. At Dartmouth 75 percent of those admitted are athletes of one sort or another. A fourth of all Princeton freshmen are high school letter winners. At Harvard every freshman is obliged to pass a swimming test! Selective campuses sometimes seem like one big playing field with the entire population suited up for anything from frisbee playing to volley ball. Fred Glimp, who was dean of admissions and dean of the college at Harvard, says that athletes "give the place a tone it needs," a tone of health, vigor, joy, competition, grace and physical control.

Al Quirk of Dartmouth admissions points out that without athletics an American campus would explode. Sports relieve tension and get the mind off the books. But what of the nonathlete? Walking may be just as constructive as competition on the playing field. There is a bit of mystique about sports. Does football build character? Certainly, but not exclusively. So does playing the violin, or doing anything requiring concentration, sacrifice and the development of skill.

Some young people have become suspicious of the claims of coaches, and it is significant that star athletes, once they are in the selective colleges, may choose to drop the sport that takes up so much of their time. Perhaps we are seeing, in the selective colleges at least, the coming end of what Henry Steele Commager, Amherst's distinguished professor of history, called higher education's "mucker pose" of anti-intellectualism and pro-athleticism. But it will die hard.

Selective colleges for the most part are not hysterical about athletics, but they are enthusiastic. Generalizing is dangerous. At Stanford football is more important than it is at Brown, and at Chicago the game is not played at all. Cornell is a national hockey power. But Satch Sanders, the great Boston Celtics star now coaching Harvard basketball, says of his players: "These gentlemen are so competitive in the classroom you'd assume it would apply to basketball as well. I didn't know how many things would be pulling at their time. We don't have students who walk around dribbling a basketball six hours a day."

Which brings up the second distinction between the colleges that heavily subsidize athletes and the colleges we have been chiefly concerned with: the Ivy athlete does have an academic commitment to meet. He may come in at a level below the class average, but he is expected to earn a degree, possibly go to graduate school, but probably not be a professional athlete. In some cases he will become a coach or a secondary school teacher/coach. New York Knickerbocker star Bill Bradley, no classroom whiz when he entered Princeton, became a Rhodes Scholar. Most selective college athletes graduate, while only 50 percent of other college athletes graduate. Moreover, if a Yale athlete, say, quits the team, he is not going to lose his scholarship, as he will at colleges where in effect he is being paid to play. There are even cases of injured athletes losing the subsidy from some ungrateful places.

So an athlete who is sought by many colleges and chooses a selective college is making a sacrifice of $2,000 a year or more, and he is deciding that he wants a rigorous education. He will not be forced to take gut courses or major in phys ed. Some coaches at sports-power colleges will not let a player be an engineer because it takes too much time away from athletics. This cannot happen at Columbia, or, to say the least, MIT. The academic records of athletes in such colleges show a consistency and staying power arising from their esprit de corps and self-esteem.

The Ivy Dilemma

Winning is not everything in the selective colleges, but it is damned important not to lose too often. We noted how Nathan Pusey, a classics scholar, insisted that the Harvard football teams must maintain a certain level of quality. The fact that Harvard president Derek Bok played basketball for Stanford and that the president of Princeton, William Bowen, was state tennis champion of Ohio is an indication of the sympathy coaches and alumni rooters have in Big Three administrations.

Bok sprained an ankle playing basketball not long after his inauguration, and Bowen's squash playing with the best woman squash player in the game, who just happens to be a Princeton student, has not gone unpublicized. Kingman Brewster, president of Yale, publicly stated that he wants better Eli athletic performances all around. Brown alumni have been assured of administration support for higher coaching salaries and a renaissance in football. Athletic competition is intense in these supposedly genteel institutions, and inevitably abuses arise and the specter of overemphasis floats above stadiums, rinks and gym floors.

Anxiety to get into an Ivy college may have led a number of people to collaborate in somehow helping a high school athlete improve his

SAT scores by an unbelievable 200 points. Investigation by the College Board was fruitless and the athlete is now an Ivy Leaguer. Admissions officers are embarrassed by such shenanigans and there is a certain tension between some of them and coaches and alumni. When teams lose it is the fault of admissions, and when they win it is because of the brilliance of the coaches.

But admissions officers admire athletes. They are liable to have been athletes themselves, and they are amused to hear that a new headmaster at a leading prep school is shocked by the attention the athletes in his school draw from colleges. "When admissions officers get together, they seem to wind up talking sports," says Fred Newberger of Middlebury, an enthusiastic skier. Dick Moll, who used to be on Yale's admissions staff and now runs Bowdoin's, makes no bones about trying to bring in the athletes that Yale and other Ivy colleges are after.

One limitation on recruitment of athletes by such colleges is the requirement that they offer no admission before April 15 (unless the applicant has opted for Early Decision, which few athletes do, because they want to keep their options open). Imagine the embarrassment of the college which romances a linebacker and then sees him rejected by admissions on April 15. Well, when so much is at stake, there are subtle ways around this difficulty, and around other rules about putting pressure on candidates.

Everyone is sore at Penn these days, including members of Penn's admissions staff, several of whom quit in 1973 in disagreement with the policy regarding athletic recruitment. No Ivy League official wants to be quoted, but it is no trouble to find admissions and athletic directors who will object to the tactics and academic standards that allow Penn to walk off with so many honors on the playing fields and gymnasiums. John Horan, sports editor of *The Daily Princetonian,* a Philadelphian, with affection for Penn, wrote on October 25, 1973:

> During the last full fiscal year, Penn reportedly operated at a $2 million deficit. About one half of this deficit was due to the athletic department subsidy. Perhaps not coincidentally, Penn did not have a varsity team with a losing record. Princeton, by comparison, had an overall budget surplus, though slight, and only $500,000 of it was due to athletics. It takes money to recruit and train good athletic teams. Another reason

I have no love for Penn athletics is the length to which their admissions department will go to admit an athlete.

There are Princeton alumni who wish Nassau Hall would go to the same lengths. One former member of the football coaching staff claims in the early seventies that academically weak players were admitted to Princeton through a subterfuge, a charge vigorously denied by both the admissions office and the then head coach, Jake McCandless.

Compared to the national scene, of course, Ivy sports are lily-white. It all comes down to the rules of the game. If, as Vince Lombardi said, winning is everything, then rules and regulations of all sorts may appear to exist only as a veneer. AN UNPRECENTED ECO-NOMIC AND ETHICAL CRISIS GRIPS BIG-TIME INTERCOLLEGIATE SPORTS, the *Chronicle of Higher Education* announced on September 24, 1973. The article by Richard Starnes of the Scripps-Howard papers cited the madness of big-time college football: nearly 3,000 games seen by 400 million Americans (that's twice the population!) involving 50,000 players and staff, bringing in a $150-million gate and $13.5 million in TV contracts.

There were 32,318 college basketball games in 1972, and the NCAA finals between UCLA and Memphis State were seen by 38 million on TV. In the recruiting process, jet planes are at the disposal of coaches, who say, "You fly or you die." The hoopla about sports requires some college bands to be flown to games at enormous expense. The business of athletics is at odds with the purposes of education.

When John Silber, now president of Boston University, was a professor of philosophy at the University of Texas, he spoke out against the overemphasis on football, and someone threw a heated can of oil through his bedroom window that exploded without hurting him only because he was not close enough to it. Texas' athletic budget currently is $1.6 million.

The selective colleges are bucking a national hysteria as they try to keep athletics in perspective. "I'm afraid there has been far too much creeping change, i.e., schools going a little beyond the rules," John Embersits, business manager of Yale and its football captain in 1957, told the *Boston Globe* in 1974. He mentioned Penn specifically. "I would like to see the Ivies re-examine and restructure the Code and embrace it. If a Penn cannot live with it, let it leave the league. I think there are other schools who would like to join."

Staton Curtis, dean of Physical Development Programs at Boston University, points out that only the Ivy League involves its college presidents in League rule-making. Other leagues and athletic groups are run by athletic directors, who make the rules and then are responsible for enforcing them. But perhaps only if there is a commitment to keep athletics within bounds can college presidents allow themselves to be part of sports governance.

The Ivy League itself came into existence in part because of the college scandals of the fifties, when basketball players took gamblers' money to throw games. Columbia's basketball coach, resigning in the winter of 1974, warned that unless recruiting practices are reformed, another wave of scandal may recur.

George Hanford, vice president of the College Board, has prepared a report for the American Council on Education suggesting what would be involved in a long study of college athletics, similar to the Carnegie Report of 1929, which condemned professionalism and overemphasis. Does it seem likely that if such a study is made, taking several years, it will change a sports mad TV audience into blue-stockings? Even Yale men thrill to see Calvin Hill run for Dallas, and when Ken Dryden is in the nets for Montreal, you can bet that there are plenty of Cornell eyes glued to the tube. Bread and circuses in America mean beer and Superbowls. Selective colleges can no more escape this syndrome than the rest of the country. They can only try to keep the fever down.

The Rise of the Jockette

Billie Jean King notwithstanding, big-time athletics are dominated by men, and this reaches down from the Astrodome to the peewee rink. With coeducation almost universal and with the rising percentage of women on campus, the selective colleges are encouraging their co-eds to engage in competitive sports and to exercise regularly. *A girl who has been active in sports in secondary school, who is a horseback rider, skier, sailor or golfer is going to get special consideration in admissions offices.*

Granted the culture she grows up in does not favor her as it does her brother. High school athletic budgets are built around boys' varsity sports mostly. Stanford warns prospective co-ed tennis players that the college has no budget for women's tennis! But it is encouraging to see a picture in a school bulletin of the daughter of a former Yale football star practicing mountain climbing on the side of a building. Already the formerly all-male colleges are publicizing the superstars among their girl students. There seems to be no escaping an emphasis on athletics, pride in the winner, the high achiever. But if girls can relieve the anxiety over a losing men's basketball team with a winning performance on the squash court or in the Olympic pool, it is going to make sports a more sensible campus activity.

Why so much emotion over sports in this country? We have mentioned upward mobility, which provides a strong stimulus to the athlete. But the community support in America is unique. Other countries devote only a fraction of their energies to big-time sports, which are organized outside the education systems. Here we condition our children, boys for the most part, to admire O. J. Simpson or Hank Aaron or Arnie Palmer, create Little Leagues and peewee hockey teams, so that by the time college rolls around, the student expects some kind of athletic excellence to be there. It has been suggested that only a team or a star can create a sense of community in a country that changes as rapidly as America. For a while Brooklyn *was* the Dodgers.

When alumni get together, the one thing that they have in common is a shared interest in athletic teams. A Harvard–Yale football game brings people together in a way nothing else can. Athletics is the visible side of education. You hang the athlete's picture in the local tap room, not the Phi Bete's.

Athletic excellence has received a new emphasis in the selective colleges as the result of the radicalism of the sixties. Athletes reassure both alumni and parents. They appear red-blooded, normal, positive thinking, in contrast to intellectuals who are querulous, critical of the status quo, alienated and breeders of radical thought. Drugs, riots, thieving and other antisocial aspects of a campus are not associated with athletes. Athletes tend to be conservatives.

If You Are an Athlete

Athletes applying to selective colleges are sometimes called scholar-athletes to distinguish them from those who simply would not be able to get by academically. Does this mean that if you run the hundred in 9.9 you also must have SATs in the 600s, rank in the upper tenth of the class and have all As? No, a scholar-athlete may be more athlete than scholar and still get in. You might say that the stronger his (or her) athletic prowess, the lower down into the academic barrel the admissions office will dip. There are, remember, three categories of candidates who are looked at separately and made to compete only among themselves: athletes, minorities and alumni children.

Using the Princeton rating system, an outstanding athlete will get a one rating on the personal side, and this allows perhaps a five on the academic side. But the scale can slide down considerably in some selective colleges for an athlete they want badly. He is admitted as "a high risk," but actually there are ways to make sure he does not flunk out. And sometimes an academic dud is turned on, challenged and performs very respectably in the classroom.

In giving an athlete a break that might not be given to an alumni child, the selective college is doing all it can for him. The maximum-aid package will still oblige him to work at college and during the summer. So it follows that you really have to want the education more than you want the money. And so, too, state universities are preferred by some athletes admitted to Harvard or other Ivy colleges.

We wish more athletes would reflect deeply about the choice, not because it will make that much difference to the quality of selective college athletics, but because we think an athlete who is admitted to a selective college will in the long run benefit more from the experience and he will escape from some of the professionalism and exploitation of the great sports powers.

David St. Pierre, Harvard captain and All-Ivy safety on the varsity football team and first marshal of his class, 1974, said in an interview: "I know I'm a member of the University first and the team second. . . . There are all kinds here. Freshman year too many people put on false fronts. Kids who give sherry hours in their rooms as if they'd been doing it all their lives. Guys who have to go running through walls of beer cans every weekend. . . . Harvard has made me much more liberal minded, more tolerant of different living styles and ideas. . . . Too many people pick out guys as jocks, preps, or some other category, but it's not that simple." He is now at Tufts Medical School.

The athlete who is not a standout should still make sure that the admissions office knows of his activity. He may not be big enough to play varsity football in college, but he could play for the 150-pound team or engage in intramural sports. He might be recruited on campus by the crew coach even though he has never rowed. In creating a well-rounded class, the admissions office wants a certain number of active people to keep up that campus tone Fred Glimp speaks of.

This is true now for girls as well. It is a real advantage for a co-ed applicant to be a good figure skater or a member of the high school gym team. As a Radcliffe admissions officer said, "We have a strong athletic program and wonderful facilities and we don't want them wasted." A top athletic record will more easily increase the rating on the nonacademic scale than almost any other extra-curricular activity.

Needless to add, none of the foregoing is meant to suggest that someone without athletic interest or talent should suddenly go into training junior year in the hopes of helping his chances of admission. Nor should the nonathlete feel that he or she will be out of place in a selective college. On the contrary, it is just this mixing of various types of these campuses that helps make the selective college experience so meaningful. But someone who is marginal academically and fails to make a varsity team is going to be one unhappy student. It is just such a student whom counselors should steer away from the competitive colleges.

11

Selective Colleges, Selective Minorities

The civil rights movement opened white colleges to minority students, but where admissions are selective, minority students compete among themselves for places. Minority students, meaning mostly Black but including Latinos, Chicanos, American Indians, disadvantaged Orientals, Eskimos and disadvantaged whites, in the selective colleges are bright and talented and tend to have "white profiles." On the average they score in the high 500s on the SAT. At Harvard the average for blacks is around 630, while the average for all freshmen is around 670.

"Our black students are not disadvantaged," says Franklin Moore, who handles Black admissions at Princeton. "We don't recruit kids standing around on the corners of the ghetto." Competition is intense among minority students. Only a third who apply are accepted by Harvard, and a fourth by Yale.

Of the total pool of students headed for college, about 13 percent are nonwhite, according to figures based on 784,848 students who filled out the optional Student Descriptive Questionnaire of the College Board. Of these 7 percent are Black, 1 percent Latino, and 2 percent Oriental (many are not disadvantaged). Other minorities in fractions of 1 percent make up the total. When we talk about minorities we are essentially talking about Blacks. Blacks are the most numerous minority and the ones who led the civil rights fight, the ones who are usually the most racially conscious on campuses. At Dartmouth, American Indian students have their own cultural and counseling center and were strong enough to eliminate the Indian as a team symbol and mascot.

Minority admissions procedures and standards have become more sophisticated. In part this is due to improved secondary school education for some minority children. In 1968, only 10 percent of Blacks taking the SAT scored over 400 and only 2 to 3 percent scored over 500. Many Blacks entered college unprepared for higher education. Selective colleges took the best, but still they often took what they called "high-risk" students who required all kinds of assistance to get through college.

At Brandeis an expensive tutoring program was necessary until minority students with stronger academic backgrounds could be recruited. Princeton refused to take any student who could not get by somehow on his own, but even so there were rough times in the beginning for Black students because they were so few that they were sometimes mistaken for townies and questioned by proctors on the lookout for burglars.

Orde Coombs recalled in *Change* magazine (June 1973) his feelings on returning to Yale 10 years after graduating: "When I had walked this street at this season as an undergraduate at Yale, a stupor brought on by physical and mental exhaustion had descended upon me." He was one of 11 Blacks in the Class of 1964 admitted out of 37 applicants. There are 144 Blacks in the Class of 1975 and he found in them a self-confidence that was impossible in his day. Only a fourth of those in one course he checked on in Afro-American Studies at Yale was Black!

There was a white backlash among liberal students on occasion in the past. When a selective college turned down the number-one student in a high school and took a minority student of far lower academic achievement, white students who supported civil rights could be outraged by what seemed patent favoritism. A girl we know graduated with a good record from Bronx High School of Science and had 600s in the SAT, but she could not get into Cornell, while Blacks with 300s in the SAT were admitted. Some of this may still occur on occasion, but the problem in general has been solved by recruiting more minority applicants with good academic records. Fair-minded people recognize the handicap minorities are under in getting decent schooling and will not object to giving them some break in admissions. Colleges now are pretty successful in spotting minority students whose record is only fair but who show promise of catching up in a year or two. But it is essential to recruit actively or applications will fall off. At the University of Chicago, Latino applications rise and fall according to the number of visits the admissions office makes to schools in Spanish-speaking communities.

Minorities change selective colleges in many ways. For some whites their first contact of any kind with Blacks may come in their freshman year; they may even be assigned Black roommates. For other whites the places their families think rightly belong to them have been given to minority students. David Evans, of Harvard admissions, says: "Total enrollment at selective colleges is stable. When the minority students increase on campus, it means some whites did not get those places." This does not bother the white students on campus, but it does upset the parents of white students who have been rejected. Perhaps 10 percent of the enrollment of the selective colleges is made up of minorities.

Recruitment of Minorities

Selective colleges rely greatly on the list of semi-finalists of the National Achievement Scholarship Program for black students run by the National Merit Corporation in Evanston, Illinois, in their search for candidates, and in awarding aid they use the National Scholarship Service and the Fund for Negro Students in New York. White alumni, especially in the South, have been very helpful in the recruiting of Blacks. One Harvard alumnus from Michigan comes to Cambridge four times a year to discuss Black candidates with the admissions office. Yet finding qualified minority candidates is not easy. Brandeis reports a falling off in such applicants in 1974 because of the preference for professional training over a liberal arts education.

Selective colleges are helping minority students not only by enrolling them, but in some instances by preparing high school students for other colleges. Dartmouth took the lead in creating an off-campus house for some Black high school students who attend local schools but are tutored and supervised by college students and faculty. Amherst has a similar program. At Brandeis there is an Upward Bound summer program for minority high school students, a few of whom enroll at Brandeis. A unique service is Harvard's referral system that places many of the minority applicants rejected by admissions in 150 colleges around the country. It was originally funded by the Taconic Foundation in 1971, but is carried on now from general funds of the college by the man who initiated it, David Evans.

Evans came from a large family in Tennessee, attended Tennessee State University because he could not afford a Black college, got a master's in engineering from Princeton, and while at work for IBM in Alabama helped to recruit Black students for selective colleges. His efforts were so impressive he was offered a number of jobs in education and settled for Harvard, where by coincidence he finds four Black classmates from Tennessee State on the faculty and in administration.

Evans has placed about 2,000 students outside of Harvard including non-Black minorities and even disadvantaged whites. At one Midwestern college he ran into a snag when they tried to reject two students he had placed with them, on the grounds that they were white! The scholarship program called for nonwhites only, and so Evans had to persuade the college to take the whites on some other basis, to come up with the money from elsewhere.

Minorities are actively recruited, and from the minority point of view there are still too few of them on campus. Minority students are aides to the admissions office often and prepare brochures, like *Black at Wellesley,* which begins:

> Since Wellesley has a limited enrollment, admission to the College is necessarily selective. However, each student's personal and academic background is taken into account to try to determine how she has taken advantage of the opportunities available to her in the high school and local community.

And ends:

> If you decide you want to attend Wellesley for well-thought-out reasons, then you owe it to yourself to apply.

A Mount Holyoke brochure by black students concludes:

> But perhaps the most important of all, there is enough blackness around Mount Holyoke to carry a black weekend, form an Afro-American Society, and support a feeling of "family." However, there is never enough blackness here to cease struggling for more.

Separatism

Minorities keep pretty much to themselves socially after freshman year, frequenting Third World and Afro-American Centers. Black separatist tendencies led a Black, Martin Kilson, professor of government at Harvard, to write an article for *The Harvard Bulletin,* the alumni monthly. It was adapted for publication in the *New York Times Magazine,* September 2, 1973, and caused much grief on several campuses. Kilson maintained that "At Harvard, as at most major white colleges, black students have reached a crisis, one that has coincided with their rising enrollments and one that has been created in large measure by black separatism and militancy." He charged that militant Blacks are often marginal academically and are anti-intellectual and "anti-achievement in orientation." . . . "No ethnic group in American society has ever advanced its standard of living and status without accepting achievement-orientation as a desirable life-style."

Kilson's comments were too much for the Black students themselves, who replied in *The Harvard Bulletin:* "We submit that such an absurd and total mimicry by blacks of the dominant American culture would not only be antithetical to the purported American ideal of cultural pluralism, but also (and more so) antithetical to every natural and human inclination toward love of self."

Neil L. Rudenstine, dean of the college at Princeton, wrote a letter to the *Times* refuting Kilson's charge that Blacks at Princeton perform poorly and have a 32 percent freshman dropout rate. "None of the Registrar's data regarding black 'dropouts' in recent freshman classes bear any resemblance to Professor Kilson's figures," wrote Rudenstine, who offered figures to show a *flunk-out* rate no higher than 10 percent. In his letter the dean also addressed the question of why Black College Board scores are lower than those of whites—

poorer secondary school training—and why Princeton (and presumably other selective colleges) should take Black students when they appear less qualified than other applicants.

> It is far from clear, however, that a policy of this kind [denying blacks admission on such evidence alone] would constitute genuinely "higher" admissions standards or yield better educational results in the long run. In all probability, it would simply mean that significant numbers of able black students with high academic potential, capable of making valuable contributions to university life and to society as a whole, would have been excluded from the best universities because they had previously failed to receive the best in primary and secondary school education.

But Rudenstine tempered his reply by saying that Professor Kilson "has raised issues very worthy of serious analysis and debate." His letter was followed by a letter from the wife of a Black MIT graduate student beginning: "Thank God for the article on blacks at Harvard."

What disturbs some Blacks more than the merits of the controversy is the airing of it in the *Times*. They fear it could weaken the position of Black students among generally supportive whites.

The Kilson controversy was confined to newsprint. The "IQ" article by Professor Richard Herrnstein of Harvard in *Atlantic* (September 1971)—expanded into the book, *IQ in the Meritocracy* (Atlantic-Little, Brown, 1973)—brought out Black student pickets denouncing the racist character of its thesis that Blacks are genetically of lower intelligence than whites. The physicist William Shockley, a Nobel Laureate, who has views similar to Herrnstein's (said to be a popularizer of the studies of Berkeley education professor Arthur Jensen) was to debate the question with Roy Innes at Harvard, but the student objections were so vehement that the administration canceled the debate because it could not guarantee that the meeting would not be disrupted.

Transferred to Princeton, the proposed debate aroused so much animus among Black students that it was in effect closed to the public and open only to members of the Whig-Clio Society, a campus debating group. President Bowen indirectly implied that Shockley's argument is ridiculous but that the right of free speech had to be upheld. To a Black man whose forebears were brought to this country in chains, the mere presence of anyone who holds Blacks to be inferior in any way to whites can scarcely be less than inflammatory.

Blacks know all too well how many there are who would like to justify their feelings about Blacks by "scientific proof" of their genetic weakness of mind. Professor Norman Daniels of the Tufts philosophy department has shown how empty of any scientific validity are the claims of Jensen, Herrnstein and Shockley in "The Smart White Man's Burden" (*Harper's*, October 1973), an article that should be read by anyone tempted to wonder if after all there is not something to these claims. Those who have not the time for reading it can settle for *Esquire*'s riposte to Professor Shockley's request that some Blacks give him blood samples for testing so that he can prove how intelligence increases according to the percentage of white blood Blacks have.

Said *Esquire* (December 1973), "Oh shut up!" The intolerance of Black students to airing the issue may not be in the best tradition of the First Amendment, but it should be recalled that in order for the First Amendment to have any meaning at all for American Blacks, there had to be a Civil War and a civil rights movement.

Black Colleges

Why do not more Black students attend Black colleges and avoid the racial tension? In fact, Black applications are not on the increase at many selective colleges, but those who do not apply to white colleges probably will not go to Black colleges because the scholarship money is scarce and tuition is high. Many Black colleges are financially on the ropes and some Black students believe that the good white colleges will probably give them a better education and a better start in life.

More or less dependent on the tuition of their 160,000 students, the nation's 100 Black colleges face extinction or merger with other institutions as enrollments decline. There are now 310,000 Blacks in white colleges. Black colleges cannot compete for top students with a Harvard, which has so much to offer including liberal financial aid for minorities. The Wellesley recruiting brochure assures applicants: "In no way does an application for financial aid enter into the admission decision." A minority student who is admitted to a selective college will not be denied necessary financial aid. Seventy-four percent of Black students in the College Board statistics already mentioned can count on a parental contribution toward their education of no more than $625 a year. No other ethnic group among college applicants is so poor. Only 51 percent of American Indians who responded to the questionnaire fall in this category.

Selective colleges have the money to do justice to Black studies. Mount Holyoke offers 17 courses in Black studies, including African Political Systems, Patterns of Minority Politics, America as a Bi-Racial Society, Caribbean Political Systems. Afro-American seminars at Princeton cover Economics of the Ghetto, Black American Writers and Improving Urban Education.

From the white point of view, the opening of the once exclusive campuses to minorities is praiseworthy, even extraordinary. That the son of a man who waited on students in a club is now a trustee of Princeton seems like a quantum jump in racial progress. If Blacks are still not satisfied, if they are looking forward to the day when it is not necessary to have separate admissions consideration of minority folders, it only means that even the brightest whites must learn that no one should have to be grateful to any institution for the opportunity to compete on equal terms for the best in education.

However, the DeFunis case clouds the picture of minority admissions. "The painful DeFunis case raises the specters of racism and anti-Semitism," said the *New York Times Magazine* (April 14, 1974). Marco DeFunis, Jr., a Jewish Phi Beta Kappa graduate of the University of Washington, sued the University for rejecting his application to the law school, on the grounds that Blacks with weaker academic credentials than his had been admitted. The Supreme Court of the United States rendered no verdict because DeFunis was subsequently graduated from the University of Washington Law School.

But the dissent of Justice William O. Douglas may be a harbinger of the end of admissions offices giving special consideration to anyone on minority grounds alone. A new criterion might then be economic and social disadvantages of the applicant. It is noteworthy that the challenge to minority admissions policies came in a public institution which has never been exclusive of any group.

The problem is really no longer one of institutional prejudice. The cost of expanding facilities to accommodate the demand for places cannot be met now by private or public institutions, so in the competition rejections are inevitable. It seems unlikely that minority students are going to be forced to compete on equal terms with those who have had superior training. But it is evident that it will be increasingly difficult to reject good students who are academically stronger than admitted minority applicants.

Despite the increased competition among minority students for selective places, the well motivated continue to apply while ignoring the fact that 600,000 openings were available in 1974–75. Minority students should be mindful to keep their options open, so first if they are turned down at one or more selective places they still have a college that will accept them. Many selective colleges, too, are taking minority transfers from less prestigious institutions—including the community colleges in some cases.

12

Old Grads and Selective Admissions

There is a subtle difference between the graduate of a college and an alumnus.* The word "graduate" is neutral and unemotional, denoting someone who has been granted a degree; "alumnus" is a warm word, signifying a person with a continuing attachment to an institution he has *attended*—it is not necessary to graduate to be an alumnus. Frank Miller, as a young headmaster of the Hackley School in Tarrytown, New York, was shocked to hear a father pleading with him to get his son into Yale even though it was certain he would quickly flunk out. "That's all right," the father said. "The important thing is that he'll be able to join the Yale Club."

Needless to add, most alumni did graduate from their alma maters, and alumni of selective colleges seem to feel particularly warmly about them, even to the point where they frequently get hot under the collar when their children are rejected by the admissions office.

One of the myths about selective colleges is that they always take their own alumni's children. Another myth is that alumni children have more difficulty getting in than minority students. To deal with the first myth it is only necessary to cite the figure of 15 to 20 percent

---

*Alumnus, a Latin word meaning "pupil" or "foster son," from *alere,* "to nourish."

alumni children in most of the selective colleges; 80 to 85 percent of the enrollment of selective colleges is made up of nonalumni children, children whose parents, if they went to college, went elsewhere. And to deal with the second, let excerpts from the following Letter to the Editor, from Tim Callard, Princeton's director of admissions, stand as a statement that applies to most selective colleges. It appeared in the *Princeton Alumni Weekly,* July 3, 1973, and chastens that publication for misleading its readers in a previous issue:

> The most notable example of the problem is the statement that "the percentage of alumni offspring applying to Princeton who are actually admitted has dropped from 75% for the Class of '63 [Callard's class] to 45% for the Class of '76." What this statement neglects to make clear is that, while the percentage of alumni children admitted over the last 15 years has gradually declined, this decline has merely reflected the increasingly more severe competition for *all* applicants to Princeton during the same time period. In the case of the Class of '63 (with which I have more than a statistical acquaintance), 38.87% of the total applicant group received offers of admission, whereas only 23.90% of all the applicants to the Class of '76 were admitted. One should note, however, that in the case of each class *an alumni child had just about twice as good a chance of admission as the average applicant.* Thus while the percentage of alumni children admitted has indeed declined over the past 15 years, the alumni son or daughter continues to have approximately the same competitive advantage vis-a-vis non-alumni children in applying to Princeton. [Italics added]

The sensitivity of alumni in matters affecting their college is that of quasi-proprietors. Loyalty to alma mater is a matter of conditioning. For those who are not alumni sons and daughters it begins freshman year, and for those who are it may begin in infancy when the baby gets his first Dartmouth bib. The feeling is akin to patriotism. A *New York Times* reporter, looking Princeton over, found the fanatical spirit of loyalty to be almost mystical. David Evans of the Harvard admissions staff came upon alumni in Long Island who began indoctrinating their sons "in the sand box," and who were paralyzed by the possibility—the impossible nightmare—that their sons might be kept out of Harvard by the competition.

The Value of Alumni Support

The selective colleges themselves are at times as aware of the alumni as they are of their students, since much of the administration of these places is run by their own graduates. Alumni are a constituency whose favor is wooed and whose support is critical. Some alumni are irked by the extremely efficient annual giving solicitations conducted by all private colleges and public colleges. Contributions run from five dollars to the thousands. As many as 70 percent of Dartmouth alumni contributed to annual giving in the 1960s. Now the percentage is 56. At Princeton it is 59 percent, and at Harvard 36 percent, but nationally the average is only 18 percent.

Typically, angry alumni threaten to withhold contributions unless the administration mends its ways, and almost invariably it turns out that such people have given little or nothing in the past. It is the generosity, not the stinginess, of selective college alumni that is remarkable. Some annual-giving figures in 1973 were: Yale $4.9 million, Princeton $3.96 million, Dartmouth $3.25 million, Harvard $4.8 million. The number of alumni volunteers raising these sums varied from a corps of 2,000 Princeton grads to 3,800 Dartmouth grads.

Annual giving is unrestricted money and may be used as the college sees fit. Restricted gifts, though, are also welcome. The Mellon Art Center at Yale, a gift of Paul Mellon, and the Loeb Drama Center at Harvard, a gift of John Loeb, are examples. In 1961, the "X Foundation" gave Princeton $35 million for its Woodrow Wilson School building and programs. Twelve years later it was revealed that the donor was Charles S. Robertson '26 and his wife, Marie Hoffman Robertson. A remarkable instance of posthumous alumni benefaction is the Jadwin athletic cage at Princeton, built in 1969 with $28 million from the parents of L. Stockwell Jadwin, who graduated in 1928 and died a year later. For more than a generation Mr. and Mrs. Stanley Palmer Jadwin kept in continuous contact with Princeton through a series of scholarships they provided to young men who became almost foster sons to them.

Public colleges also have their loyal alumni and their endowments, with the University of Texas leading with half a billion dollars. Gifts to public colleges enable them to enrich programs above and beyond funds provided by the legislature. At the University of Washington, alumni make contributions to the business school in exchange for useful research. Alumni children have recently been the subject of attention by some public college admissions offices. All educational enterprises need some of that intangible thing called alumni spirit to keep them vital.

Alumni are not loved for their money alone. Colleges like to bask in the reflected glory of their illustrious graduates, and they like them to come back to the campus for reunions. Alumni magazines reflect the fellowship of classes in the most read section, the class notes. During the upheavals of a few years ago alumni leaders were invited to campuses to hear the administrations' side of the story, to meet students, and then to reassure, it was hoped, other alumni back home. The moral backing of alumni was a key element in the stabilizing of unsettled campuses.

Some graduates of course are left cold by alumni activity and resent the amount of mail they get from their college. A Smith alumna was turned off by a classmate's card with this jingle and note:

> There was a young lady from Smith
> Whose existence was almost a myth.
> She wrote her class sec
> Saying, "I'm here by heck!"
> Sharing news of her kin and her kith.
>
> So why don't you follow her example and do the same!

Yet thousands of alumni turn up for class reunions, and more recently alumni are paying to attend *alumni college,* a week of faculty lectures and discussion of a topic. For example, in 1974 Scripps College in Claremont held an alumni college on the art of the film.

One characteristic of selective college alumni would appear to be longevity. Harvard's Class of 1912 has 146 living members in 1974 out of 602 who entered as freshmen in 1908 (498 received degrees), almost 34 percent of the graduating group going strong in their eighties! The tradition of keeping Harvard classes together is almost as old as the college itself. In 1884 the Class of 1829 held a reunion for which Oliver Wendell Holmes wrote a poem called "The Girdle of Friendship" that concluded:

So, link by link, our friendships part,
So loosen, break and fall,
A narrowing zone; the loving heart
Lives changeless through them all.

A college "class" has a life of its own, and that is why a college education that involves transferring from one college to another or piling up credits at night is a different thing from a four-year span on a residential campus with the same group of classmates who remain in touch sometimes for a lifetime. Many a group of classmates has rallied discreetly to help the families of one of their number in times of trouble.

At some colleges alumni have the inside track on doing business with the place. If you show up at Harvard to sell something, sooner or later the question will come out: "What did you say your class was?" If it was Yale '56, better try your luck in New Haven.

Alumni as Recruiters

Given this spirit it is understandable that alumni would volunteer to help admissions offices recruit applicants. In the past the recruitment of athletes, particularly football players, was traditional but informal. An alumnus would spot a good high school halfback, money would be raised to send him to Exeter, or perhaps Hun School in Princeton for a year of seasoning, and then he would go to Dartmouth or Yale on a scholarship from the college or from a local alumni club. When the huge number of high school applications began to swamp the admissions offices, they turned to alumni clubs around the country for help in assessing the quality of the high school and of the applicants. Gradually the alumni committees have assumed a fundamental importance in helping admissions officers identify candidates and in persuading them to accept invitations to enroll. Alumni thus become auxiliary staff that broaden the sweep of admissions offices. The table of organization of Princeton admissions (p. 178) was sent to some 2,200 alumni schools committee members. It is worth noting that undergraduates are now being brought into contact with alumni committees for the purpose of helping explain and promote the college to candidates.

TABLE IV
PRINCETON UNIVERSITY • ADMISSION STRUCTURE

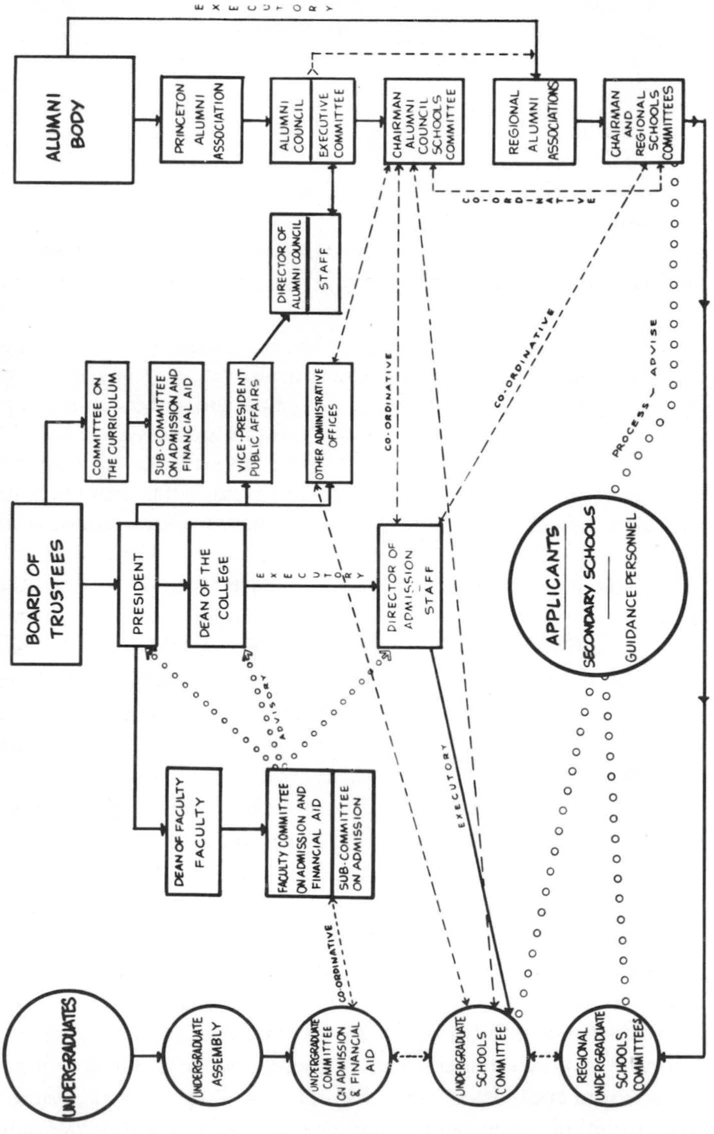

We have earlier noted how helpful alumni can be to a candidate in the admission process. Here is an alumni interview statement that helped a candidate who did not submit test scores get into Bowdoin:

> His inner strength, determination and independence undoubtedly provide the tools to permit his success in all efforts. For example, he likes to hike and camp, but no one he knows can keep up with him—thus the bulk of his trips are alone with two dogs. And he is now a vegetarian, after a careful study of foods.

A Princeton interview report went like this:

> The personal impression one gets from Erik is probably very much like the impression one gets from his school records and board scores. He is a bright and mature young man who could without question perform successfully at Princeton. He has apparently done well in every and any activity in which he has been involved. His attitudes like most of his peer group are level headed if somewhat cynical. His interests are broad but as yet unfocused. I feel I can recommend him for admission, but I am not sure that I can say he is much better qualified than the many qualified applicants who cannot be accepted.

An alumnus may spend several hours a week on this work during the school year, calling on students, visiting schools, arranging for visits on campus and holding candidate meetings with undergraduates. Someone like George Kovatch, a Ph.D. who works for the U.S. Department of Transportation in Cambridge, Massachusetts, is on the Princeton Schools Committee for the pleasure it gives him, even though only 120 of 563 applicants in the Boston area are accepted and only half of these actually go to Princeton. Kovatch, who graduated in 1955, said in an interview, "I'm not sure I would have gone to Princeton if it had not been for the alumni attention I received." He remembers that Robert Kinehart of the Class of 1904 came from New York to Scranton to see him. George was an honor student and football player who turned down attractive financial offers from other colleges to go to Princeton on more stringent terms.

Alumni committees pay no particular attention to applicants who are alumni children, which irritates some alumni, naturally. Alumni children are assessed in a separate category by the admissions offices

—they compete among themselves for a certain percentage of places. An alumni interviewer makes his judgment of such candidates on the same basis as the others and it is up to the admissions office to weigh the comments along with the other material in the folder.

One selective college that is trying to do something about the agony caused by rejecting alumni children is Amherst. Its admissions office invites alumni to bring their sons in for an early assessment of their chances *junior* year. No one is prevented from applying, but those who look weak are urged to apply elsewhere, and most alumni are realistic enough to accept this verdict. Some express gratitude for the help they have received, which may include a suggestion of the right college for the boy. A few stubborn alumni force their sons to hope against hope and try to exert pressure to get them in. "This is painful to watch," says Ed Wall, admissions dean, "because it hurts the boy and embitters the parent."

Columbia takes the bull by the horns in explaining its policy regarding alumni sons.

> Five years ago, an alumnus's son would be admitted to the College and told of his admission well before other applicants, provided he met minimal academic standards. This is no longer so. Instead, *any* applicant may request an early notification, and if he is admissable and has informed the Admissions Office he wishes to attend Columbia, he will be guaranteed both a place in the entering class and a financial aid award.

So says Columbia's report to schools.

Changes in admissions policy at the selective colleges have riled some alumni not just because it is harder for alumni sons and daughters to be admitted than it use to be, but also because of the changed composition of the student body that is no longer drawn from the old narrow group to which these alumni belong. Dr. Chase N. Peterson, former dean of admissions at Harvard, in his report on the years 1967–72, observed:

> *Harvard has always been grateful for its traditional clientele and remains so.* But an optimum match between faculty resources and intellectual goals required the continual enrichment of the undergraduate body. In the early years of Dean of Admissions Bender's administration there

were few applicants from what is now called the third world who were able to be interested in coming to Harvard College or qualified to do the work. Quite likely, to use Ralph Ellison's phrase, the third world was "invisible" to Harvard as it was to itself in intellectual and cultural terms. [Italics added]

Unhappy Alumni

Not all the traditional clientele are happy with the democratizing of selective campuses from Harvard to Stanford, but only in a few cases have they protested openly. The most prominent protest group is one calling itself *Concerned Alumni of Princeton*. Of all the traditional colleges, Princeton has changed the most. The old "northern college of the South," all male, with no Blacks and few Jews, has gone co-ed, and Blacks and Jews probably add up to 30 percent of the student body. Dorms are co-ed, half the clubs are gone, most of the faculty voted for McGovern. Lordy! What a list of reasons to be concerned about.

CAP, as it is known, is highly visible and highly vocal because of its very attractively put together 32-page monthly magazine *Prospect* (the name of what was once the president's handsome mansion, and is now the faculty club). *Prospect* is mailed free to perhaps a third of Princeton's 50,000 alumni. CAP has the backing of Shelby Cullom Davis '30, a distinguished diplomat now U.S. Ambassador to Switzerland and a man who has given $5 million to the university as well as serving as an adviser to the history department. He is co-chairman with the well known Asa S. Bushnell '21. T. Harding Jones '72 edits *Prospect*.

Alumni contributors are solicited to help support the work. As an undergraduate, Jones founded USA, which stands for Undergraduates for a Stable America, a conservative political group of 25 students that claims credit for bringing ROTC back to Princeton. *Prospect* has been frequently critical of admissions policy. In the October 1973 issue, John H. Thatcher, Jr., '53 wrote as follows:

> Any time a university like Princeton has nearly five candidates applying for every one it accepts, it is patently obvious that *both* diversity and high character can be achieved within the student body. That Princeton

hasn't quite done this, despite its good intentions, can be traced to three main factors; (1) shifting priorities and faculty-administration pressures on the Admission Office, (2) faulty staff evaluation of candidates at the working levels of the Admission Office, and (3) relegation of the formerly large role alumni schools committee men played in the admissions process to one that currently consists largely of information-servicing and recruiting. Personal evaluation and character estimation made on the basis of familiarity with local schools and conditions as well as the applicants themselves, has been de-emphasized.

What CAP seems to want is the kind of place Princeton was 20 years ago. Some of the supporters of CAP wore buttons to reunions reading: BRING BACK THE OLD PRINCETON. The collapse of the Princeton football team has intensified the dismay of CAP, which sees admissions as inhospitable to athletes. T. Harding Jones, who has a picture of William F. Buckley, Jr., on his desk, feels that coeds at Princeton add nothing to the place, and he says that Princeton is now little different from a state university.

In an interview he told us that the admission office seeks activist students, left-leaning, and that young alumni on schools committees help to recruit them. One result of this claimed tendency, in his view, is that the club system has been undermined, since left-wing students decline to join. When it was pointed out that many admission officers are private school graduates and would hardly be leftists themselves, Jones said: "People in Brooks Brothers suits are likely to be people with a conscience to purge."

Many Princeton alumni seem to share some of CAP's concerns, but few are actively criticizing the administration, and *Prospect* tends to rely on the same few people to write its material. Jones runs letters critical of CAP, including one from pro-basketball star Bill Bradley resigning from CAP's board, but his approach is that of advocacy journalism. One Princeton class refused to release its mailing labels to *Prospect* after a class officer pointed out that CAP had made serious misstatements about President Goheen. The administration policy has been one of refusal to engage in polemics, but CAP's needling forces administrators to spend valuable time replying privately to alumni asking for verification of or comment on CAP criticism.

Lacking a T. Harding Jones, conservative alumni groups elsewhere have a somewhat ad hoc character. In the fifties, Harvard had its *Veritas,* right-wing alumni expressing anger over the number of alleged leftists on the faculty, and this led to some hesitancy among donors to contribute to Harvard until they were persuaded that Harvard was not an agency of the Kremlin.

At Yale, whose motto is *Lux et Veritas,* a *Lux et Veritas* group put out a critique of admissions policy in a blue-and-white brochure that looked as though it came from an official university office. There was talk of a suit for misrepresentation, but like Princeton, Yale simply would not reinforce the antagonists' dissatisfaction by reacting, and as the behaviorists predict in such circumstances, the irritation was "extinguished." There have been rumblings of revolt among Dartmouth alumni, and Denison University has a group called CFAD—Concerned Friends and Alumni of Denison.

All these opponents of changing admissions policy and of the new character of the American campus (Jones should know that state colleges have in some respects changed even more than private colleges) have in common a conservative political philosophy and a deep feeling for their alma maters. They deplore, but they remain "a loyal opposition." They do not want to tear the ivy walls down, they want to put some barbs on them that would make it impossible for certain applicants to get a foothold.

Their capacity for making a college reverse directions is pretty limited, because a college administration is working every day and few alumni attacking it can make the full-time job of it that Jones has at Princeton. But by giving vent in an extreme way to misgivings shared by many alumni who are more subdued about their dissatisfaction, this "loyal opposition" may make college administrators more cautious and more aware of risks they run in alienating old grads by introducing innovation without adequately involving alumni leadership. For this reason administrators are spending more time and money cultivating alumni these days.

Alumni and Candidates

Applicants to selective colleges are often urged to talk to an alumnus not only for an interview but to deepen their knowledge of the college. Alumni can of course "blow it" by creating a bad impression. "If he's typical of that place, I wouldn't go there on a bet!" is the reaction admissions officers watch for, and then they have the delicate job of getting the volunteer alumnus off the committee or trying to train him to be more tactful. A serious difficulty is persuading alumni not to scare off a group of potential applicants by beginning with: "I assume you all got 650 or better on your SATs."

Alumni failure to cultivate counselors, coaches and others in the secondary school administration can turn a school against a particular college. "It's not worth applying there," a counselor will say. "They'll only break your heart. A bunch of snobs. Haven't taken any of our students in years. They even turned down the valedictorian." Students, the best of them, are quixotic and easily misled. When a student gets down on a good college because an alumnus turned him off, wise parents will wait a bit and then quietly help him to make a less emotional evaluation. But there may be as many unwise parents as there are clumsy alumni.

One way of forming some impressions of any college is by reading the alumni magazine. It is possible to get past the obvious puffery in some of them to serious articles and alumni notes. The *Dartmouth Alumni Magazine* in December 1973 ran a series of statements by undergraduates on "Why College?" One student explained why he came back to Dartmouth after a year in Colorado camping and skiing: "I eventually figured, however, that Colorado would remain for quite a while, whereas my 'threshold-of-life' youth and willingness to endure the strains of academia would not." Another explained that Dartmouth was his second choice and that he was hoping to transfer to his first choice, only to be hooked by a philosophy teacher and just having to major in that department. "I discovered that college doesn't teach you; it encourages you to teach yourself."

Alumni notes tell you something about what the graduates of various places become, being breezy reports by class secretaries on the successes of their classmates—who is vice president of what, who published which book, who has six children. They do not report divorces, nervous breakdowns, alcoholism, financial failure, or crimes of the graduates, and so the picture is rosier than reality. A prominent West Coast lawyer in response to a questionnaire for his 25th reunion at Harvard wrote: "I have not won my H in life." He later became a district attorney.

Alumni club scholarships are worth inquiring about. They are limited in number and not always large, and in parts of the country there is no club big enough to create scholarship funds. Their scholarships generally become part of the aid package awarded by the finance office. What is nice about these scholarships is that they are usually limited to students in the club's region and they must be given out. Sometimes they come as a windfall to a student and actually increase the aid package. Generally it is impossible to get both a college and alumni scholarship. If the aid package is only a loan and a job, the alumni scholarship can provide more than the college was willing to give by itself. The Harvard Club of New York City awarded 19 scholarships in 1974, including six to students outside of New York. One award went to a Black student who had won his school history prize and headed the school council; another winner was active in Ukrainian community affairs in New York; two were football players.

Alumni continue to look for good athletes for their colleges and are not unwilling to spend money as well as time at it. The practice is frowned upon by the Ivy League. "No more dinners for football players," is one interpretation of the rules. A former Dartmouth football player recalls how Harvard tried to recruit him. "I got an invitation to come to an alumnus's house in Cambridge, an impressive place, swimming pool and all. And who should happen to drop in? A member of the Harvard coaching staff, pretending to be surprised to see me there."

The non-Ivy selective colleges have their alumni scouts too. Most Amherst men are proud of their former players in the National Football League. A Princeton fund-raiser has said: "When we have losing football teams there isn't a falling off in giving, but when we win there is an observable increase." With fewer undergraduates coming to see football games, younger alumni may be less interested in the admissions problem of attracting athletes. But some alumni are long-lived and they are liable to be better heeled. So for the foreseeable future any athlete capable of being admitted to a selective college has friends in the alumni, and if he does not cultivate them, they will cultivate *him.*

For any candidate to win an alumnus' support is no more guarantee of admission than it is to be the child of an alumnus, but it cannot hurt and might make a difference. An alumnus can turn an evaluation around by providing something for the "folder" that is eye-catching

—a news-clipping perhaps, a comment from someone who knows the candidate, or simply a strong insistence that the college take a second look. And even if it does not work out, a relationship has been established. A boy turned down by Princeton and accepted at Harvard wrote a Princeton committeeman: "Even though I did not eventually attend Princeton, I feel very fortunate indeed to have visited such a fine school and met so many outstanding people. . . . I have gained true friendship, and in the long run that is what is really important."

13

Money, Money, Money

Selective colleges are the most expensive to attend. In 1974, the annual cost ran over $5,000 a year.* Some private colleges may cost $1,000 less and public colleges $2,000 less, including room, board and expenses. But tuition for out-of-state students in public colleges is rising to as high as $2,800 at the University of Michigan.

How to pay for college is now the biggest educational concern we encounter among parents and students. It is also one of the chief concerns of higher education as a whole and of selective colleges in particular. For what is happening is that the selective colleges, which have always been financially comfortable and in some cases very rich indeed, are no longer able to provide as much scholarship aid as they once did and are turning to loan programs as a principal source for helping students and their families.

To put it another way, the treasuries of these colleges in the past were able to finance much of the burden of needier students, thanks to the generosity of alumni and other benefactors. Now because of rising costs—salaries, fuel, security, insurance, etc.—this burden is going to have to be shared with someone else, chiefly the student

*Typical student budget at Princeton, 1974–75: tuition $3,500, room and board $1,675, personal expenses $650, plus transportation.

and/or his family, through loans, which may eventually be backed by the federal government.

This new situation calls for some new habits. Americans are used to borrowing money to pay for homes, cars, appliances, even vacations. They are now going to have to mortgage their future to some extent to pay for the best in education. That they are willing to do so is evident from the increase in applications to colleges like MIT and Princeton, which rose in 1974 by 20 percent and 14 percent respectively. Amherst and Williams are examples of small, selective colleges that have the highest number of applicants ever.

We would like to underscore the need for able students and their families to approach this problem with as little emotion and as much reason as possible. A sense of panic is the inevitable result of punitive inflation. To have to pay out more for college for your children than for your home is indeed a shocking situation, and more sacrifices than anticipated will be necessary in many instances. But the colleges we are talking about are determined to enroll large numbers of students from moderate-income families. *No one who is qualified should fail to apply to a selective college because of the cost.*

This is not to guarantee that every admitted student at every selective college will receive sufficient financial aid. When the money runs out, some students admitted to some colleges will not get the help they need. But there are other sources of funding. At Mount Holyoke, which is not as heavily endowed as Dartmouth, for example, 40 percent of the students require aid, but only 17 percent have scholarships from the college's own funds. The rest are finding other means to pay their way.

But some students admitted to Mount Holyoke went elsewhere for financial reasons. Dartmouth, on the other hand, has not so far had to turn away any needy admitted student. Only a few institutions are in Dartmouth's position. But we firmly believe that one way or another a student admitted to any of the highly selective colleges can find ways to pay for the highly desirable education offered. Families and students should not give up hope without long consultation with the college in question, for an offer of admission is a sincere wish of the college that the student enroll.

The University of Chicago has one of the most generous financial-aid policies, and it appeals to families to explore ways to pay for their children's education. "We particularly invite middle income families therefore to apply for scholarship assistance for their children, and to work with us in determing a sensible and just parental contribution based on individual family circumstances," reads a Chicago brochure. Other Chicago material worth quoting includes this encouraging statement: "All admitted students who need financial aid will receive it. . . . With a reasonable investment of time and energy, and with some reasonable parental sacrifice, every student can find a way to pay for an education at the College of the University of Chicago."

Having made this point, that at the selective college it is possible for almost every admitted student to come up with a financing plan for his education, we must now admit that the burden is getting heavier and heavier. Before discussing specific ways financial aid is applied for and administered, let us look briefly at what has occurred to change the financial posture of even the richest colleges.

Inflation Plus

Inflation alone will not explain the enormous rise in operating costs of today's colleges. A Sloane Foundation consortium study of nine colleges (Amherst, Brown, Dartmouth, Harvard-Radcliffe, MIT, Mount Holyoke, Princeton, Wellesley and Wesleyan)* shows that their operating budgets rose on an average by 147 percent between 1962 and 1972—Wesleyan's went from $5 million to $17 million, a 240 percent increase. In this period these nine institutions went from a combined surplus of $6.2 million to a combined deficit of the same amount. This occurred during the post-Sputnik era, dubbed the Golden Years in college circles. Much of the increase was for new programs, new courses, student aid and operating costs of expanded facilities. At the height of this growth the per-student expenditures increased by more than 10 percent in 1970 (this was also when student antipathy to college administrations crested). But revenues could not keep up, and the seventies have become a period of belt-tightening.

William G. Bowen before he became president of Princeton wrote a paper, "The Economics of the Major Private Universities," in which he concluded that there is a "productivity problem" in higher education that accounts for much of its rising costs. Salaries and wages rise

* *Paying for College*, The Consortium on Financing Higher Education, Hanover, New Hampshire, 1974.

but college output cannot be much increased by technology, as it can be in a steel mill. You can increase the enrollment while not increasing faculty and staff, but this will hurt quality and it can occur only once.

To pay for part of these increased costs the nine colleges and most others must use funds that would otherwise be used for student aid. One of the interesting aspects of selective college economics is that the students who receive no aid nonetheless receive a hidden subsidy: their tuition is considerably less than what it costs to educate a student. Taking $2,800 as the average tuition in 1971, the actual educational cost for a student was $4,700 at these colleges. It is this $1,900 differential that puts the quality into selective college teaching and the whole campus experience.

In addition to the hidden subsidy for all, there is the actual student aid and these colleges have been generous in their distribution of aid, to say the least. In the decade mentioned, scholarship expenditures tripled—$6.2 million to $18.6 million—the percentage of scholarship students rose from 28.6 to 37.9, and the colleges' own expenditures on scholarships as a percentage of tuition income went from 18.4 to 25.9.

But then look what happened. In the year 1971–72 the average tuition at the nine colleges went up $300 and the scholarship per student went up only $75, so the student and/or his family had to make up the difference. This tells the story of why it is going to cost more from now on at selective colleges even for those on aid: the student or his family has to find the money the college no longer can scrape together for him without cheating him of the quality education he wants and deserves. But it can be told in a more depressing way by the following table from the consortium study:

TABLE V
PARENTAL CONTRIBUTION FOR A 3-CHILD
FAMILY WITH 1 CHILD IN COLLEGE
1968–1973

ANNUAL EFFECTIVE INCOME	EXPECTED CONTRIBUTION		DOLLAR DIFFERENCE	PERCENT DIFFERENCE
	1968	1973		
$10,000	$1270	$ 830	−$440	−35%
15,000	2300	2670	+ 370	+16
20,000	3810	5460	+1650	+43

Effective income is formulated on after-tax income, less some minor deductions plus an income equivalent based on the family's net assets. The study comments: "Middle-income families typically have incomes too high to qualify for substantial financial aid, and if they choose to purchase high cost private education rather than public education, they often face a considerable revision in their pattern of living. Many may be finding that choice increasingly difficult."

Applying for Aid

Financial aid has become so widespread that a central clearinghouse called the College Scholarship Service (CSS) has been established by the College Board in Princeton to screen applications on a national basis even-handedly. *Eighty percent of a group of 670,622 taking the SAT in 1973 reported that they planned to seek aid.* Aid comes in a package consisting of some combination of scholarship, loan and job. What CSS provides is a recommendation to the college of the amount the family should contribute. It is then up to the college to provide the package as best it can. If the college costs $5,000 and the family is expected to provide $1,500, then the package may be a scholarship of $2,000, a loan of $1,000 and a job worth $500. But if scholarship funds are low, the package may only be $1,000 in scholarship and $1,000 in loan, making the family borrow another $1,000 or if possible liquidate assets in this amount.

Applying for aid involves filling out the Parents' Confidential Statement, but before this is done *a frank family discussion is essential.* Parents owe it to their children to let them know their financial position. Yet most children have very vague ideas about family means. Some students deliberately pick the least expensive college education because they do not want to burden their families, but they might very well have done better by themselves had there been more rapport within the family. Grousing about the high cost of living, a perfectly warranted complaint, may be interpreted by teenagers as a signal that the family cannot afford an Ivy college, when in fact the family may well wish to make the sacrifice.

To the student we say, screw up your courage and let the family know your ultimate desire, and if there is an explosion it will only make a loud noise. And to parents we say, screw up your courage and let your children know where you actually stand financially. You cannot help them get better grades or higher test scores, but you can help your children plan for college. The difference in cost between a selective college and a state college may in the end be repaid in terms of the satisfaction that will come from the special kind of education available only at a selective college.

In estimating what the family can contribute, a close look needs to be taken at discretionary expenses and at available capital. It will save anguish and argument later if the possible sacrifices are enumerated. Perhaps vacation plans must be altered. The summer camp bought for a thousand dollars years ago may now be mortgagable. The home mortgage that has been amortized may be refinanced. The summer baby-sitting job may turn out to pay too little and a less appealing but more lucrative form of work by the student will have to be undertaken.

Once the bare-bones budget has been prepared, it is time for the parents to fill out the Parents' Confidential Statement. The Parents' Confidential Statement has a formidable look at first glance, but its 16 pages include work sheets, instructions, separate forms for farmers and proprietors. It asks for income, expenses of the family, income taxes for two years plus the estimated tax for the current year. Assets and liabilities must be listed, and college expenses anticipated. There is no need for children to see this form, so long as they are aware of the general situation.

All the circumstances of the family are considered—the number of children, number in college and so forth—and economists and mathematicians work out the individual situation with the aid of a computer, relying on government figures on the cost-of-living.

CSS gets it in the neck on the issue of short-changing middle-income families. But their formulas are worked out in conjunction with the colleges themselves, and it is to the college an aggrieved family must appeal if the aid package seems impossible to live with.

While awaiting word of the aid package, which is not announced until April 15 by the selective colleges, there should be an exploration of all possibilities for obtaining scholarships and loans outside the college. We have provided a guide to scholarships and loans in the Appendix, but it is impossible to know all the many local funds for education that are available. It will pay to make the effort to discover sources of grants and loans from churches, lodges, college clubs and civic groups.

When the aid package is known, emotions can run high and it is a bad time to decide on a college just because its aid is higher than another college's. There is plenty of time for reflection and conferring with the colleges to which a student has been admitted. The Ivy group compares its aid lists and adjusts them if necessary so that there is no competition among them in distributing aid. Colleges that recruit athletes strenuously can do better financially by potential stars than the selective colleges. We believe an athlete is foolish to turn down the chance of going to an Ivy college for monetary reasons, but of course there may be extenuating circumstances. The athlete has to determine his commitment to an academically demanding environment.

How much any one family will be expected to contribute cannot be estimated, since each family's circumstance is unique. There has been much criticism of CSS expectations of sums such as $1,200 from a family with a $12,000 income. We can only sympathize with the complaints while observing that up to now the selective colleges have been oversubscribed, as it were. Somehow families manage. But whether these colleges will be able to draw the same mix of affluent, modest and poor families a decade from now is a question.

"We don't want a campus polarized between a large group of full paying students, and a smaller group of poor students more or less completely on financial aid," Clara Ludwig of Mount Holyoke says. Dartmouth now expects every student on aid to provide a minimum of $1,400 a year, and Dartmouth alumni clubs around the country find jobs for students when they are off-campus.

In Debt for Alma Mater

A scholarship is a grant, a gift, free and clear. If the amount of tuition money available for scholarships diminishes and there is no other source of scholarships, such as the federal government, then there are three ways to make up the loss: family savings and other assets ("You mean I have to sell some cows?" a dairy farmer father of an applicant asked a Dartmouth financial aid officer), student jobs on or off campus, and loans. In the Sloan study a survey indicated that only 6 percent of the Class of 1952 borrowed; less than 1 percent owed $2,500 or more at graduation. But 32 percent of the Class of 1970 borrowed, and a third owed $2,500 or more at graduation; 8 percent owed over $5,000.

Borrowing occurs essentially because colleges have less grant money to distribute. A basic principle now is that families must contribute more heavily to higher education, especially families who are not poor, yet are not affluent. When the family is told it must come up with a certain sum of money that seems excessive, the only recourse is a loan.

"It's often a matter of how discretionary income is spent," Alfred Quirk of the Dartmouth admissions office told us. "Maybe a club membership will have to go." And maybe to keep the membership is essential for business or social life, in which case the parents look into the lending mechanism.

There are three kinds of educational loans, those the college makes, those that banks and other lending institutions make, and those the government (federal and state) underwrites.

College Loans

These come from the college's own funds and they revolve as students pay back what they borrowed. The selective colleges announce such loans in the aid package, so it is unnecessary to apply for them. They are limited to $1,000 to $1,500 in most cases. Interest rates can vary from 4 to 7 percent, depending upon family income. Repayment is worked out after graduation and may take many years; interest continues on the unpaid balance.

Emergency loans repayable within a year may be had to tide a student over a tough financial period. Sometimes the interest may be higher than the long-term loan.

Only Duke and Yale have tuition deferrment plans of 30 and 35 years respectively. These are long-term loans with insurance features and some interesting tax breaks. For a number of reasons no other colleges have followed these leads, and they remain a long-term experiment in educational financing.

Bank Loans

Educational installment loans are available to families with good credit and work the same way any other installment loan works. Interest rates are about 8 or 9 percent. The borrower pays a monthly sum, starting prior to enrollment, and the bank or credit company pays the college out of the prepayments. This is in effect forced savings with insurance. The amount is generally $10,000 repayable in six years from the time the note is signed.

Federal and State Programs

Four programs may be identified. the National Defense Student Loan Program, Guaranteed Student Loan Program, Loan Programs of 35 states, and Private Programs.

National Defense Student Loans of up to $1,000 a year and not to exceed $5,000 altogether are available to those students who show need. Federal funds are allocated to colleges for administration under the Higher Education Act of 1968. Only the college can authorize these loans, which are *interest free* during college years. Repayment begins nine months after graduation and must be completed in 10 years, during which time interest of 3 percent is charged on the unpaid balance. Those who go into teaching will be forgiven 50 percent of the debt and those who teach in designated depressed-area schools are forgiven 15 percent a year up to 100 percent. These loans are part of the college aid package and cannot be applied for directly.

The Guaranteed Student Loan Program (GSLP) is primarily for middle- and upper-middle-income families and is administered largely through local banks under the Higher Education Act of 1965, which guarantees vast amounts—$5.8 billion in eight years loaned to 3.5 million students. Included in this program are Federal Insured Student Loans (FISL) administered directly by the federal government for those who have no access to private institutions. No more than $7,500 may be borrowed in undergraduate years. Repayment begins nine months after graduation and for those with an adjusted income of $15,000 or less the federal government pays the interest. For others the charge is 7 percent simple interest. Some 140 institutions of higher education have become eligible lenders.

Tight money has meant that not all who are eligible to borrow will get funds, but steps have been taken to loosen this type of credit. The Student Loan Marketing Association, known as Sallie Mae and paralleling Fanny Mae, Federal National Mortgage Association, is making it possible for lending institutions to refinance student loans and increase their lending power. But just as mortgage money can be short, so too with education money.

State Scholarship and Loan Programs are sponsored in 35 states independently of colleges, and applicants must apply to a central state agency. Inquiries should be made to the state's department of education. In the Appendix we have described the excellent Massachusetts Higher Education Loan Plan (HELP).

Private Programs include loans available through a variety of organizations: Unions, churches, PTAs, civic and fraternal groups, employers, professional organizations and industrial associations. Such information is generally available through schools.

It is easier to describe a loan program than to obtain a loan, and it is easier to obtain a loan than to pay it off. But it appears that borrowing for education is going to increase. The Sloan study, called *Paying for College,* turns out to be a report on borrowing with recommendations for reforming present practices.* The subject is complex, but no doubt bright graduates of selective colleges will master such problems as consolidating hybrid loans (loans from different programs on different terms). There will be heavy responsibilities for many young people to bear, especially after also borrowing for graduate school. The default rate on GSLP loans has run at 10 percent, but it is unlikely that many who declare bankruptcy are graduates of selective colleges.

*

Scholarships

Emphasis on loans should not be taken as a sign that scholarships no longer exist. It is simply that grants tend to be given to students from the least-well-off families, and the colleges are still actively

---

*In a seven-year period students at the nine colleges took out 24,000 loans worth more than $25 million.

recruiting at the lower rungs of the economic ladder. In 1971–72 Harvard gave out scholarships in the amount of $4.2 million. About 2,236 undergraduates received some form of aid. This is 46 percent of Harvard's enrollment. Scholarships come from three sources: the college's own funds, federal and state government, and miscellaneous private groups.

College Scholarships are awarded as part of the aid package. No special application is necessary. They are given on a need basis, whereas formerly the size of the scholarship depended on academic performance. The brightest got the biggest award. Now college education is not deemed a reward so much as a right. To be admitted to a selective college is itself a reward for achievement. The key concept in the words of the Sloan study is: equal access without regard to economic background.

Government Scholarships are designed for low-income families. The most notable federal scholarships come through the Basic Education Opportunity Grant program (BOG) that gives a student $1,400 a year minus a family contribution, depending on financial circumstances. Some $475 million was appropriated by Congress for academic year 1974–75 to be distributed only to freshmen and sophomores. It is studying a proposal to provide $1.3 billion in 1975–76. BOG scholarships are part of the college's aid package and no separate application for this money is necessary.

State scholarships vary and must be applied for separately in many instances.

Other Scholarships are: National Merit Scholarships based on tests taken with the College Boards. Students are made aware of these scholarships by their secondary schools. These four-year awards based on need range from $100 to $1,500 and become part of the aid package at the college attended.

National Achievement Scholarships are given to 250 Black students each year. The four-year grants range from $250 to $1,500 annually.

National Honor Society Scholarships are awarded to members of the Society.

Alumni clubs have many scholarships. Generally amounts are small. Other sources of scholarships are the same as loans, i.e., local churches, PTAs, etc.

Jobs

Working your way through is not what it used to be. Campus jobs are limited by the academic workload to 10 hours a week at selective colleges and return about $500. Some enterprising students do go into business and earn more than this, and certain jobs consume more time and pay better, particularly editorships of daily papers. The range of jobs may be greater than in the past, particularly social service jobs, but the rate of pay is generally low. Traditional dining-hall jobs have been greatly reduced by money-saving cafeteria service. Summer jobs, as everyone knows, are not easily found.

The Money Crunch

There is a depression in higher education that promises to close down many private colleges. It is estimated that 60 percent of them now operate in the red. For the moment the selective colleges do not face bankruptcy, although Columbia's momentary slide into a $16.5 million deficit shows that only careful management can keep the best colleges solvent. Choice of college must now include the query: Is this place good for four more years? The chief cause, of course, is lower tuition at public colleges.

"We're moving toward government monopoly of higher education," says Miller Upton, president of Beloit College in Wisconsin.

The pressure on public colleges to increase their tuitions in order to save the private sector comes largely from the private sector—the Committee for Economic Development and the Carnegie Commission are two examples of outspoken critics of low state-college tuition. Selective colleges which charge the most have had the least to say publicly about this situation, but they are unnerved by the prospect in the 1980s of a diminishing applicant pool. They fear that middle-class students will be driven increasingly to low-tuition public colleges.

"It will be easier to get in to Brown then," we were told by a Brown admissions officer, and no doubt it applies across the board. The money crunch is bound to make selective admissions less selective, but how much less selective is anyone's guess. What admissions

STUDENT ESTIMATES OF PARENTAL INCOME
AMHERST COLLEGE CLASSES 1970 THROUGH 1976

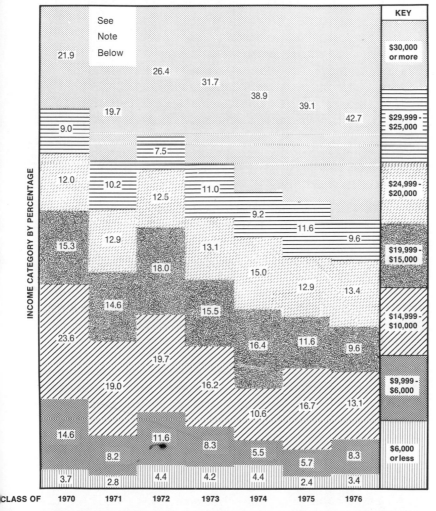

Note: In the Class of 1971, 12.6% of responding freshmen were unsure of parental income

A glance at this chart shows what is happening at Amherst. In the Class of 1976, 42.7 percent come from families with incomes over $30,000. This represents the upper 5 percent of the national population.

officers dread is a return to upper-class predominance among the student body. If those who can afford to pay their way become a vast majority on campus, the Ivies and other selective colleges will be back to square one.

And if more and more applicants come from the affluent sector, as Bowdoin has noticed is the trend, academic standards will be threatened, because there are only so many bright people among the affluent. At the University of Chicago one admissions officer said that rather than lower standards they would close their undergraduate departments and train graduate students exclusively, a solution not open to small colleges without graduate schools.

Edith Green, who represents Oregon's Third Congressional District, is one of the leading advocates of federal aid to higher education. Addressing the 29th annual meeting of the National Association of College Admissions Counselors in 1973, she said:

> Education at a private college is fast becoming out of reach to all but the sons and daughters of two distinct elite: The children of the very rich and those of the very poor who can qualify for full scholarship aid. Such polarization is not healthy for education and it is not healthy for our country. It seems to me that major government efforts should be directed to decreasing tuition so that the choice of a college is within the reach of more and more students rather than fewer and fewer. I do favor institutional aid for both private and public colleges for this reason.

Federal aid for the so-called disadvantaged middle class is most likely in the near future to come in the form of loan money. The next generation of selective college graduates might well be dubbed the Debtor Classes.

Is It Worth It?

An astute businessman who recruits students for his selective college has come to the conclusion that the reason for the rise in applications to selective colleges in 1973–74, despite their cost and despite recession prospects, is that "They're worth it. They give you more than your money's worth." He believes that parents reason: *It's going to cost a lot wherever our children go. Why not pay a little more and get the best?* We have said all along that a good education is available at many places, but it is up to the student to get it.

When students describe their own state college as a zoo, no matter how many great professors there are on the campus, it will be more difficult to learn something from them than at a selective college where classes are small and faculty mingle with students at meals and on social occasions. Princeton, for example, makes it possible for faculty to live near the campus in what are expensive residential districts just so they will be available to students at night and on weekends. John Hersey in his *Letter to the Alumni** states flatly "that Yale is, at least at the instant I set this down, quite simply the best private university in the country." One may question the hyperbole, but who can doubt Yale's qualities? Who would ever say that Yale is not worth the price you must pay to attend?

The point is self-evident. So many of the best students believe it is worth it, that they deluge these colleges with their applications. Selectivity may vary in degree, but it will continue despite the cost. And who knows, the whole cost problem may add a new status to these institutions, and it may become a matter of pride to say, "I'm staying home for my vacation. I still owe Oberlin four thousand dollars and that obligation comes first."

*New York: Knopf, 1970.

14

For Parents Only

A New York psychiatrist, the late Dr. George K. Pratt, discovered that in trying to help mothers by giving them lectures on child-raising, he tended to make them ill at ease and less sure of themselves as parents, and so he quit lecturing. We have no lecture for parents on how they can help their children be admitted to a selective college. If we were to prescribe a series of steps parents could take, the prescription might appear to work in one instance and not in another, and there would be no way to prove that in either case the prescription was a cause of success or failure.

But we do know that parents are a factor in college admissions, and we go so far as to say that on every application to a selective college there falls the shadow of the applicant's parents. In a sense they too are applying, and the "college of your choice" is often the college of family preference. Few students rise to the challenge of the competition for places in the top colleges without considerable encouragement at home. If parents decide, "Jack's not the studious type," you can be sure that Jack will bring home more Cs than As. If parents are determined that Gill will go to Radcliffe, Gill is liable to be an academic achiever. She still may not be accepted by Radcliffe, though.

We know of no formula that will guarantee to parents admission of their children to any particular college.

By the time a student is a junior in high school and considers himself in the running for acceptance by a selective college, parents have already made their major contribution to their child's development and preparation for highly demanding college training. There is little they can do to assure that he will get into the college of his choice. The parental role at this point becomes semipassive, because things are happening to the student and not to the parent. The student is being tested and evaluated. It is impossible for parents not to feel that they too are being evaluated. It is possible to suppress the expression of this feeling.

Donald Barr, headmaster of the Dalton School in New York, has pointed out in a stimulating collection of his writings, *Who Pushed Humpty Dumpty* (1972), that most young people no longer have several adults in the family to talk to—no maiden aunt, no grandparents in the house—and the small "nuclear" family is a rather emotional one. It is important for parents to control themselves during a period when their child is going through a time of self-scrutiny, trying to answer the question: *Who am I?* by deciding on a small group of colleges to apply to, always wondering: *What if I'm rejected, then who am I?* The more tense the child, the more important it is for parents to be models of calm.

We asked Tim Callard, Princeton admission director, what he would tell parents if they asked him how to get their child into Princeton. He replied:

> I'd say, create a home environment of strong support in which a kid can be himself. At the same time parents ought to show their high expectations for things of value. My father was an educator, a private school teacher, but he left it to us to grow. I don't remember any great pressure at first. I did not perform very well in grade school, but I was not made to feel that I was letting anyone down. Then my father took us to England for a year when he was on an exchange program. Something happened to me and when I came back to school in Baltimore, I had a greater sense of what learning is all about and I did well enough to get into Princeton.
>
> It's a dialectical thing. You have to let the child go his own pace, but let him know if he sells himself short. The atmosphere should be *free*, not permissive. A child needs exposure to models he can imitate, good teachers, older students who are outstanding.

It's important for parents to look at colleges, several of them, to get a realistic perspective. I am amazed how some parents realize what the situation is, that their children must lead their own lives. Others seem *unable themselves* to lead their own lives and try to live through their children, and they are so emotional they can hardly control themselves. Parents really should walk very carefully.

We all like reflected glory, but it is not easy to find it nowadays by sending our children to the most prestigious colleges, because their chances of not getting in are four or five to one. A realization of the *probability* not the possibility of rejection is the most desirable state of mind a parent can achieve. For example, in 1973–74, applications to most of the Ivy League and Seven Sisters rose by over 10 percent, while enrollment remained more or less stable. That meant more rejections than the year before, more disappointments naturally.

The most common mistake parents make is failing to realize how aware a child is of their expectations. When he does not get into the college of his choice, his own disappointment is apt to be mingled with a feeling of fear that he is letting his family down. And while the first shock will soon disappear, a lasting sense of inadequacy may dog him, building resentment that will leave him dissatisfied with himself and less able to accomplish realistic goals. What parents must be prepared for and help their applicant children to accept gracefully is rejection by the college of their choice.

The prospect is not so bleak as the odds suggest. Because a large majority of applicants are outstanding, and if for reasons that are not their fault they are turned down by one or more colleges, there are literally dozens of good colleges that will accept them. The temptation to heap scorn on the colleges that turn down our children must also be seen for the sour-grapes attitude that it is, and one that has no constructive value for young people, who thereafter go through life sneering at Ivy Leaguers. To what purpose?

Our own experience leads us to make these suggestions:

(1) Do not fix your attention so exclusively on one or two selective colleges that you will be shattered if your child is rejected. Satisfy yourself that there really are some good colleges that you just may not be aware of or up-to-date on. Hedge your bets, as Callard urges, by exploring a reasonable range of colleges. Avoid building up pressure

and anxiety around any single institution. Remember that students who do well in a good college may in the long run have the advantage over those in the top colleges whose record was only fair.

(2) Be careful how you talk about colleges, especially if you have more than one child. George may be headed for Columbia where his father went, but Sally may love animals and want to go to a state agricultural college. Invidious comparisons are abhorrent. It is better to talk about education, learning, subject matter, than about institutions.

(3) Relax! What are you worried about? Have faith in yourself that you have done your best by your children. They will not let you down. By being true to yourself, you have shown the next generation how to be true to itself.

Is there anything practical you can do, like helping fill out applications? No, not really. Since the child is going to college, the child must assume the responsibility for meeting deadlines for registering for College Board tests, for completing the applications, getting teachers' recommendations and for all the other procedural matters. If you visit colleges with your child or encourage visits on his own, if you let him or her know the limits of your financial contribution to college costs, if you do not badger or nag your child about problems arising from the trying business of "getting in," and if you are sympathetic and supportive without encouraging self-pity, then you have done your duty in this instance.

What about calling up a college trustee in the hopes of improving the chances of your child's acceptance? Well, such a maneuver will do no harm but it probably will not do much good either. The danger lies in your child's reaction if he finds out. Suppose you do talk to a trustee or even the president and the child is accepted, how will he rid himself of the idea that he got in not on his own merits but by pull? Long experience has proved to us that the admissions process is a fair one. Mistakes are made. Your child could *mistakenly* be rejected by one college, but probably not by two. If you will play the rules of the game and avoid the temptation to try using your influence, you will automatically be showing your respect for your child's right to be what he is. By letting the chips fall where they may, you are strengthening your child's sense of independence.

The rules of the game, however, should be studied, and there is nothing wrong with pointing out things *an applicant can do* to help his chances. Key people in the admissions process a candidate can legitimately contact are: coaches, faculty members, alumni—especially those on admissions liaison committees—and important friends of the college. If a trustee happens to know the candidate, *let the candidate talk to him* if he thinks he might write a letter that would go in the folder. One exasperated admissions officer being badgered by a father finally exploded: "Who is applying, you or your daughter?"

You can overdo a good thing. Getting too much praise into the admissions office can lead to the suspicion that the candidate is really a bit weak, in need of more supporting documents than most. There is wisdom in the saying, "The thicker the folder, the thicker the candidate."

Candidates often hold off until the deadline to submit their personal statements after filing their applications. Parents can help clarify ideas that are difficult to express, but the statement must be the candidate's own. And it should be neatly written. We know of cases when the final decision turned on a sloppy personal statement. Sloppiness shows a lack of serious interest in the college. A warning about this from parents is quite appropriate.

We have tended to assume that parents are liable to get too emotionally involved in the admissions process for their children's good. But another reaction that is not helpful, either, is total withdrawal in order to avoid conflict.

A professor we know assumes his daughter would not want to go to the college where he teaches (thereby saving him the tuition cost) because she would not want to live at home and be around a faculty member constantly. He has not dared to discuss this subject with her. Would she have to live at home and not in a dormitory? Would she see much of him on campus unless she took one of his courses? Does *he* not really want her on *his* campus? Until the two of them talk about their own feelings, their assumptions will determine "the college of her choice," and the assumptions may have no validity whatever.

Parents have a huge stake in the college training of their children. There is little they can do when the kids are 16 or 17 about getting them into a selective college. But they have every right—not to say an obligation—to know how their children perceive their future. It may surprise some parents how much common sense they will uncover in their children with a little subtle probing.

15

Who Gets In?

On Monday, April 15, 1974, the mailman delivered five letters addressed to Valerie Cumings (not her real name) from Radcliffe, Princeton, Williams, Yale and Stanford. Trembling with anxiety as though she were playing Russian roulette, she began to open the envelopes in reverse order of preference.

(1) Stanford—admitted. Relief! She got in *somewhere*.

(2) Yale—rejected. Well, she didn't like Yale anyway.

(3) Princeton—rejected. A sinking feeling. Princeton wasn't her favorite, *but* if Princeton turned her down, did that mean . . . ?

(4) Williams—admitted. She expected this. Well, between Stanford and Williams she would pick Williams.

(5) Radcliffe. She paused. Radcliffe was her first choice. But now if Yale and Princeton said no, naturally Radcliffe would turn her down. She tore open the envelope. Admitted!

Valerie proves our point that each selective college actually *selects* its freshman class according to *its* lights. Stanford, Williams and Radcliffe saw in this applicant qualities they wanted. Princeton and Yale, comparing her folder with others, chose others and not Valerie.

Here is her record in private secondary school: in the top 10 percent of the class; SATs—700 verbal, 700 math; Achievements—English 770, Math I 660, French 630; president of the debating team, literary magazine editor; a sculptress, she sent slides of her work to each college she applied to. The following comments were made by her teachers: "An extremely intelligent girl with a powerful personality . . . the most brilliant student in the class . . . an excellent math student . . . cheerful, friendly and open . . . handles abstractions easily . . . interested in philosophy."

For two summers she went to a summer school and she was abroad in the Experiment in International Living. The school commented: "Although this list is long, Valerie is by no means a dilettante. We give her our highest recommendation." The school gives its highest recommendation to only a handful of its graduating class.

We do not know why Yale and Princeton turned Valerie down. The impressive thing is that three outstanding colleges accepted her. The teachers' comments and the school's support were of fundamental importance to her admission. To teachers who wonder if they are saying the right things to help their favorite students get into college, here are two actual reports on behalf of Monica Ruben (not her real name), who was admitted to Dartmouth, Bowdoin and Middlebury. We present them in full.

I

I am writing to display a special interest in a student who is applying to your college for admission as a freshman in the fall of 1974. Monica Ruben has been in my Physical Education class for two years. I have also known her in many other settings and by elaborating upon these, I hope to show you what a fine asset she would be to your program.

Part of my work includes various coaching responsibilities. Monica has participated actively in our hockey and tennis programs. She is a thinking player who develops during each season. Her considerate manner and competitive drive are quite harmonious. She enjoys working and achieving and both have become part of her style. Please note that my comments do not attempt to offer you an exceptional athlete but rather, a well-skilled participant, who works deliberately. These have fantastic carry-over value in her daily experiences.

Monica has a delightful sense about movement. She enjoys exploring people and places within a physical medium. She has been receptive to diverse class projects and has become interested in the local student center, which helps to interweave the numerous motifs of education.

Monica recently participated in a workshop with teachers from many schools. She was on the Seminar staff and was able to give to and gain from all the groups.

During the early fall, Monica was one of eight students selected to assist in the seventh-grade Outdoor Orientation Program. During the four days she displayed a keen understanding of children, enormous enthusiasm and consistent sensitivity. Following the experience, her evaluative perceptions were helpful to the faculty.

My other contact with Monica is as one of my counselees. She is vibrant and warm about people and programs. She has been touched by your college and feels that she will be comfortable with its environs. She also feels that your school will be challenging and meaningful. If I can be of any further assistance in your decision, please feel free to write me through the school. In summary, I recommend her without hesitation and would encourage you to act positively on her application.

II

Monica entered as a new student in the eleventh grade, and was faced with the choice between placement in a mathematics section where her background would be deficient, or one in which she would have to repeat some work. She chose the accelerated section, worked hard to make up for missed work, and did very well. Because of the handicap, she chose to take the course pass-fail, but would have had an A for the third trimester and a B+ for the year. She has a powerful ability to analyze, and works accurately. I would not call her a creative mathematics student, but very few are. She has a sophisticated sense of humor, and was vastly amused when I read the class a spoof on sequences and series from *Mathematics Made Difficult.*

I had the pleasure of the company of Monica and a friend of hers camping last summer, and can report that she is cheerful even when cold, tired and hungry, more than cooperative in pitching in with the work, and a perceptive observer of the passing scene. I was much interested in her reflections on the Asian history class trip to India.

Monica is an ardent skier and excellent athlete. She completed the summit climb of Mt. Washington with energy to spare. She seems to me an unusual combination of very attractive all-American girl with a good deal of seriousness and purposefulness underlying. She is enthusiastic about Dartmouth and is, I think, an excellent candidate.

And here is the full report of the college counselor:

Monica is one of the most winning young women I have come across in a long time. The School is encouraging her early decision application because we feel we can give her our extremely enthusiastic support. She and Dartmouth appear to be well-matched.

Her academic record speaks for itself. She is patently capable of doing demanding and scholarly work and is eager to learn. Although her 11th-grade accelerated math "pass" grade appears to be a blotch on her escutcheon, her math teacher's comment at the end of the year is illuminating. She says, giving her an unofficial "A" in the final trimester, "I had to put that A up there even if Monica is taking the course pass/fail! The conics notebook was excellent and so was the determinants exam. Monica is a marvelous addition to the school."

This year in our student description summary, she was the only student out of the forty whose forms I have seen who was judged truly outstanding by all of her teachers in *every* category, both academic and character/personality ratings. This was reinforced by the observation of her Asian History teacher. Last spring he led part of his class on a three-week trip to India (for which Monica worked to earn all her expense money, including airfare). The group had the usual predictably trying experiences with inefficient travel arrangements, unaccustomed cultural adjustments, and inflammatory new foods. Monica was endlessly cheerful, accommodating and even-tempered and apparently capable of infecting her less joyful fellow voyagers with a positive outlook. After the trip her teacher stated: "An anthill couldn't be nearly as industrious, or Miss America half as engaging as Monica. She has been a very competent and valuable addition to the class in all respects. It was wonderful to have that extra spark along on the trip."

Last summer she helped a teacher drive to Quebec via New England. Stopping to climb Mt. Washington, she reports that they started their 6,000-foot ascent at six o'clock in the morning. She and a friend then traveled down the coast and wended their way back, climbing and camping out whenever possible. Once home, she worked at a local ski store, resumed her domestic responsibilities of cooking and sharing in the cleaning, managed a week at Hockey and Lacrosse camp with thirteen girls and rounded things off by assisting on a four-day camping trip attended by eighty 7th-graders at the opening of school.

If I were condemned to a week on a desert island with any member of this class, I would pick Monica. She brings an "élan vital" to everything she does, and she and Dartmouth could benefit immensely from each other.

Alex Agostino (the name has been changed) was admitted to Yale and Penn. Here is a report about him:

Alex is a soft-spoken boy whose intellectual potential when he entered our school was classified as very superior to gifted. With this most felicitious endowment, he has blazed his way through the School. As his record will show, he has performed on a consistently high level and found great joy in stretching his intellect. Last year he did some translations of *The Catullus* which were described by his Latin teacher as "fine and sensitive." During the same trimester he also did an independent and difficult project for French IV combining his interest in linguistics with that language.

In all of his vigorous academic searching, he is supported by a warm and loving family. Dr. Agostino is a professor of biology and Mrs. Agostino, having recently received her Ph.D. in social work, is teaching. They have broad artistic and cultural interests and a strong concern for our contemporary social problems, which has been transmitted to Alex.

Aside from being a scholar, Alex is also a major force in the choir, chorus and madrigal groups. The director of these groups (the head of our music department for 30 years) describes him as a "brilliant boy and a fine musician with a real musical gift." He is the leader of the tenor section in the choir, a selective group of about 40 students. When the choir toured England, Scotland, and France last spring Alex emerged as one of the leaders, earning the strong respect of his fellow singers.

As minor interests he is involved in enough other things to make a less energetic person yearn for his couch. Aside from tutoring a 9th-grader in math and doing part-time work for the chairman of the math department, he finds time to do editorial work and write for both the newspaper and the yearbook.

Strongly motivated, with a history of successes behind him this attractive and gifted boy deserves only the most challenging and stimulating college experience. We send him forth with a keen sense of anticipation for what he will give back to all of us in the future.

Eloise Sichard only made Princeton's waiting list. She received an Early Evaluation of Possible and was rated 3 academically and 2 nonacademically. Eloise listed a dozen extracurricular activities, of which the one that counted most was editor of the school paper. She ranked 11th in a class of 100. In her character and personality ratings by the school she was in the top 2 to 3 percent in all but warmth of personality and sense of humor. Her counselor recommended her strongly but not enthusiastically. With a record of As and Bs, 680 in both math and verbal SATs, and Achievements just below 700, she fell into that large group of applicants about which it is so difficult to make a decision. The fact that she was put on the waiting list is clear evidence that Princeton knew she could do the work. Unfortunately, there were few places open to those on the list, so Eloise was never offered admission to Princeton.

A Black candidate, Jean Carter, got into Penn, Mount Holyoke and Vassar from a private day school, where she had a full scholarship. She had As and Bs and ranked in the upper fifth of a competitive class. Her SATs were 480 verbal and 500 math, with Achievements of 490 in English composition, 510 in Math I and 590 in French. Comments from teachers: "A fine young lady who is rapidly overcoming a weak background. . . . Did competent work in the Honors class. . . . Speaks out in class discussion." The school recommended her without reservation.

Thomas Hadley was second in a large class at a big city high school and had a 96.4 average over four years. SATs were 680 verbal, 670 math; Achievements were Spanish 700, English composition 680 and Math I 630. He edited the school paper and was active in student government. Outside school he tutored Spanish-speaking children. He was admitted to Dartmouth, Brown and Cornell, which turned down many students with higher test scores.

But higher test scores did not hurt Porter Brandt, who got into Princeton, MIT, Cornell and Georgia Tech. He had a verbal SAT of 770 and a math SAT of 740, with Achievements of 740 in English composition, 730 in Math I and 800 in physics. He was in the top 2 percent of a suburban high school. Comments: "Possibly the most well-read student I have encountered . . . brilliant boy . . . a rarity . . . exceptionally bright . . . doesn't flaunt the fact that he's an A student." To top it all, Porter had completed the four years work in only three years! But the school counselor reported: "Porter Brandt is ready for college."

Students and parents who are interested in other examples ought to ask counselors and admissions officers to cite them without reveal-ing names. Knowing who got in where is helpful in assessing a can-didate's chances, but remember, the same college never seeks to create two classes that are exactly alike. So if a candidate appears to match the model of a particular freshman, it may be that the college will not need that type of person in the upcoming class.

The Waiting List

We have said little so far about waiting lists. Every selective college creates a waiting list of students who may possibly be offered admission after it has been determined that there are still freshman openings. The reason for waiting lists is that no college can precisely predict the number of admitted candidates who will decide to accept their offer. We mentioned that in 1973 Amherst unexpectedly had 56 more freshmen than expected, and that in 1974 the number of those admitted was reduced accordingly. It still could happen that a higher percentage would accept than Amherst counted on, but in actuality there were 20 openings and these places were filled from the waiting list.

To be on a waiting list is to be in limbo. Chances are that you will not be offered admission. Take Grant Miller, admitted to Penn, Trinity and Hobart, and on Yale's waiting list. He has elected to enroll at Penn. But if Yale should beckon, he will probably accept. Where does that leave Penn? It must turn to its waiting list for a replacement. This game of musical chairs can go on as late as September, at which time some college ends up with fewer freshmen than they want. Even the wealthiest college wants a full enrollment for the tuition revenue. Princeton lost a hockey player in September 1973 to Yale, which called him from the waiting list.

On the other hand, from the student's point of view it is nice to hold this lottery ticket and thrilling to be a winner. And if your name isn't called, you have that waiting-list rank as sort of a consolation prize.

16

The Changing Campus

We find that there is a lag in the perception of today's campuses. Many adults are looking at them through yesterday's glasses, so to speak. Either they remember the headlines about violence and changes that were occurring in the sixties, or they remember their own days in college and find the changes intolerable. And you do not have to be an old grad to be disoriented. Members of the Class of 1965 are disturbed by new buildings, or worse, by what has happened to very old buildings, whose interiors have broken out in a rash of semipsychedelic colors. A Victorian chapel has become a student center. A beer garden appears in what was an old library. You would think young Americans would be used to change and take it as it comes. But campuses have a sacred character for all of us, and what is an improvement to an undergraduate is a defilement to a graduate.

Parents in particular are uneasy about sending children off to what sometimes seems like another planet: the college world of crime, sex, drugs, radical politics and atheism. Although all of these are prevalent in their own communities, they think of them as particularly concentrated in colleges. They forget that the most serious problems tend to occur in adulthood. *Kleine kinder, kleine sorgen* ("Small children, small troubles") is still a good proverb for parents of college students, especially of those in the selective colleges. This is not to make light of the overcharged atmosphere of the past that resulted in serious difficulties and even in tragedies. But those days are for the moment over and Harvard Square is quiet—if somewhat scruffy looking.

There is an uneasy stability on campus as the chief issues of the sixties—Vietnam, the draft, curricular and college administrative reforms, drugs and parietals—have vanished. Only racism occasionally surfaces to trouble the otherwise tranquil groves of academe. There are those who find this new quiescence disturbing and retrograde. Today's students are so concerned with careerism that social issues fail to touch them deeply. Young minds may be set in a conservative mold before they have developed exalting ideals. A callous indifference to injustice and the suffering of others could be one outcome of the present mood. When Mickey Mouse is chosen as the theme for the 1974 Dartmouth Winter Carnival, does it reflect nostalgia, cynicism or a spirit of innocent fun? The ambiguity is troubling.

Here is how things look on selective campuses in the midseventies:

On Crime and Violence

In 1973, a woman on the Radcliffe faculty was murdered at twilight in Longfellow Park near the campus, and a Columbia professor was murdered on Morningside Heights. Such horrors make the small-town campus seem safer, but in fact there is no longer any place to hide from crime and violence. Beloit hired Martin Security, Inc., to patrol the campus in 1970 and had to install special locks on dormitory entries to discourage strangers on that quiet hilltop campus above a small manufacturing city.

The ivory tower may be the place from which a demented student mows down passersby with an automatic rifle. The campus is just one more place where you have to be careful. It probably never was as safe as it was thought to be. Recall the 18 football players who died in 1905? In the thirties some 16 students in a fraternity house at Dartmouth died in their sleep due to a faulty draft in a coal furnace. Hazing has disappeared, and so has one cause of tragedy and death at colleges.

A recent letter to the *Princeton Alumni Weekly* recalled the suicides of two campus homosexuals a few years ago before the Gay Revolution brought a modicum of acceptance to that reviled minority.

The likelihood of being assaulted, raped or murdered is no greater on college campuses than it is anywhere else. But, of course, violence has greatly increased in America since the fifties. Girls on urban campuses, if they are sensible, walk in pairs at night and avoid dark streets. Their parents should be mindful that muggings elsewhere occur in broad daylight, and bank robberies occur in shopping centers. There have been episodes of rape due to hitchhiking, but find a campus where no one has to hitchhike. College students in Boston hitchhike in the city, and college students outside the city hitchhike to the city, or just to a shopping center.

Crime and violence have increased on America's campuses obviously, but so have security precautions. Proctors and campus police are now a substantial budget item for any college. Beloit's security costs have gone from $50,000 in 1970 to $100,000 in 1974. There are outside agencies staffed with ex-FBI men who specialize as consultants to colleges and advise them on strengthening security. Some college dorms even in small communities are guarded against strangers entering. An issue that arouses student furor is the arming of campus cops. The cop's point of view is: "Why should I go into a building unarmed when I may be facing someone with a knife or a gun."

Burglaries are prevalent because of student casualness about locking their rooms. Students themselves are caught stealing in the college bookstore or the library. Amherst's Frost Library lost $30,000 in books in 1974. The phone company finds it impossible sometimes to collect phone bills of students who have skipped town by dropping out. Not every crime is committed by "street people" or professional criminals. Co-eds have been known to belong to prostitution rings, and of course for a time drug-peddling was a widespread occupation of a student underworld. While these extremes have all but disappeared, two varsity wrestlers at Columbia were indicted in 1973 for selling cocaine. Conviction carries a life sentence.

Mere worrying about crime and violence on the campus will not help reduce their incidence and parents can unnerve their offspring by casual remarks of concern over safety. Advising students to be prudent is the most constructive course in the face of present conditions. The belief that Black students have brought crime to the campus has little substance.

That the best colleges should have the worst conditions in any respect came as a terrible shock during the period of student unrest. But even in the fifties the University of Chicago's only strategy for keeping up its small undergraduate enrollment was to help finance a massive slum-clearing project that improved the campus neighborhood. Still several rapes have occurred in recent years and security costs $1.3 million a year. In meetings with groups of parents and their college-bound children we have frequently had to spend time combating rumors that make the campus seem more bizarre than the station house in a TV cop serial. Such rumors, based on events of the last decade and greatly embellished, can be checked out by a phone call to the college in question. For instance, Harvard now has a standing crime committee and a student guard force of 65. Magnetic card locks keep strangers out of dorms, and burglaries have diminished. Officials of any good college will frankly answer queries about campus security.

On Drugs

The hysterical period is over. Hard drugs never got very far on selective campuses. "These kids are too smart to get involved with any of the addictive drugs," Dr. Willard Dalrymple, chief of Princeton's medical services, told alumni in 1971. Pot is widespread but it is not considered a problem except in those states like Maine and New Hampshire where there is what amounts to a no-knock law and college authorities cannot intervene if the police move against students. There are few student pushers these days. In New York they risk life imprisonment. By the time they get to college today students have experimented with pot and alcohol, are pretty blasé and beyond the thrill-seeking that now goes on in some junior high schools.

A questionnaire filled out by Dartmouth seniors at graduation time shows that the high point of whatever hard drug-taking there was occurred in the late sixties. All Dartmouth students are advised that New Hampshire law allows a bust in dormitories without warning to college authorities, and there is a mandatory prison term if anyone is caught with pot. The college itself has no patience with pushers and expels them. In 1973–74 no such cases were reported at Dartmouth.

On Sex

Burt Honea, an Episcopal minister and Concord Academy college adviser, accepts the figure that 30 percent of college undergraduates, male and female, have sexual intercourse by sophomore year. Where this figure comes from is opinion sampling and guesstimates of observers. Susan Williams, an undergraduate columnist for the *Princeton Alumni Weekly,* said it was true among Princeton boys and girls, but her opinion is disputed among students themselves. Kathleen Squires, head of Princeton's Orange Key hospitality organization, doubts it. Landon Jones, editor of the *Alumni Weekly,* accepts Ms. Williams' report as reliable because it was based on interviews.

In any case who today questions the fact that Victorian sexual standards have vanished? The problem for parents—and for young people too—is simply a question of *when* sexual experience begins. For some it starts in high school and for others in college and for others even later. The ethic no longer concerns the unacceptability of premarital intercourse but the responsibilities involved.

Take co-ed dormitories. Girls and boys live on separate floors, or in separate entries. But then an affair begins, and a suite that is male or female becomes *de facto* co-ed. Cohabitation, they call it, and there is no word for the distress this situation can cause impressionable roommates. We could cite a number of cases of girls in their freshman year at Ivy colleges who have been thrown for an absolute loss by such things as a senior adviser (female) sleeping with four different boys in the course of a term; or a roommate inviting a boy to move in with her.

It is said that when Robert Goheen was president of Princeton he returned from a trip remarking that he had seen co-ed dorms in Australia, and that that was too much for him. One of his classmates at a reunion came out of the shower in a Princeton dormitory and found a girl and boy standing in their bathrobes at the sink. Without a word he crossed the tiles stark naked, took his towel off the hook next to the nonplussed couple, and walked out. A couple of years later *Newsweek* ran a picture of an undergraduate unmarried couple at a dorm sink and captioned it: "More like brother and sister." Bryn Mawr, an all-girl college, has co-ed bathroom facilities because of visiting Haverford students.

The response of the colleges to sexual activities is somewhat two-faced. It has to be. On the one hand, a staff gynecologist is available to provide information, birth-control advice and to deal with women's health problems. At Wellesley there is a Sexuality Information Service. On the other hand, a college must reassure parents that it neither encourages nor condones premarital sexual relations. Administrators are caught in the conflict of generations and indeed in the conflict among students, since more of them than less appear to be engaging in cohabitation. But no administrator is fool enough to believe that the sexes can be segregated when they do not choose to be. Remember what happened to Noah when he forbade mating on the Ark, and the cats were followed onto Mount Ararat by a litter of kittens. "How did it happen?" he asked. His wife replied: "Remember the night those two cats were fighting so furiously? Well, they weren't fighting."

A particular problem the colleges seem helpless to rectify is the genuine gripe of a student whose roommate brings in someone of the opposite sex to live with them. "I'm paying for a room for two. Now I'm crowded," the student will complain, but to little avail. Some day there will be a suit in equity that will force colleges to pay a rebate in such cases, and once it starts costing the college money, cohabitation is liable to be permitted only on payment of a fee.

Another tension arises from the pressure to conform. The tyranny of the peer group, real or imagined, can be less compassionate than that of adult authorities. Sexual intercourse has become a necessary achievement in some young minds, and great anxiety occurs if this is not fulfilled. Susan Williams of Princeton reported to alumni that a junior told her: "I know one girl who tried all freshman week to get a man to sleep with her because she wanted to be able to approach men on an equal level; they would have a hold over her if they thought she was a virgin."

In other cases students turn to the campus counseling center for advice on their feelings of sexual inadequacy in the midst of what they believe is the total sexual freedom and a student activity of their peers. For some students the pressure today is far greater than it was on past generations of college students, who, though benighted by puritanism, at least had the comfort and security of an enforced value system and corresponding set of guidelines. The 10 o'clock curfew was a great aid to the girl under hot pursuit.

Even an all-girl campus like Wellesley has no parietals. Boys are free to visit in the dorms and some stay all night, sometimes to the annoyance of the roommates.

On Emotional Problems

The appearance of the campus psychiatrist in the sixties may be viewed as a symptom of an underlying social disorder, or as the advent of a useful health service to meet a new situation. Years ago the *Harvard Lampoon* carried a cartoon showing a faculty adviser bidding goodbye to a freshman in his office, saying: "Glad you stopped by, Frothingham. Come back again, say, fall of senior year." The homogeneous campus just was not as uptight as today's mixture of meritocratic students who look so much alike but have less in common than they may appear to have.

Vance Packard in *A Nation of Strangers** was appalled to find that large percentages of college students said they had no close friends. David Riesman, the Harvard sociologist who has studied the college-age population in great depth over the last decade, reports that today's students have fewer friends and greater feelings of alienation. The selective college's competitiveness can be disturbing to students, especially since so many have been outstanding in secondary school and are startled to find themselves in the middle of the pack rather than in the lead. The pressure is such that almost all good colleges now allow students to interrupt their undergraduate years by taking a year off, with or without credit. Stopping out, it is called—instead of dropping out, which few students in selective colleges do.

Students in selective colleges have a special problem in dealing with stress, because of the high expectations they have for their own performance. One girl we know in an Ivy college is getting good marks but feels like an outsider. Characteristically she blames herself and not the institution. *Colleges with great prestige can provoke a great sense of personal inadequacy.* The reasoning goes: "Everyone else seems to be enjoying it here; it's a great place but I can't live up to it; there must be something wrong with me." But when a student is unhappy in a place lacking prestige, he generally blames the college, its administra-

*New York: McKay, 1972.

tion, its students, its faculty or its lack of facilities and atmosphere. If there is something wrong with him, he doesn't see it.

At Wellesley there is recognition of the emotional strain that develops there, and a series of seminars called "The Wellesley Crunch, Coping and Noncoping in the College Environment," brings girls together with counselors to discuss their problems. Twenty-nine sources of tension were identified at the first session, including the academic pressure *coming from students not faculty,* lack of intellectual conversation in the dorms and the inability to relax.

One way a student can avoid emotional problems is to have the good sense to choose a college where he will be successful. To go to Harvard and find yourself in what has euphemistically been called the "happy bottom quarter" when you were valedictorian in your high school can be ego shattering, and the Harvard B.A. will mean less to you than a degree with honors from a less intensely competitive school. Parents who can assess their children's capacities candidly will know that for the reflected glory of sending them to name colleges they may pay a price in prolonged suffering.

Fortunately, college administrators want no part of the problems emotionally disturbed students can cause them, and the selective admissions office tries its best not to admit anyone who looks obviously unhappy and insecure. In 1973, Harvard lost only eight of its freshmen because of bad grades. (Remember, most everyone Harvard *rejects* is capable of getting passing grades, so theoretically no one *admitted* should flunk. Those who do generally have some emotional disturbance rather than an intellectual deficiency.) An advantage of the selective colleges is that their student body is, in general, emotionally healthy.

It would be a mistake to assume that, because the volatility of the campus has vanished, mental health problems that do crop up are less severe. On the contrary, Stuart Pizer of the Harvard medical service finds that the occasional eruptions of demonstrations and even violence enabled disturbed students to release their frustrations. "Lacking the outlet of protest," he says, "today's depressed student is more likely to turn his feelings inward against himself in a dangerously destructive way." A majority of college counselors support this concept.

On Radicalism

Rockford College, in a widely distributed brochure, promises "the chance to attend a college whose policies are consonant with and supportive of the American form of government and the private enterprise system." In the thirties it was said that the way to Washington was to go to Harvard and turn Left. Now almost every campus has some activism, though it is terribly subdued and academic these days, and the faculty tends to be in the liberal camp. At Princeton, 83 percent of faculty in a poll said they voted for McGovern. In the forties the faculty was split more evenly among Republicans and Democrats.

There has been a shift among alumni too, and more Princeton alumni of the sixties say they are Democrats than Republicans. Students were prepared to hate both parties under the circumstances of an unpopular war. They appear now to be anti-Republican but not terribly pro-Democrat and scarcely radical at all. They no longer question the system, and are working furiously to get their feet on the rungs of the system's ladders, the graduate schools.

A good way to sense the political tone of any campus is to look at the student newspaper. What you generally find is a pale reflection of national politics. There is no Movement any more, no political force on campus like SDS, the Free Speech group of Berkeley, no Mark Rudd, no Timothy Leary. All this vanished after Kent State and the bombing of Cambodia. The McGovern debacle completed the disillusionment of impatient youth. Columbia graduate James S. Kunen, writing in the *New York Times Magazine* (October 28, 1973), reported a 25-year-old law student saying: "I'm not committed in the same way I was in college. It's such a youthful thing. I thought things then were—not so much worse, but—more disgusting. Now I just think things exist." A college freshman in 1975 will have difficulty trying to understand such a statement. For him commitment means doing whatever you do with all you've got.

Are the campuses again as they were in the fifties, the era of the Silent Generation, which was deplored until the noisy sixties made silence preferable? Time does not run backward. The seventies are cool and if the greening of America was prematurely announced, the red, white and bluing of America is for hard hats, not college students.

Campuses remain an occasional rallying point for social justice, but the peak of their influence has passed and this has lessened the political influence of their faculties. Colleges now count less politically because they deliberately avoided the polarization that can threaten academic freedom.

Politics for the faculty now means not imperialism but guarantee of tenure and unionization. Teachers still want to influence their students, but they no longer want to turn them into an army that supports with demonstrations some political hobby horse they are riding. In short the hysterical radicalism of the campus has evaporated, leaving a small remnant of no visible significance. The students are in their libraries, not going to mass meetings.

What has replaced radicalism is prudent preparation for a career via graduate school. Gone are the go-go years of affluence, and for the first time since the 1930s college students face the prospect of unemployment. It was one thing to rebel against the family materialism by taking a job as a bartender or cab driver. You could, it seemed, always change your mind, go to law school, teach, enter the family business. Now there may not be a first chance, let alone a second chance, so the best insurance is to earn the grades that will get you to graduate school.

Much radicalism was traceable to activist faculty. But the faculty is also threatened by the financial crisis shaking the foundations of many private colleges, and so its concerns are with professionalism and tenure. Unionism is still negligible among the selective college faculty.

Parental attention to their children in college is closing the generation gap. Family relationships seem closer, as college attendance becomes a cooperative effort in meeting college costs. The sacrifices are now so obvious that students seem determined to make them worthwhile. Such seriousness leaves little room for extreme, emotional positions on political issues. The American Council on Education reports a shift of liberal opinion among freshmen in 1974 toward the center of the road.

On Restructuring

The turmoil of the sixties forced necessary changes on every campus, but nothing fundamental was abandoned. Students now have as much power in the governance of their colleges as they have time for or interest in. Student representatives are listened to, and both administration and faculty are much more sensitive to their clientele's interests. Student trustees are commonplace. The old arrangement was patronizing. Jacques Barzun, former provost of Columbia, deplores the passing of deference and civility that put students in a hierarchy below their teachers and deans. The story is told of the difference between Goethe and Beethoven when they were walking together and a nobleman passed. Goethe tipped his hat and bowed; Beethoven pulled his hat down over his ears. Students stand somewhere between these extremes in their relations with faculty.

At selective colleges it is recognized that for the high tuition they must charge, the faculty and administration cannot be faceless and remote. Teaching by graduate assistants is infrequent, and college presidents are making it clear that research obligations cannot be fulfilled at students' expense. The reduction in available federal funds has also cut down the trips to Washington that take professors away from their students. Today's student is not necessarily put off by a certain old-fashioned authoritarianism.

A professor of English in a New York private college starts off each term by declaring: "I don't want to hear too much from you because you know nothing about what I am here to teach you." Zbigniew Brezinski, head of Columbia's Russian Institute, believes that he needs at least an hour to develop an idea and does not wish to be interrupted.

Relevance and restructuring were two of the demands of the student movement. Relevance is almost a forgotten word and was probably born out of the agony of Vietnam, which made nothing seem very relevant. But there has been restructuring of college governance and of the curriculum. College governance is a specialty, of interest to only a few students now, but each student is interested in the fact that most college curriculums give him the chance to cut his own educational cloth to suit his needs. Not every student knows what his needs are.

For example, at many selective colleges in the midseventies half the students are hoping to become doctors, but only about a fourth will finish a pre-med program. Most students enter college without a clear idea of what they want to accomplish. The elimination of required courses makes it possible to explore more widely than used to be possible to discover where interests and talents really lie. Sometimes this takes four years. Benson Saler, professor of anthropology at Brandeis, majored in sociology at Princeton and developed a passion for anthropology only in his senior year.

Major curriculum changes include no fixed course requirements except for English composition for those who need it; pass-fail options that allow students to take subjects that interest them but which they might not have time enough for if they had to worry about keeping up a grade point average; more interdisciplinary majors (one example is child care in Russia, requiring psychology and Russian civilization); credit for study abroad or off-campus experience; creation of new courses as students ask for them; establishment of Afro-American studies, courses related to women, courses related to non-Black minorities.

College level or advanced placement courses in high school allow students who take three of them to skip freshman year if they wish to. Those with the drive to compete for selective admissions generally take many advanced placement courses but they seldom skip freshman year, preferring to gain the full impact of four years of college. The American undergraduate stint seems destined to remain at four years. A move to reduce it to three at Princeton was strenuously resisted by the faculty. But at a rapidly increasing number of colleges, students can graduate in three years by intensifying their course load or fulfilling credits by advanced placement, achievements, or college-level-examination placement testing.

Faculty resistance to change should be taken into account by those who feel that liberal faculty are leftists opposed to the American system. A professor may be liberal in matters off-campus and conservative about his professional standards and habits. Robert Reinhold reported in the *New York Times* that at Brown liberal curriculum changes put through by students in the late sixties have been successfully resisted by the faculty, and the reforms "are struggling for survival against heavy odds."

Students always balk at requirements, so the selective colleges recommend rather than require four years of a foreign language and four of math in secondary school. Those who enter without fulfilling these requirements will probably find that they must use valuable time in college making up this educational deficit in order to meet the demands of a major. A distribution of one course in science, one or two in liberal arts, and one in social science is generally required before graduation, but the student is free to choose the courses.

This is the heart of the liberal arts tradition: a reasonably broad exposure to the basic foundations of our heritage and knowledge before moving on to more specialized and concentrated areas of study. Scientists and engineers are expected to know something of the liberal arts and social sciences, and the nonscientists must bridge C. P. Snow's "two cultures" by taking some science. Robert Goheen, a classicist, said, while president of Princeton, that liberal arts students needed more math than they were getting. Four years of high school math enables the student to take a college math course and move into statistics or computer science even if he is majoring in history.

Four courses a term or quarter remain the normal load, and teaching still is taught in lecture halls, classrooms and laboratories, and the library, greatly modernized, is central to undergraduate education. The use of language laboratories, film slides, microforms and TV have added other dimensions to pedagogy. A foreign film can be the basis for a modern-language conversation course, and students may be encouraged to deepen their classroom experience off-campus, speaking Spanish in a Spanish section of town, for example, or spending a semester in Mexico or Spain. Social sciences are also extended beyond the classroom to the field. Today's campus is more like a home base from which one explores a subject wherever necessary. Most selective colleges have programs in foreign countries or in urban centers these days.

But basically, college education is still taken up with reading enormously and writing papers. The modern curriculum is far richer than it used to be. The growth of graduate education has had its impact on undergraduate offerings and on the marking system. In graduate school a C is a failure and many undergraduates expect no less than a B. The numbers of honors students has greatly increased. To interpret this as a lowering of standards is not justified at selective colleges where the academic level is so high. The test of standards came during the activist years when those who put in too much time in demonstrating flunked courses and had to extend their time in college or drop out.

Poetry, painting, music and other creative arts are flourishing on campuses that once considered these "practical" subjects outside the liberal arts teaching tradition, too unscholarly to qualify as academic learning. Manual arts are encouraged for relaxation, not credit.

At Dartmouth, students have free use of a magnificent shop where they can make furniture just for a change of pace. Journalism is still not considered an academic discipline at most selective colleges and only Penn has an undergraduate business program. Vocationalism is not making inroads at the liberal arts colleges, where the belief in a sound foundation in an academic discipline is the best basis for later training even in disciplines like painting and acting.

On Going Back

While all of the changes make today's colleges seem superficially unrecognizable to parents of applicants, they have only to look around them and see contemporaries, particularly women, going to college for both undergraduate and graduate degrees. The self-deprecating notion that "today's kids are so smart that I couldn't compete with them" is belied by the success of middle-aged students. But the amount of work that is asked in any course is punishing to one settled in his habits. The dean of a large evening degree-granting school said that leafing through his catalogue made him decide to take an economics course one fall. A Columbia Ph.D. and former political science professor, he admitted that his administrative work did not allow him to keep up with the assignments and he finally dropped it.

17

Applicants and Selective Admissions

The number of applications to selective colleges rose on an average of about 10 percent in 1974 over the preceding year. Because enrollments are stable, this means the chances of being admitted were that much diminished. But the competition should not discourage the qualified student. Some applicants are wasting their time, taking a flyer, as they say. Counselors have pointed out how improbable admission will be for them, but they have to find out for themselves, and this is their right. No one should prevent anyone from filing an application anywhere. Just to encourage the doubters, here are a few cases where we know that "lightning has struck":

- A student at an unaccredited college, after spending a work semester in the Black ghetto, dropped out and remained in the ghetto two years, keeping a diary. He submitted the diary to a top college and was admitted as a freshman more or less on the strength of the diary.
- The graduate of a junior college with average grades took up pottery while living in a commune. Her father was sent by the government to India, where she worked with native potters for a year. She then applied to one of the Seven Sisters and was admitted as a junior.
- A man in his twenties who had become a champion archer was admitted as a special student at one of the Big Three.

• An unlikely candidate won the support of some alumni who were able to show the admission office at Princeton qualities that had not been in the folder. He was admitted.

None of these cases involved a genius or an extraordinary person. There is a spectrum in selective admissions. One percent of the Unlikely candidates is admitted. He who hesitates is lost. When in doubt, apply to the college you would like to go to and take your chances on being rejected.

How can you increase the possibility of being admitted? The first thing is to make sure that you are doing the necessary things to make your folder a true report of your capabilities and personality. Look over the following schedule (used by the Educational Consulting Center at Howard Greene Associates). Depending on what point you are at in the admissions process, follow its suggestions as much as possible. You will note that it makes no reference to selective colleges. No applicant should limit himself to applying only to the most selective places, and it is a good idea to be prepared to attend a college that is not necessarily your first choice.

COLLEGE ADMISSIONS SCHEDULE FOR STUDENTS

JUNIOR YEAR:

October:

Take the combined Preliminary Scholastic Test/National Merit Qualifying Test (PSAT/NMSQT)

January-February-March:

(1) With results of the PSAT/NMSQT in hand and questionnaire previously handed out, meet with your college adviser for a first session to explore personal interests, abilities, interpretation of test results, goals and appropriate college plans or alternatives. Arrive at a tentative broad list of colleges to explore.

(2) Discuss senior year curriculum with college adviser and teachers as it relates to academic interests, strengths, and post-high school programs.

(3) Discuss your College Board testing schedule for March, April or May. Plan to register for appropriate tests.

March-April-May:

(1) Review thoroughly catalogues from those colleges on your recommended list. Learn especially about course offerings, outstanding features or programs, size, location, requirements for admission.

(2) Plan to visit several of the colleges that seem of interest to test out their appropriateness as a type of college for you. Consult the "Guide to Visiting Colleges" which you have received from your adviser. It explains how to arrange for a visit and interview, and what factors you should be investigating during your visit.

(3) Following your visits meet with your college adviser again to review your reactions to the colleges. This session will help confirm or reject your earlier thinking. Additional recommendations can be made at this time.

(4) If you are considering applying Early Decision to a definite first-choice college, be sure you are signed up to take SATs and appropriate Achievements, if required, by June at the very latest.

June-July-August:

(1) Have a wonderful summer, one that will help you to expand your interests and experiences. If you are considering particular colleges or technical programs because of a specialized interest or talent, use the summer to gain greater exposure in the field.

(2) Talk with practitioners, students, people at appropriate colleges that are in the area.

(3) Visit any colleges of strong interest that are especially far away.

(4) Take June SAT or Achievements if you failed to do so in April (for SAT) or May (for Achievements).

SENIOR YEAR:

September-October:

(1) See your adviser if you need to consider a major change in plans and/or type of college. Otherwise, make appointments to visit the re-

maining colleges on your list. Discuss with your adviser additional colleges you have learned about from friends or other sources.

(2) Register for the November SAT at least four weeks in advance of the test date.

(3) If you have determined to apply on the Early Decision program, plan to have your application submitted by November 1. Be sure to give the teachers their recommending forms and the guidance office the secondary school report form at least two to three weeks prior to that date.

November:

(1) Begin working on college applications. Some important reminders:

a) Be sure to meet the individual college's application deadline for submission of your personal form. The earliest deadline normally is January 1. Most are later.

b) Be sure to give teachers the appropriate recommending forms if they are required by a college. Always provide a stamped, addressed envelope for the teacher.

c) Be sure to have the Educational Testing Service in Princeton, New Jersey, forward your test results to all the colleges. If you did not list all of them on the last test registration form, use the request form available from your adviser to have test results forwarded.

d) Be sure to give the guidance office the secondary school report forms, again with a stamped, addressed envelope, at the earliest possible date. This will ensure your transcript and recommending letter reaching the colleges on time.

e) Be sure to notify your adviser of the complete list of colleges to which you have applied. He can check that your records have been sent to every college and he can review whether you are protected in terms of admission with your group of colleges.

(2) Register for the December SAT if it was not taken in November and for appropriate Achievement Tests if required by the colleges.

(3) If you are applying for financial aid, have your parents complete the Parents' Confidential Statement and submit it to the College Scholarship Service in Princeton, New Jersey, prior to December 31. Be sure to list all the colleges to which you want copies of the PCS forwarded.

December-January:

(1) Complete applications to the colleges.

(2) If your grades and/or test results from November and January have changed dramatically, discuss with your adviser possible changes in your applications.

February-March-April:

(1) As decisions on admission are announced, discuss your final choice with your adviser and parents. You may need to revisit one or more of your choices before making a final decision if you are unsure.

(2) Please, please write to those colleges in which you are no longer interested requesting that your application be withdrawn. This could possibly help a classmate who wants to attend that college. While most institutions do not have quotas from any one school, they do find it difficult to select several from among a large number of qualified students.

May:

Take any Advanced Placement examinations for which you are prepared. These may result in extra credit for a college course or placement in advanced sections of a subject.

By following the steps of the admissions procedure scrupulously you are doing your best to help yourself, because in selective admissions it is critical that the folder carry all the necessary elements on which a committee judgment can be based. The most essential of these are: the application itself, the school transcript, test scores and comments from teachers and others. You alone can fill out the application. The transcript must be sent in by the school *at your request.* The comments of teachers and others must be mailed by the individuals *at your request.*

Mechanical mistakes, delays in the arrival of teachers' comments, foul-ups by the computer will not influence your chances of admission to a selective college, so while it only makes sense to take time enough to do everything right, you should not go into a panic if the admissions office indicates that something is missing in your folder, that a check has not been received. Any number of little things can go wrong, including the failure of a college to receive SAT scores from the College Board (colleges will not accept the report as official from any other source). But selective colleges are prepared to take the time to sort everything out and to judge each applicant on the merits of his case, and not on some picayune error of his or somebody else's.

We wish to reassure every applicant that he or she will get a fair shake by the admissions committee. Long hours are spent going through each folder. Selective admissions means that selection is made on the basis of studying each applicant's folder. There are certain key documents you are responsible for.

The Teacher's Report: This is scrutinized closely by the admissions office. Any reservations the teacher has about a candidate are quickly spotted. A student should therefore pick carefully the teachers he plans to ask for a recommendation, and he should not be afraid to say something like: "I am applying to Vassar, Swarthmore, Dartmouth and Reed. Will you recommend me highly to these colleges?" Applicants should be aware of the amount of work they and others are asking of their teachers. If a teacher gets overloaded, he may write a report too carelessly. Since a recommendation will not be needed until senior year, a candidate can determine for himself what teachers are most likely to say the right things about him, and be conscientious about their reports.

Coaches will also write recommendations even if you are not college varsity material. Their comments on your drive, competitiveness, team spirit and sportsmanship will add weight to your folder. But of course, if you are in no way athletic and just went out for a sport without putting your heart in it, no coach is going to write anything useful about you.

Faculty advisers are good people to write recommendations for you if you have done outstanding work under their supervision in dramatics, publications or other school activities.

Some schools write summary reports about candidates based on reports they have from the faculty. These reports will be enthusiastic. There is no need to fear that a school will spoil your chances by negative comments.

It is the candidate's responsibility to see that the teacher's report reaches the college. A subtle hint rather than a direct, "Have you sent in my report to Yale?" will tell you whether it has been mailed. "Do you know when Yale sends out its Early Evaluations?" will remind the teacher if he has not sent in his report, and if he has, he will probably say so. Delay in a teacher's report will result sometimes in the admissions office requesting it.

Other Recommendations: A candidate may ask others to write to the college on his behalf, but this should be done only if the writer can add something significant to the folder. For example, a camp director can add a dimension to a candidate by describing what an excellent counselor he has been. The local clergyman can help only if he has had a chance to measure your capacities for responsibility against others. To say that a girl has a good character is not very informative, since this is assumed. Employers are good people to recommend the way you did your job, but you should get the report from your supervisor. If you worked in your uncle's plant and your uncle writes the report, it is not going to be taken too seriously.

Portfolios: Exhibits may be sent to the admissions office with the proviso that the material has already been tested and is outstanding. A published short story, yes; a short story for a creative writing class, no. Photos only if they have been in an exhibit or published and have been adjudged excellent. The taped *performance* of a concerto solo at school (if documented as genuine) is probably better heard by the music department than the admissions office, which may not have the time to ask for a professional appraisal. Any faculty recommendation a candidate can obtain is highly desirable, but this is rare.

The Personal Statement: The personal statement should be neatly written, and honest. The candidate's attitude should be: "This is the way I am. This is how I feel." It is best to take some time not only in writing the statement, but in putting it aside for a week or more and then rereading it to see how it strikes you.

Influence or Pull: Most candidates know enough to bend over backwards before they try to use influence or pull on an admissions office. To have your famous alumni aunt badger the college president is not going to help you if you have a weak academic record by comparison with other candidates, and no extracurricular standout qualities.

A Word of Caution

Likely candidates in the nine Ivy Group colleges using Early Evaluation should be aware that not every Likely is admitted. There *can* be slips between cup and lip. We are not referring to avoiding a drug bust or flunking courses. Obviously, admission is contingent on continuing to maintain the record that won you the Likely rating. We are referring to overconfidence, cockiness and insolence. Such attitudes have a way of getting back to the admissions office. We know of one brilliant Likely candidate who blew his chances by saying too often he wasn't sure whether he would accept admission to a certain Ivy college. With today's competition an admissions committee can find among those it rated as Probable hundreds of enthusiasts who will accept admission. Why should they accept someone who might turn down their offer?

We should add that many candidates are accepted even though it is certain they will go somewhere else. Yale and Princeton accept many Harvard alumni sons and Radcliffe daughters sure to enroll at their parents' colleges. But they have to do this to encourage applications from others in the same school for years to come. Otherwise, the word would get around: "Don't bother to apply to Yale; they turned down Marcia. Radcliffe is the best bet for you."

If a candidate has gone by the book, his folder should be in order and there is really nothing more for him to do. But it is a long, long time from January to April, and on cold nights many a high school senior worries and wonders. One candidate recently said to us: "Suppose none of the seven colleges I applied to accepts me." It is normal to worry occasionally, but it is foolish to waste much time at it, because it cannot change the situation and it can only make the candidate (and his family) miserable. If a candidate has been well advised, he has applied to at least one college that will accept him. But even if he has not, believe us when we say once more that there are a number of excellent private colleges just waiting for him to apply.

April 15 and After

And now it is April 15 and all the results are in. The candidate must make his choice if he has two or more acceptances. And it is on the colleges that accepted him that he must focus his attention. He must forget any that rejected him as quickly as possible. We realize how much a rejection hurts, and only a Pollyanna can say, so what? it won't mean a thing in the long run. But as Adlai Stevenson said after his defeat by Eisenhower: "It hurts too much to laugh and I'm too old to cry." The acceptance is the thing, not the rejection. The disappointment is real, but the reality is the college where the next four years will be spent, not the one that was hoped for.

Young people are often hypersensitive and feel responsible for letting others down—the family, the school, the coach—when a college rejects them. But even the most disappointed parents have other things to think about, and most will snap out of it when they have to do something about the acceptance—like writing a check! Most animosity is directed not at the candidate but at the institution that turned him down. But invariably the candidate blames himself and wonders where he went wrong. It is not worth trying to figure it out. That is behind now. What counts is what comes next.

Is it possible that the letters could get mixed up and the wrong candidate be rejected? Absolutely not, because each college has its lists of admitted freshmen and if there is no reply from any accepted student, he will be contacted. But it has happened that an acceptance went to someone who had been rejected. In such a case the college honors its acceptance, but if it is felt that the student will flunk out or be unhappy in the college, the admissions office says so frankly and leaves the choice up to him.

Do admissions officers of selective colleges compare notes and trade off candidates with each other, saying: "You take Jim, I'll give you Alex"? Absolutely not. Even if there were time to compare application lists, what would be gained by such exchanges? Each college knows what it is looking for to make up a class and no two colleges have the same class in mind. The only information exchange occurs among financial-aid officers after all admissions are announced, and this happens only among some of the selective colleges like the Ivy Group and Seven Sisters to prevent competition in giving aid. This procedure allows candidates to decide among colleges they have been admitted to on their merits and not on financial advantage. It also prevents the colleges from being forced to engage in a competition they can hardly afford.

18

Scaling the Ivy Wall

Our examination of selective admissions has been limited to a particular group of colleges that might be described as "over applied to." Williams, with 888 admits to offer, had 4,500 applicants in 1973–74. But the prestige colleges are not the only places where applications are overflowing. We have not mentioned the military academies, art schools, drama schools, music schools and engineering schools that turn away many applicants. Within large universities like Boston University, Pittsburgh and Georgia Tech that are not highly selective in liberal arts, there are programs open only to very highly qualified students.

Each one of these situations represents an "ivy wall" to be scaled, and of course the professional graduate schools, particularly medical schools, are so much in demand that many discouraged candidates are studying medicine abroad. We wonder whether this trend toward studying medicine will continue under these conditions. Engineering, we suspect, will be making a comeback. Here is a report to us from Marquette University:

> Engineering enrollments have declined for several years and we can now expect only 30,000 engineering graduates in 1975. The supply will decline from a graduating class of 42,000 in 1973. Looking at the demand,

as projected by the U.S. Department of Labor, Engineering Manpower Commission and the Bureau of Labor Statistics, estimated needs are for 48,000–58,000 engineering graduates per year.

Note too that engineering graduates are sought after for such related jobs as programmers, technical writers, industrial designers, systems analysts, urban planners, and more, in addition to specific engineering fields. Others use their engineering backgrounds to enter such professions as law, medicine, dentistry, business management, and college teaching.

Engineers are and will be in short supply. Engineering graduates are hired at salaries averaging well over $900 per month. The situation for engineering manpower is tight and will get tighter.

It makes sense for parents and teachers to make young people aware of this particular opportunity offered for careers in engineering. It is easier now to get into the engineering program at a selective college than it is to get into the liberal arts program. Furthermore, engineering degrees can be as useful in business, law and medicine as a B.A. A B.S.E. from a predominantly liberal arts college means that the student has been exposed to a broad range of nonscience subjects.

Applicants from Abroad

So many students want to take a year of college abroad that it may surprise some to hear that Americans who live abroad very much want their children to go to college in the United States after secondary education in a foreign country. The international involvements of the United States have greatly increased the number of American families abroad, particularly in Europe. Here a group of private schools have banded together to help increase understanding of their programs among selective admissions directors back home. Called the European Council of Independent Schools, it has arranged to finance trips for admissions officers to inspect schools in England, France and Switzerland. The problem for the admissions officer at times is to evaluate the academic level of the school abroad.

The American applicant living abroad falls into no special admissions category, as the foreign applicant does. He joins the competition on a par with the mass of applicants back home. But being so far removed from what is going on, he or she, and the family are more ill-at-ease about the process. Visiting colleges may not be feasible, or it may be possible only during a home leave at a time that is not the best for such visits. There are few alumni to talk to about a particular college. You cannot pick up the phone casually and chat with the admissions office. All the more important that the school be up-to-date on the admissions picture and able to provide adequate college counseling. Some schools in England, recognizing the problem, have retained professional counseling services that bring someone directly from the United States in contact with college applicants.

So long as the secondary school is sound, there is just as much chance of an American applicant from Europe, Mexico or Southeast Asia being admitted to selective colleges as from home soil. If the schooling has been inadequate, it may be necessary to take a fifth remedial year to prepare a bright candidate for the competition. One of the tests of any school, of course, is its record of what colleges its graduates attend.

But even a good record ought to be checked, because many European schools are proprietary, dependent on enrollment for income and willing to expand enrollment to meet demand. You can get ambiguous or misleading answers to the question: How many of your graduates go to highly selective colleges in the United States? A problem at some overseas schools is turnover of faculty with a resulting lack of stability in the program. American-government-operated high schools are liable to be less strong than the better suburban schools back home.

All the admissions testing apparatus is available abroad, so that it is unnecessary for a candidate to come home for tests. Obviously, interviews cannot be required, but if the candidate plans to be in the United States, interviews can be arranged ahead of time. Since interviews provide the chance to ask questions about the college, it is often the candidate who has been out of the country who benefits most from one of these sessions in terms of learning about the college.

Selectivity Abroad

If selective admissions in America seems elitist, English and European admissions procedures are positively mandarin. The American college student lucky enough to take an undergraduate year at Oxford, the Sorbonne, Heidelberg or any other European university, will sit beside the academic crème de la crème, who have risen to the top through rigorous competition. In those systems there is no "personal side" to consider in the admissions process. You either score at the appropriate level in national examinations, or there is no place for you at the free public universities. The potential university student is segregated as early as age 11 and prepared in public high schools to take national examinations at age 18. In England, 60 percent passed in 1972. Somewhat fewer passed the following year in France.

Unlike the American system, there is great rigidity in the selection of college students abroad. Failure of the national examination (which can be taken over) definitely limits a young person's future, for there is not the huge spectrum of colleges from which a degree can be earned. Britain has 81 universities. With roughly four times the population, the United States has more than 200 times the number of degree-granting colleges. There are 1.5 million American freshmen and 65,000 English freshmen.

In France, the university system is supplemented by a number of *hautes écoles,* higher schools, the equivalent of our graduate schools. "To graduate from any of these schools is to have doors open up for you. Your future is assured," a teacher in a private preparatory school near Paris told us. The system so obviously favors the educated classes and particularly alumni children, that a graduate of the École Polytechnique, the training ground for those destined for brilliant careers in government and business, has written an exposé calling the graduate-old-boy network a Mafia. Despite intense competition generation after generation turns out *polytechniciens.* Rarely does anyone from the lower classes penetrate this sanctum of French preference.

One of the reasons for European student unrest is disgust with the narrowness of educational opportunity. This has caused public support of higher education, all of it paid by taxation, to diminish, and there simply is not the enthusiasm for college education that you find in America. In England, 2,700 places went unfilled in 1972 because students felt they could not live on the small grants provided by the government.

Excellent as these old universities are, many are overcrowded, and there is little student faculty contact. Hence Americans abroad are willing to sacrifice the money it costs to send their children to college back home.

The Best and the Brightest?

So for better or for worse, American higher education seems best for Americans, and we are chauvinistic enough to say it is the best in the world. We will even go so far as to say that its selective admissions processes, for all their complexity and shortcomings, still offer more opportunity to those deserving of intensive college training than any other means of selection up to this time. Perhaps the greatest virtue of the selective colleges is that they are not monopolistic. They do have prestige but there is no agreement that they are the best American higher education has to offer, and a degree from them does not open doors automatically, nor does it by any means assure the future of their graduates. In short, privilege now plays a minimal role in admissions at colleges that were formerly dominated by the upper classes. At the same time, meritocratic principles have become so deeply accepted as American articles of faith, that outstanding graduates of almost any college whatever can compete for jobs with Ivy graduates and win.

The Pulitzer Prize-winner David Halberstam calls his massive impressionistic account of the men who were responsible for American military involvement in Southeast Asia, *The Best and the Brightest* (1972). A Harvard graduate himself, he goes to some lengths to show that Ivy League backgrounds, including the best prep schools and the best graduate schools, may help get men to the top, but such advantages cannot give them scruples, moral sensitivity or just plain common sense.

In some circumstances "the best and the brightest" are more proud than good, and far from bright in the application of their knowledge. Goodness and brightness are not to be found in *any* college. It is ironic indeed that Halberstam's title first appeared in a religious poem called "Epiphany," by an English clergyman who became bishop of Calcutta in 1882:

> Brightest and Best of the sons of the morning,
> Dawn on our darkness, and lend us thine aid.

Some of the best and brightest will always be associated with the prestige colleges, but it is more important for men and women to be truly good and truly bright in whatever college and in what they do thereafter.

Reports on Admissions

Admission to Amherst College in 1973

Twenty-Seventh Annual Report to Secondary Schools

I would like to begin this report by calling your attention to some changes in our deadline for receipt of applications, timetable for interviews, degree requirements, and curricular offerings, and by making a special request.

A NEW APPLICATION DEADLINE

Beginning with the Class of 1978, our DEADLINE for receipt of applications for admission and financial aid will be FEBRUARY 1.

THE INTERVIEW TIMETABLE

This year, except for transfers, we shall not conduct any personal interviews in March and April. Seniors should visit the campus for personal interviews before March 1; juniors not before May 1. During the month of April, however, we plan to hold group sessions for juniors twice daily at 10:30 A.M. and 2:30 P.M.

Whenever possible, we request that you provide juniors with unofficial transcripts of their high school records prior to their visits to the campus. This will assist us in giving candidates an estimate of their chances of admission at the conclusion of the interview.

FOREIGN LANGUAGE REQUIREMENT DISCONTINUED

In a time of reform, experiment, and change in higher education, the Faculty, at its meeting last February, voted to discontinue proficiency in a foreign language as a requirement for the Bachelor of Arts degree. In assessing a candidate for admission, however, we shall continue to recommend a minimum of two years of one foreign language at the high school level with some preference given to applicants who present three or four years of one.

Breadth and depth of study in English, mathematics, history and the social sciences, the natural sciences, and a foreign language will continue to be of primary importance in the selection process.

A NEW PROGRAM: NEUROSCIENCE

Thanks to a grant of $400,000 from the Alfred P. Sloan Foundation, a new program to develop undergraduate study and research in the neurosciences will go into operation this fall. According to a recent article in *The New York Times,* many leaders in the field of biology feel that "the mysteries of the central nervous system and the brain present the greatest challenge in science today."

A SPECIAL REQUEST

In recent years we have been disturbed by an increasing tendency on the part of hundreds of applicants, many of them outstanding candidates for admission, to submit their credentials on or very near the deadline. Many of these procrastinators force us to place their names on our alternate list or are rejected outright when they might very well have been offered admission had they filed their applications earlier. We request, therefore, that you urge your counselees to submit their applications as soon as possible after our forms reach them and that you submit the necessary supporting documents as soon as possible after our NASSP transcript form reaches you. In this way, all of your counselees will be assured of receiving the fairest possible treatment by the selection team.

THE MECHANICS OF THE SELECTION: HOW WE DO IT

The actual mechanics of selection vary from college to college. At Amherst, the Admission Committee consists of: the President, who is an ex-officio member; the Dean of Admission as Secretary; the Associate Dean of Admission; the Assistant Dean in charge of Financial Aid; the Registrar, who is also an Associate Professor of Psychology; four professors representing the departments of Chemistry, Romance Languages, Music and English, the last of whom is Chairman of the Committee; and four students, three of whom are elected by the student body as a whole, one by the Afro-American Society. This group meets infrequently during the year to establish and review policy, set guidelines and align priorities. It is not a folder-reading committee; most of the members simply do not have the time. It takes about 300 hours for an experienced person to read fifteen tubs of admission folders.

The selection of the class, therefore, rests firmly on the shoulders of the four members of the admission staff—the Dean, the Associate Dean and the two Mayo-Smith Interns. Each application is read and rated at least once by the four of us. Once in a while, we are joined by other members of the Committee whose comments are often very helpful. Once the applications of candidates seeking financial assistance have been approved by the selection team, they are read by our Assistant Dean in charge of Financial Aid who, with the help of the information contained in the Parents' Confidential Statement and our own financial aid form, determines the amount of demonstrated financial need, if any.

Folders are rated A+, A, A−, B+, B, B−, and C. We also use two other ratings: A+/− and A+/C. Students with pure A+ ratings from all four members of the Admission Staff are admitted without discussion if they are Early Decision applicants; they become definite alternates and possible acceptances if they are regular applicants. All applicants with two or more A + ratings are discussed at length by the selection team as are all Early Decision applicants with four A ratings or better including those with two or more A+/− or A+/C ratings.

Each rating is a reaction on the part of each reader to the objective and subjective material presented to us in a folder—the application itself, an optional statement of some sort by the applicant, often an interview report by either a member of the staff or one of our alumni advisors on admission, a transcript of the student's record in high school, his CEEB or ACT scores, usually a statement written by the counselor which almost always is a compendium of comments from individual teachers over a 3 or 3–1/2 year period, letters of recommendation, most of which are not very helpful, and all of the correspondence we have had with the applicant and/or his family.

When we dive into the tubs between trips in mid-October, we find that very few applicants present academic credentials we even attempt to criticize, but naturally some are more impressive than others.

An applicant's academic credentials consist of the quality of his academic program, the number of honors or advanced placement courses, his actual performance as measured by rank in class, numerical or letter grades or written evaluations, and his CEEB, ACT or other test scores.

Students with poor records and test scores (and there aren't very many) are eliminated quickly. Next to go are students with poor records and high test scores. Once in a while we gamble on such an applicant and admit him because of some special talent, interest or achievement which he seems to have, but this is pretty risky business, and experience has taught us not to take many chances of this sort. These applicants are often rated A+/C and sometimes turn out to be some of our most interesting candidates.

An A+/C rating means, in essence, that the candidate could either be potentially great or a complete bust.

A C rating indicates that the candidate simply isn't in the running. His marks and test scores and his overall constellation of interests and achievements are simply not up to the competition. We make a special effort to send early rejection letters to as many as possible of these applicants.

A B rating is simply a middle-of-the-road applicant in all ways in our particular applicant pool. A B− is a B with negative connotations; a B+, a B with positive connotations. There is often a fine line between a B+ and an A which usually boils down to academic considerations. Upon a second reading a B+ sometimes becomes an A+.

Any student who has taken a strong academic program in high school, has performed well in that program and has done a reasonable job on the required standardized tests, will almost always be rated in the A group.

When our folder reading is completed in early March, there are usually somewhere between 1300 and 1600 applicants in the A− to A+ range. Approximately 200 to 300 end up with A− ratings; 400 to 500 with A ratings; 750 to 800 with A+ ratings; and a handful with A+/C and A+/− ratings. The A+'s consist of our Early Decision acceptances which total 150 to 175 and the 500 to 600 finalists who comprise our regular acceptances and alternates. Separating these finalists in March is the most difficult part of the selection process.

Every candidate with a rating in the A range—plus, straight or minus—and many of the B+'s are clearly qualified academically.

An A− is a candidate about whom we have no doubts as a student but toward whom we have some substantive negative feelings as a person. An A is a candidate about whom we have no doubts academically or personally but, who in the opinion of the selection team, lacks that "something extra" or "distinguishing factor or quaiity or excellence" which might separate him from the several hundred other well-qualified applicants. An A+/− is an A + about whom we have minor reservations.

In other words, once we are satisfied that an applicant is on firm ground academically, we look for something in an application that will tip the scales in his favor. Every one of our 450 to 500 or so acceptances and our 250 to 300 alternates possess "something extra" in the opinion of the four readers. The difference between those accepted and those who make the alternate list is minimal.

Examples of something extra are: demonstrated intellectual brilliance above and beyond marks and test scores; scholarly achievement in some field; keen interest and achievement in the offerings of an underpopulated department at the College; corroborated talent in art, drama, music, writing or sports; sincere social commitment; the extent of the candidate's interest in Amherst; membership in a minority group or an underrepresented socio-economic class (i.e. blue collar or working class background); being the son of an alumnus or a faculty or staff member; unusual background or experience; geography; our relationship with a particular school—an especially sensitive area because there are nearly 1500 secondary schools represented in our applicant pool each year!

All other things being equal, one or more of the above factors can, and usually does, make the difference. We don't have a crystal ball. We don't have a ouija board. We don't throw the folders down the stairs, picking only the ones that land right side up. We don't select on the basis of marks and test scores alone. We can't take all the stars. We have many difficult and often painful choices to make. In the end, we make every effort to bring to bear on each case a combination of 17 years of experience in the profession, make those agonizing decisions and prepare ourselves for the phone to ring two days after the letters go out.

WHO SHOULD APPLY FOR EARLY DECISION?

Unlike some colleges with rigid formulas for Early Decision applicants, we feel that any student who has performed well in a challenging academic program, who, in your opinion, has that "something extra" we seek and who, above all, really wants to come to Amherst, should be encouraged to file for Early Decision.

SPECIAL PROGRAMS

We have noticed in the past year or two an increasing preoccupation with "special programs." When we visit your schools, many of you ask us "What special programs has Amherst initiated in the recent past?" A student we accepted this year chose to go to a larger university because "they had many more special programs and it didn't look like Amherst was doing as many exciting things."

We have, of course, read about a number of these innovations at other schools. Some of them seem to be examples of educational gimmickry. Most of them seem to be exciting and valuable attempts on the part of cumbersome educational bureaucracies to increase the options through which students can fulfill their individual needs. In the midst of this proliferation, we hope that counselors and students alike will remember that the strength of small liberal arts colleges like Amherst is their ability to provide the space in which each student's program can potentially be "special."

Our offerings in Field Study and Independent Study; an Honors Program where every participant writes a thesis; January Interterm of four weeks open to all; the Freshman Seminars; the Junior Colloquia; Special Topics or reading courses for individuals or small groups—over 200 last year—available in each department, not to mention the many opportunities available through Five College Cooperation, all strike us as "special" and we hope that you will agree.

The Year in Retrospect

DEFERRED ADMISSION

Among the 514 students accepted into the Class of 1977, 10, including one young man who has decided to take still another year off, have elected to delay their matriculation at Amherst until September 1974. Two of the nine deferrals in the Class of 1976 decided to enroll elsewhere this fall; one decided not to attend college at all! We shall continue to offer this option to all accepted applicants.

THE "4–0–4"

The "4–0–4" calendar, judged a success for the second year in a row, will be continued. The highlight of the January Interterm of "voluntary and self initiated educational ventures on the part of students and teachers" was the Copeland Colloquium, a week of lectures, discussions and films on controversial topics in government, science, the arts, and society whose theme was "What's Worth Doing?"

THE FRESHMAN SEMINARS

The Freshman Seminars, voluntary courses for first semester freshmen intended to introduce new students to the intellectual life of the college and an attempt on the part of the college to combine the teaching and advising functions, "worked out superbly" according to the co-ordinator of this new program. Morale was high and a "less formal and perhaps more trusting relationship" between teachers and students seemed to prevail throughout the term. Each instructor was assisted in the planning and teaching of each seminar by an undergraduate upperclassman, usually a senior. Both the President of the College and the Dean of the Faculty taught Freshman Seminars last year and served as faculty advisor to 15 students each.

EMBARRASSING MOMENTS

Our target for the Class of 1977 was 300. On May 15 we had a class of 346. When freshman orientation began on September 4 there were 336 on hand! My staff has suggested that I enroll in a course in remedial mathematics!!

CO-EDUCATION

On October 28, 1972, President Ward made public his recommendation to the Board of Trustees that Amherst become a college for men and women by admitting transfer women in September 1974, freshmen women and additional transfers in September 1975. Citing "concern about size, student-faculty ratios, finances and effects on co-operation with other nearby colleges" and the fact that "no condition or circumstance forces the college to become co-educational now," a "sharply-divided" Board at their winter meeting in late January decided that the President's recommendation "should not now be approved." President Ward suggested further that "the question not soon come formally before the College again in order that energies can be directed to other matters." The issue of co-education at Amherst is still very much alive, however, and the Trustees have charged the President to "pursue actively the many ramifications . . . so we may return to the question and come to a conclusion." We shall keep you posted.

THE STAFF

My partner, Michael C. Behnke '65, new to the field of admission in 1971 and now an established professional, has been promoted to Associate Dean of Admission.

We shall be joined by two Mayo-Smith Interns, Stephen G. Dibble and Jeremiah E. Smith, both members of the Class of 1973. Steve, an English major, came to us from Mariemont High School in Cincinnati, Ohio; Jere, a Black Studies major, from La Grange High School in Georgia and the ABC Program at Phillips Academy, Andover, Massachusetts. Stephen R. Gang and Wayne M. Wormley, last year's "junior executives," have departed for

Harvard Law and Stanford Business School, respectively. Steve will be a John Woodruff Simpson Fellow in 1973–74, his first year in a new joint law-business program. Wayne, who will be working on his M.B.A., was one of twenty-five students accepted into the optional Urban Management Program in conjunction with the M.B.A. Program and, if all goes well, may be able to qualify for the Doctoral Program in Education. We shall miss this talented twosome.

"Skip" Routh and Pat Mullins will be back at their familiar posts in financial aid. Lorraine Carey, clerk par excellence, left us early last year for bigger and better things in the Deans' Office. In Jeanette Smith, who joined Marion Siroskey, Ruth Dunn, Carole Laliberte, Chris Evans, and Bev Contois on July 30, we think we have found a first-rate replacement. Marion Siroskey, the axis on whom this operation rotates, has also been promoted and has a new title: Supervisor-Academic Administration.

My personal thanks to each of them for seeing us through another challenging year. Additional copies of this report are available upon request should you want them.

This report carries with it our best wishes for a pleasant and profitable 1973–74.

Statistics of the Class of 1977

1. VOLUME

Total Applicants	2412	
Accepted	514	21% of those who completed applications (includes 10 whose admission in 1973 has been deferred until 1974)
Matriculated	336	65% of those accepted (includes 4 whose admission in 1972 was deferred until 1973)

2. DISTRIBUTION OF THE CEEB SCHOLASTIC APTITUDE TEST SCORES

	Verbal			Math		
	Applied	Accepted	Matriculated	Applied	Accepted	Matriculated
700-800	413	128	65	828	230	139
600-699	1027	215	152	1001	187	134
500-599	622	117	87	387	59	39
400-499	232	28	18	107	17	12
300-399	60	9	6	34	4	4
200-299	7	-	-	3	-	-
No Score	51	17	8	52	17	8
	2412	514	336	2412	514	336

3. RANK IN CLASS

	Public	Private and Parochial
First Fifth	162	62
Second Fifth	8	17
Third Fifth	3	6
Fourth Fifth	-	1
Fifth Fifth	1	1

Not Listed	11	64
	185	151

4. SECONDARY SCHOOL DISTRIBUTION

	Public		Private and Parochial	
Total Applicants	1471	61%	941	39%
Those who Matriculated	185	55%	151	45%

5. FINANCIAL AID

Completed Scholarship Applications	969	
Accepted with Amherst awards	128	
Total Amherst grants and loans to acceptances	$365,150	
Matriculants with Amherst awards (88)	$230,600	
Average award from Amherst to matriculants	$ 2,621	
Percent receiving Amherst grants and loans	27%	
Outside awards (55)	$ 42,500	
Percent of class receiving aid from all sources	36%	

Distribution of Amherst Awards

$ 100- 500	7
$ 501-1,000	7
$1,001-1,500	9
$1,501-2,000	11
$2,001-2,500	10
$2,501-3,000	6
$3,001-3,500	13
$3,501-4,000	6
$4,001-4,500	8
Over $4,500	11

6. GEOGRAPHICAL DISTRIBUTION

New York	66	Missouri	4	Oklahoma	1		
Massachusetts	40	Wisconsin	4	South Carolina	1		
Connecticut	35	Florida	3	Tennessee	1		
New Jersey	23	Minnesota	3	U.S. citizens living			
Illinois	21	North Carolina	3	abroad	7		
Pennsylvania	15	Vermont	3	Non-U.S. Citizens			
Maryland	12	Washington	3	living in U.S.	4		
California	11	Arkansas	2	China			
New Hampshire	8	Georgia	2	Netherlands			
Ohio	7	Indiana	2	Sweden			
Rhode Island	7	Oregon	2	United Kingdom			
Michigan	6	Alabama	1	Foreign	4		
Virginia	6	Colorado	1	Canada			
Texas	6	Delaware	1	Greece			
Arizona	5	Iowa	1	Poland			
D.C.	4	Kentucky	1	Rhodesia			
Louisiana	4	New Mexico	1				
Maine	4	North Dakota	1				

7. ACADEMIC INTEREST

History	37	Language	8	Business	2
English	34	Undecided	8	Classics	2
Biology	32	Pre-Law	7	Education	2
Science	26	Bio-Chemistry	5	Music	2
Political Science	24	Philosophy	5	Architecture	1
Pre-Med	23	Drama	4	Asian Studies	1
Mathematics	23	Geology	4	Astronomy	1
Social Science	17	American Studies	3	Ecology	1
Physics	14	Anthropology	3	Engineering	1
Psychology	13	Humanities	3	Fine Arts	1
Chemistry	13	Liberal Arts	3	Journalism	1
Economics	8	Religion	3	Oceanography	1

8. OCCUPATIONAL GOAL

Medicine	78	Sociology	5	Film Making	2
Law	74	Ecology	5	Oceanography	2
Teaching	35	Economics	5	Physics	2
Undecided	25	Mathematics	5	Psychology	2
Research	23	Music	5	Anthropology	1
Journalism	9	Biology	4	Chemistry	1
Engineering	8	Ministry	4	Chess Player	1
Government	7	Science	3	Computer Programmer	1
Writing	6	Architecture	2	Curator	1
Business	6	Art	2	Historian	1
Foreign Service	6	Drama	2	Icthyologist	1
		Geology	2		

9. SENIOR MAJOR DISTRIBUTION FOR THE CLASS OF 1973

American Studies	25	Geology	6	Economics-Math	1
Anthropology	9	History	24	Biophysics-English	1
Biology	8	Interdisciplinary	6	Music-English	1
Biophysics	4	Latin	1	English-Psychology	1
Black Studies	6	Mathematics	6	Physics-Economics	1
Chemistry	11	Music	9	Biology-Philosophy	1
Dramatic Arts	4	Philosophy	6	Physics-English	1
Economics	24	Physics	5	English-Art	1
English	52	Political Science	16	History-Drama	1
European Studies	1	Psychology	19	Religion-Geology	1
Fine Arts	12	Religion	8	History-English	1
French	5	Sociology	5	Independent Scholars	22
		Spanish	1		

10. CAREER CHOICES OF THE CLASS OF 1973

Education	17%	Ministry	2%
Law	16%	Other	13%
Business	16%	Undecided	21%
Medicine	15%		

11. SONS OF ALUMNI   12. BLACKS   13. LATINOS

Applied	78	Applied	132	Applied	23
Accepted	47	Accepted	59	Accepted	11
Matriculated	39	Matriculated	34	Matriculated	7

14. EARLY DECISION

Total Applicants	407
Accepted	171
Deferred, Accepted later	14

15. ACADEMIC PERFORMANCE OF THE CLASS OF 1976 AT THE END OF FRESHMAN YEAR

Enrolled in September 1972	312
Withdrew from College	4
Failed one or more semester courses	16
(during the year 1972-73)	
Finished first year on Dean's List	62

Columbia College Report to Headmasters, Principals, and Counselors, 1973

ELITISTS *vs.* SNOBS: NEW DIRECTIONS

"To strive always for excellence, and to surpass all others" is that line from Homer chosen by Moses Hadas to epitomize what he called the "Greek Ideal." In a provocative and scholarly essay,* Professor Hadas traced the outgrowth of this ideal, and pointed out its connections with humanism.

It is the keystone on which our culture rests. In eras when the spirit behind this ideal was suppressed, whether for religious, political, or imperial motives, the results were consistently the same: a dehumanized culture. In this light, it is revealing to examine the rapidly shifting usage of the word "elite."

A short time ago, the word had a positive ring to it. Confections, type faces, businesses and so on took the word for their name. In Webster's and the *OED*, "flower" and "choice" appear as synonyms. But now it is no longer smart to be elite. In fact, the word has given birth to an "ism," propounded by "ists," both of which are accusations, hurled or dodged by academics and politicians. Most of its current meanings are pejorative in that they convey a sense of snobbery and exclusion which was much weaker in the recent past.

EDUCATIONAL ELITISM

As the word "elitism" is used to describe not only the seeking of excellence but also the forming of cliques, the former goal is held less firmly as the latter is avoided. Education, however, *must* be elitist, in the broadest and most traditional sense, if it is to retain a sense of purpose. That is, it must continue to declare the necessity of a personal quest for excellence, as Homer did. For it to do anything short of this—to prepare students for trades, to produce self-satisfied "consumers" fitting snugly into prefabricated societal roles, to assent to students' feelings that their own experiences and opinions are all that matter—is to act as the servant of an already dehumanizing mass society. It is therefore timely to discuss the ways in which the Ivy League colleges,

---

* *The Greek Ideal and Its Survival,* by Moses Hadas (New York: Harper and Row, 1966).

Columbia in particular, are elitist, by examining the principal forms snobbery may take: financial, social, and intellectual.

Despite the perennial view of the Ivy League as a wealthy gentlemen's club, this has certainly not been true in Columbia's case. At the time of filing applications for admission, students who can't afford the fee are encouraged to request a waiver. And once students are admitted to the College, financial aid is plentiful: over two-thirds of the student body receives some form of financial aid, and about one-half the student body receives outright scholarships from Columbia. To view the role of the Admissions and Financial Aid Offices as "keeping the poor out" is therefore unrealistic. The greatest challenge faced by these personnel is just the opposite: continuing to meet the financial needs of entering classes. Each year it becomes harder to do so, and the day may yet come when financially needy students cannot enroll. But this will be despite the college's efforts, not because of them.

Social snobbery, if practiced by a college, would occur in its Admissions Office. First, special favors would be granted to those whose fathers were alumni. Second, it would look kindly upon those whose parents graduated from similar institutions, or were similar in status (income, profession, residence) to those who did. Other means of selectively dispensing privileges are more subtle: to particular secondary schools, a college may leak (actually, pour!) early word on admissions, thus raising its chances of enrolling those it wishes to, and also increasing the number of applicants from these particular schools. Especially attractive applicants outside these schools may also be given early word on their "chances."

Each of the above forms of snobbery, however, has been drastically curtailed, and not simply by Columbia. Five years ago, an alumnus' son would be admitted to the College, and told of his admission well before other applicants, provided he met minimal academic standards. This is no longer so. Instead, *any* applicant may request an early notification, and if he is admissible, and has informed the Admissions Office he wishes to attend Columbia, he will be guaranteed both a place in the entering class and a financial aid award. All applicants, regardless of whether they view Columbia as their first-choice school, are given a "probable-possible-unlikely" rating as soon as possible. Parents' status, or that of the secondary school, no longer plays a role in such early notification.

Utterly inconsistent with social snobbery is Columbia's (and many others') workings to enroll and graduate students from lower-class backgrounds. Special recruitment efforts, preparatory programs, counselling, student organizations, and tutoring now function to attract students who were formerly ignored.

Intellectual snobbery expresses itself in regarding all but one's own views and beliefs as inferior. A rigid curriculum, uniform for all, would reflect this, as, too, would an educational attitude which allowed students to go through college without ever having been asked to expand their own outlooks. Columbia requires all students to take courses outside of their favorite areas, and in fields which stress the importance of self-examination and intellectual honesty (philosophy, social science, natural science, literature).

GENERAL AND CONTINUING EDUCATION

Yet, "in the midst of strong and inescapable trends toward specialization and vocationalism in the work of the University, it is essential that the humane values and concerns underlying every branch of learning be rearticulated. The humanities can no longer be thought of as limited to studies of high cultural traditions and their literary expression. They go beyond the latter in affirming that the human aspect of things should remain a central concern on virtually every level of educational and cultural endeavor." This statement is an excerpt from "University Directions II," a proposed major reworking of Columbia's educational program. The twenty-three page document, recently submitted to the University Senate by Provost and Executive Vice President for Academic Affairs William Theodore de Bary, calls for "a new kind of 'open university' within the modern multiversity—a program of general and continuing education which is open to all students and serves as a meeting ground for the disciplines and professions." Dr. de Bary further stated that "students conclude that a university which avoids questions of values and priorities is . . . incapable of facing up to its moral and social responsibilities. The university appears non-commital and 'value-free,' when, for undergraduates looking to it for leadership, it should appear 'value-full.' "

In short, Dr. de Bary is calling for a renewed dedication to excellence and accomplishment—elitism—as a means of countering narrowness and stagnation—the consequences of intellectual snobbery. In this, he is supported by University Professor Jacques Barzun, who points out that "the fusion of professional with liberal arts is designed to show the students what they have lost of the power of imagining—that is, how college education is geared to man's life in the world."

The Admissions Office has already complemented these efforts in a direct way. It seeks those students who have demonstrated a motivation for excellence using as criteria the only possible means: repeated intuitive judgments. Two different applicants with the same "numbers" may be vastly different individuals; selection is therefore in harmony with a number of personal ideals, and not according to numerical guidelines. To do otherwise (e.g., admit the first seven hundred applicants, or work on a lottery system) would be immoral when an honest transaction is called for, and a limited resource is being managed. In sum, the College seeks to enroll students who are likely to enter what Ortega has called the only true elite: those who make demands on themselves.

It is apparent to anyone associated with Columbia that, far from being snobbish, the College has actively, even aggressively, sought to open its doors to a wide range of people, and to prevent its own members from settling into a narrow parochialism. But it is not enough for students and their teachers to avoid snobbery, while still feeling uneasy about seeking excellence. Elitism is a natural drive, perhaps an expression of the basic psychological mechanism of "identification." (Even the most fervent "anti-elitists" seek the *most* radical, the *purest* ideological stance!) It should not be equated with snobbery, and shied away from, but should be accepted and harnessed positively.

We welcome any comments and suggestions.

Area Coverage

Under our regional system, each of the admissions officers has assumed responsibility for alumni and undergraduate recruiting, secondary school relations, and the processing of applications in a particular geographical area. Questions concerning applications or alumni recruiting activity should be directed to the admissions officer in charge of your area. The following areas have been assigned for 1973–1974:

Area One (Gary Cornog and Eugene Buckingham, area representatives): Alabama, Alaska, Brooklyn, California, Connecticut, Florida, Georgia, Hawaii, Indiana, Kentucky, Mississippi, New Jersey, North Carolina, Ohio, Pennsylvania, South Carolina, Staten Island, Tennessee, Virginia.

Area Two (William Oliver and Kenneth Wright, area representatives): Arizona, Illinois, Iowa, Kansas, Maine, Manhattan, Massachusetts, Michigan, Minnesota, Missouri, Nebraska, Nevada, New Hampshire, Queens, Rhode Island, Texas, Vermont, Westchester, West Virginia, Wisconsin.

Area Three (Michael Lacopo and Kevin Foley, area representatives): Arkansas, Bronx, Colorado, Delaware, Foreign, Idaho, Long Island, Louisiana, Maryland, Mexico, Montana, New York, North Dakota, Oklahoma, Oregon, Puerto Rico, South Dakota, Utah, Washington, Washington, D.C., Wyoming, New Mexico.

COLUMBIA COLLEGE

FRESHMAN FIGURES

Number of freshman applicants	3422
Offers of admission	1435
Number of freshmen registered	750

SECONDARY SCHOOL BACKGROUNDS

From public schools	64%
From private and parochial schools	36%
Number of schools from which freshmen came	464

RANK IN GRADUATING CLASS

Tenth:

Top	51%
2nd	16%
3rd	13%
4th	4%
5th	2%
6th	1%
7th	.6%
8th	0%
No information	12.4%

CEEB SCORES OF FRESHMAN CLASS

		Percent	
Scores	Verbal		Math
700–800	21		24
600–699	48		49
500–599	20		19
Below 500 and no info.	11		8
Median	660		660

GEOGRAPHICAL DISTRIBUTION

New England	85	Mountain	6
Middle Atlantic	510	Pacific	20
Southern	47	Foreign	17
Middle West	55	Number of states represented	40

Percentage from outside a fifty-mile radius of New York City   52%

PROBABLE PROFESSIONS

Architecture	12	Law	145
Business	30	Medicine	183
Dentistry	0	Scientific	62
Engineering	16	Teaching	55
Journalism	40		

SCHOLARSHIPS
   404 freshman hold scholarships administered by Columbia. These include 8
   National Merit and National Achievement, and 7 Pulitzer Scholarships.
   250 other freshmen received New York State Scholarships. All Scholarship awards from Columbia included jobs or loans or both.

TRANSFER APPLICANTS

   Applications received   340
   Offers of admission   105
   Transfers registered   91

FOR FURTHER INFORMATION WRITE TO: College Admissions Office • 212
Hamilton Hall • Columbia University • New York, New York 10027

Common Statement of Ivy Group Institutions

Over the past few years there have been a number of questions raised by applicants to and alumni of our institutions regarding the admission of students who may be interested in participating in inter-collegiate athletics. The Ivy Group institutions encourage able persons to attend including those persons who have proven themselves as athletes. However, all the institutions

• admit men and women whether or not they are athletes on the basis of their potential as students;• provide financial aid only on the basis of need;• never require that any student continue in athletic competition as a condition for continuation of financial aid.

Further, the Ivy Group agreement of 1954 notes: "In the total life of the campus, emphasis upon intercollegiate competition must be kept in harmony with the essential educational purposes of the institution."

In the process of admitting those interested in intercollegiate athletics a number of people may become involved. Alumni and coaches are eager to inform students about the academic and athletic programs and facilities at a particular institution. Admissions officers must screen and make decisions about all applicants. Financial aid officers must objectively evaluate financial need and make financial aid awards. The following guidelines established by the Ivy Group policy committee may be helpful to all those concerned with this process.

(1) In each of these institutions the Office of Admissions is the only office which has the authority to admit a student. Admissions officers will attempt to advise applicants about the likelihood of admissions, but the applicant should rely solely on two formal communications in this regard.* The first is the Early Evaluation statement, sent out before February 15 and the second is the formal admission letter which is sent out by mid-April. No other person

*There are two exceptions: applicants under the Early Decision program, and commonwealth residents applying to the University of Pennsylvania under the rolling decision program.

or office is authorized by an Ivy Group University to make such communication about chances of admission or formal admission to the applicant.

(2) Coaches at each of the institutions are the most knowledgeable about the athletic programs and are eager to be of help to an alumnus or an applicant who wishes to know about a particular athletic program. Letters to them from alumni and applicants about such programs will be promptly answered. Coaches also travel frequently across the country, meeting with alumni groups and potential applicants, to answer their questions. Neither alumni nor applicants should put the coaches in the difficult position of trying to estimate the chances for admission of a particular candidate. This is the sole responsibility of the admissions personnel.

(3) Financial aid is awarded at each of our institutions according to the demonstrated need of the student. The award is made at the time of admission and no applicant should consider or accept an offer of financial help from anyone else associated with the institution to which he is applying. Applicants intending to participate in intercollegiate athletics are considered for admission and financial aid along with all other applicants, and the same standards are used for everyone. The composition of the financial aid package and continuation of financial aid will not depend upon athletic status.

(4) In any case where an alumnus or an applicant has a question about admission, financial aid, athletic participation or eligibility, we urge that a telephone call be made to the chief admissions officer of the institution involved. That is by far the best source of information when confusion arises in this area.

ABOUT THE AUTHORS

Howard Greene, a former admissions officer of Princeton, has his own education consultancy, Howard Greene Associates, in Westport, Connecticut, with clients from San Francisco to London. He graduated from Dartmouth with honors, and holds master's degrees from Harvard and New York University. His experience includes private school teaching and coaching.

Robert Minton is a writer who has also been a secondary school and college teacher. After graduating from Princeton and Columbia School of Journalism, he was a reporter and book review columnist director of public affairs for Radio Free Europe, and subsequently was director of university relations at Boston University. He lives in Concord, Massachusetts, with his wife, Lal, a teacher of French at Boston University.

How to Read a College Catalogue

College catalogues have a deadly quality. The prose is antiseptic and impersonal. But for a reason. A catalogue is a contract. The student can hold the college to what the catalogue says. So a catalogue should be read for what it is, a description. Most of the contents can be taken at face value. Since no one reads everything in a catalogue, it is important to read selectively.

From the catalogue may be gleaned, among other things, the following: size of undergraduate enrollment, ratio of women to men, size of faculty, faculty qualifications, endowment, course offerings and academic programs, academic requirements, admissions requirements, facilities including dormitories, labs, athletic fields, etc., a history of the college, costs and financial aid, academic prizes, social organizations and fraternities.

If you list such items in a column and then put the names of colleges at the top of the page, by checking the list you can quickly compare colleges to see what they have or lack according to your own needs. College A has strong government courses but is weak in science. College B has no crew. College C seems to emphasize drama and music activities. College D will not let you live off campus until junior year.

Every catalogue puts the college's best foot forward and avoids negative comment, so the catalogue makes every college sound good. The question is: Is it good for you?

Here are a few suggestions on how to proceed:

Begin with the academic qualities. You are going to college first of all for academic training, not for the social life, athletics, glee club or mountain air. Unless you find the right academic atmosphere, the rest will be superficial and meaningless to you.

What are the degree requirements? Is there a thesis? How about interdisciplinary majors? Are there pass/fail options? The bulk of a college catalogue is taken up with course descriptions. Look for what is *not* offered to see if you might be shortchanged. If you are interested in becoming a geologist and there are only a few courses in this field, then this college, which may be otherwise excellent, is not for you.

Special programs of study offer clues to a college's strong points. Are you interested in creative writing? The catalogue will tell you just how much academic training you can expect.

The catalogue should give an indication of the percentage of faculty with doctoral degrees and what the ratio of faculty to students is. Top colleges have few faculty who lack a Ph.D., and the faculty-to-student ratio is one teacher for every 10 students or less. The catalogue will not tell you how many teaching assistants (graduate students) you will be taught by. Nor does it always say what percentage of the college's graduates go to graduate school, or what distinction the alumni have achieved.

Description of facilities should be scrutinized. Is there a swimming pool, hockey rink, tennis courts, student center? How many books does the library have? Small colleges have 150,000 volumes, while universities have one to three million. Is there a science center, a theater? Whatever a college does not list, it does not have. A catalogue is an inventory of assets.

The catalogue describes living arrangements and costs. Must the student take meals in commons? Can he live off campus? Are dormitories large or small? High-rise or low? If there are fraternities there will be extra costs.

The makeup of the student body will tell you whether you will feel comfortable there. The number of out-of-state students may be low.

Useful Books Related to College Admissions

Every school library has some books on this subject and the public library has more. Students, and parents too, should browse. Opinions and impressions will be contradictory, forcing the individual to make his own judgments. Our one word of caution has to do with those books full of caustic comments about particular colleges. If catalogues and promotional brochures are too bland and patently upbeat, some books deal altogether too casually and irresponsibly with some aspects of higher education. Here is a handful of books we believe well worth consulting:

Barron's In-Depth Guide to the Ivy League Schools, Barron's Educational Series, Inc.

Barron's Profiles of American Colleges, Benjamin Fine, Editor, Barron's Educational Series, Inc., 1971.

Choosing a Private School, John Esty, Dodd, Mead, 1974.

Choosing a College, John C. Hoy, Dell, 1967.

The College Handbook, College Entrance Examination Board, 1972.

Comparative Guide to American Colleges, James Cass & Max Birnbaum, Harper & Row, 1972–73.

The Insiders' Guide to the Colleges, The Yale Daily News, Berkeley
    Medallion, 1970.
Lovejoy's College Guide, 1970.
Student Expenses at Post-Secondary Institutions, 1974–75, College
    Scholarship Service.

Glossary

College admissions has a language all its own. To reduce confusion we offer the following guide:

Admissions, rolling	Absence of any admissions deadline is called rolling admissions. Decisions are made sometimes in less than a week after applying. No selective college has rolling admissions.
Admit-Deny	A candidate who is admitted but denied financial aid because the college has used up its aid budget.
Candidate's reply date agreement	Selective colleges give admitted candidates two weeks to accept. At the end of that period if no reply has been received, the admission is withdrawn.
Cohabitation	Unofficial rooming together of a boy and girl in a college dorm.
College night	A gathering of a large number of college representatives for a regional meeting with high school students and their families. The concept has been expanded into a college fair, held for

thousands in large halls in big cities.

Early Action (MIT)	MIT's Early Decision plan, not binding on candidates.
Early Decision	Early Decision applicant applies early in fall and indicates that the college is his first choice. He receives notice before Christmas and must agree to withdraw all other applications if he accepts admission. Harvard, Yale and Princeton have no Early Decision.
Early Evaluation	A new system started by Princeton and adhered to by the Ivy Group. The candidate is informed in January or February that it is Likely, Possible or Unlikely that he will be admitted.
Flyer	"Take a flyer" means applying to a college even though chance of being admitted seems slim.
Folder	Accumulated documents on which admissions judgment rests, such as application, transcript, test scores, recommendations. At Mount Holyoke it is called a docket.
Full ride	(1) What star athletes receive from big-time sports colleges—tuition, room and board, expenses, extras. (2) Any aid package covering all expenses.
Independent school	A private school that is not parochial or denominational. Preferred by private schools because of the connotations of "private."
Ivy Group	Ivy League plus MIT. The League is Harvard, Yale, Princeton, Dartmouth, Cornell, Columbia, Penn and Brown, and is athletic. Ivy Group presidents meet annually to discuss admissions policies, athletics, etc.
Legacy	Having a parent or other blood relative in the alumni body of the college you apply to.
Minority	Minority really describes educational disadvantage, not race. Poor whites are considered a minority. Jews are not (unless they are poor

whites). Most Blacks are minority, many Chinese are not. Puerto Ricans are considered foreign in some colleges.

Overlap

The effect of several colleges receiving applications from the same student; the overlap occurs when a student is admitted to two or more selective colleges. Ivy financial-aid officers share information at an overlap meeting to eliminate competing for students by offering aid differentials.

Pass/Fail

No course grade, just a pass or fail. Pass/fail courses are dwindling because of the importance of grades in applying to graduate school.

Pool

A particular group of potential applicants—the pool of those with high grades, requiring no financial aid, the pool of minority seniors qualified for selective colleges, etc.

Recruiting

Soliciting athletes, or simply soliciting students to build enrollment. Selective colleges recruit athletes and top scholars. Recruiting is carried on by admissions office, coaches and alumni.

Scholar-athlete

Athlete able to do the academic work of a selective college. It does not mean the athlete is necessarily a top student.

Seven Sisters

Barnard, Bryn Mawr, Vassar, Wellesley, Smith, Mount Holyoke and Radcliffe. Vassar, now co-ed, no longer accepts the epithet.

Snob

Short for *sine nobilitate,* a designation at the University of Bologna in the Middle Ages for students who had no noble blood, and hence as a defense they considered themselves superior!

Special rounds

Admissions committee meetings at which groups of candidates are considered separately from the rest: athletes, alumni children, minorities and special cases.

Stopping out

A selective college term for taking time out from academic work for a semester or more. Distinguished from dropping out by the fact that stop outs get their degrees.

Waiting list

A list of candidates who will be admitted if the class is not filled. Notice can come as late as September. Deposit made at another college is forfeited if the candidate decides to accept a call from the waiting list.

INDEX

Index

The size of the endowment may be listed. Some small colleges have as much as $56,000 per student in endowment. Obviously they have more to offer than a college where the endowment is only $10,000 per student. But some colleges with low endowments receive large donations for current operations.

The athletic programs listed will tell you whether you can engage in your particular sport. Not every college has rowing, sailing, fencing, hiking and so on. In a city college where do you work out? Is the pool open daily, and at what time?

A catalogue is no substitute for a visit to the campus, but rather, an aid to the visit. Read it before and during the visit. It will stimulate questions as well as provide answers.

In addition to catalogues, colleges put out an enormous number of brochures. Some are simply promotional and must be read with care, while others are highly informative. They are not contractual in nature like the catalogue, and may be issued by a department without central-administration control. Since many private colleges are losing enrollment, reliance on sales promotion is increasing. The intelligent student will do well to "look under the hood."

AH2K